KU-519-382

OXFORD

French Verbpack

OXFORD
UNIVERSITY PRESS

OXFORD
UNIVERSITY PRESS

Great Clarendon Street, Oxford OX2 6DP

Oxford University Press is a department of the University of Oxford.
It furthers the University's objective of excellence in research, scholarship,
and education by publishing worldwide in

Oxford New York

Auckland Bangkok Buenos Aires Cape Town Chennai
Dar es Salaam Delhi Hong Kong Istanbul Karachi Kolkata
Kuala Lumpur Madrid Melbourne Mexico City Mumbai Nairobi
São Paulo Shanghai Singapore Taipei Tokyo Toronto

Oxford is a registered trade mark of Oxford University Press
in the UK and in certain other countries

Published in the United States
by Oxford University Press Inc., New York

© Oxford University Press 2000

British Library Cataloguing in Publication Data

Data available

Library of Congress Cataloging in Publication Data

Oxford French verbpack / [edited by Valerie Grundy].   p.   cm.
1. French language—Verb.   I. Grundy, Valerie.
PC2271.O97 2001   448.2'421—dc21   2001036190

ISBN 0-19-860338-X

6

Typeset by The Read Setter, Osney, Oxford
Printed in Great Britain by
Clays Ltd, Bungay, Suffolk

Contributors

Edited by	Valerie Grundy
Verb directory	Isabelle Stables
Verb patterns	Philip Gerrish
Proofreading	Cathy Riqueur
Text management	ELLA Associates Ltd

Contents

Introduction

How to use this book

For quick access to essential information, look up the verb in the *Verb Directory*. There are over 4000 verbs in the directory, most of them in common use. For each verb listed in the directory, the following information is given: whether it conjugates with *avoir* or *être*, the principal translation, the model verb that gives the conjugation pattern the verb follows, and the number of the model verb.

The verb directory is not intended to be used as a dictionary, but as a reference tool to take you to the appropriate conjugation pattern. Many verbs have a considerable number of different meanings and it does not fall within the scope of this book to list these. The directory also contains those forms of irregular verbs which are not readily identifiable.

The verb patterns are at the front of the book. There are 79 of these, 77 of which are laid out on double-page spreads for easy access to the information provided. They are clearly numbered and are in alphabetical sequence, apart from the defective verbs **déchoir** [78] and **gésir** [79], which come after the others.

On the left-hand page are tables showing the conjugation patterns for the principal tenses: *present*, *future*, *imperfect*, *perfect*, *past historic*, *conditional*, *present subjunctive*, and *imperfect subjunctive*. The box at the top of the page shows the pattern verb, its number, and translation, whether it is regular or irregular, whether it conjugates with *avoir* or *être*, the three forms of the *imperative*, and the *present* and *past participles*.

Endings are shown in bold where the **stem** remains unchanged.

On the right-hand page, you will find various types of useful information, including other verbs that follow the same pattern, phrases showing how the verb works in different contexts, and a *Language in use* section showing idiomatic phrases. For grammatically complex verbs, such as **être**, **avoir**, and **falloir**, the information is laid out so as to show clearly the principal functions of the verb. These are illustrated by example phrases and expressions.

The section *How French verbs work* which follows aims to provide clear guidelines on using verbs. The grammatical terms that are used are explained in the *Glossary of grammatical terms* on pages 15 and 16.

Informal usage in example phrases is marked *.

How French verbs work

Conjugations

There are three conjugations of verbs. The first two are regular. The conjugation that a verb belongs to is determined by the ending of the infinitive and the present participle, so **aimer**, **aimant** is an **-er** verb and **finir**, **finissant** is an **-ir** verb. If you look at the conjugation tables for these verbs (numbers 3 and 34), you will see that each has its own set of endings for the various tenses and within the tenses. The part of the verb infinitive that precedes the ending is called the stem. All other verbs belong to the third conjugation. Most of them are irregular.

Within each tense, the verb has six forms, according to the subject of the verb: **je**, **tu**, **il/elle** in the singular and **nous**, **vous**, and **ils/elles** in the plural. These are referred to as the first, second, and third person singular and the first, second, and third person plural. The impersonal pronoun **on** is also third person singular:

> **j'**aime votre maison   *I like your house*
> **il** aime le champagne   *he likes champagne*
> **ils** ador**ent** les chevaux   *they love horses*

Third person subjects are, however, very often nouns rather than pronouns:

> **ma sœur** aime le chocolat   *my sister likes chocolate*
> **les chiens** aiment la viande   *dogs like meat*

Slight irregularities in -er verbs

The only verb ending in **-er** that is truly irregular is **aller** [4] but certain groups of **-er** verbs in the first conjugation show slight variations from the norm. Each of these groups is represented in the pattern verbs and marked as an irregular verb. However, the irregularities are slight, easy to grasp, and come about because of French pronunciation rules. These groups and the pattern variations are as follows:

⬦**manger** [42]

Takes an **e** after the stem when the ending begins with an **a** or an **o**:

> nous mang**e**ons   *we are eating/we eat*
> il mang**e**a   *he ate*

The **e** is added to prevent the **g** having to be pronounced as in **garden**, as it would be before these vowels, according to both French and English pronunciation rules.

⬦**placer** [54]

The **c** of the stem becomes **ç** when the ending begins with an **a** or an **o**:

> pla**c**ez les verres sur la table   *place the glasses on the table*
> elle pla**ç**ait les verres sur la table   *she was placing the glasses on the table*

This happens for similar reasons to the **e** in **manger**, that is to say to keep the **c** soft, as in **cease**, rather than hard, as in **cat**.

⬦**acheter** [1]

The **e** of the stem becomes **è** where the following syllable contains a silent or unstressed **e** in order to avoid the word ending with an unpronounced or unstressed syllable:

> nous ach**e**tons beaucoup de légumes   *we buy lots of vegetables*
> elle ach**è**te beaucoup de légumes   *she buys lots of vegetables*

⬦**appeler** [5]

For the same reason as above, the **l** of the stem is doubled before a syllable containing a silent or unstressed **e**:

> elle a appe**l**é son frère   *she called her brother*

elle appe**ll**e son frère   *she calls her brother*

✧**geler** [36]
In verbs where the stem has just one syllable consisting of a consonant + **el**, the **e** becomes **è** before a syllable containing a silent or unstressed **e**.

il va g**e**ler   *it's going to freeze*
il g**è**le   *it is freezing*

This also applies to composite verbs with this type of verb as their basic part, such as **congeler** and **dégeler**.

✧**jeter** [38]
For the same reason again, the **t** of the stem is doubled before a syllable containing a silent or unstressed **e**:

nous je**t**ons le ballon   *we throw the ball*
elle je**tt**e le ballon   *she throws the ball*

✧**lever** [40]
Similarly again, the **e** of the stem becomes **è** before a syllable containing a silent or unstressed **e**:

nous l**e**vons nos verres   *we raise our glasses*
elle l**è**ve son verre   *she raises her glass*

✧**assiéger** [8]
In verbs having **é** followed by a consonant in the last syllable before the stem, this becomes **è** before a silent **e** only:

ils assi**é**geraient la ville   *they would besiege the town*
ils assi**è**gent la ville   *they are besieging the town*

✧**employer** [28], **essuyer** [30]
In all verbs where the infinitive ends in **-oyer** or **-uyer** the **y** becomes **i** before a syllable containing a silent or unstressed **e**:

nous emplo**y**ons cinq personnes   *we employ five people*
j'emplo**i**e cinq personnes   *I employ five people*

Note that **envoyer** [29] adds an **s** in the **tu** form of the

Imperative when followed by either of the pronouns **y** and **en**:

> envoies-en à Sylvie   *send some to Sylvie*

Reflexive verbs

A reflexive verb is one that has the same object as its subject. In English, the object of a reflexive verb will be one of the -**self** pronouns, as in he washed **himself**. The same thing happens in French:

> **je me** lave   *I wash **myself***

The reflexive pronouns in French are **me, te, se, nous, vous**, and **se**, corresponding to the subject pronouns **je, tu, il/elle/on, nous, vous, ils/elles**. French also has a number of verbs which are reflexive but do not correspond to English:

> je **me** souviens de son nom   *I remember his name*

In many cases involving actions on parts of the body, where the verb is used transitively, an indirect reflexive is used in French, indirect because the object of the verb is no longer the same as the subject. The form of the reflexive pronoun does not change when it is used indirectly:

> il **se** lave **les mains**   *he is washing his hands*
> il s'est cassé **la jambe**   *he has broken his leg*

The direct objects of the verbs here are **les mains** and **la jambe**.
✧see also *Agreement of the past participle* below

A final use of the reflexive in French occurs when the reflexive pronoun is translated by *each other* or *one another*:

> ils **se** connaissent   *they know **each other/one another***
> ils s'aiment   *they love **each other/one another***

Forming the passive

In the passive, the action of the verb happens to the subject of the verb, rather than the subject performing it, in contrast to the active:

> il **a tué** sa femme (*active*)   *he killed his wife*
> il **a été tué** par sa femme (*passive*)   *he was killed by his wife*

The passive is formed in French in exactly the same way as in English, using the verb **être** *to be*:

> ma voiture va **être réparée**   *my car is going **to be repaired***
> leurs canditatures **ont été refusées**   *their applications **have been turned down***

◇see also *Agreement of the past participle* below

The passive is used a great deal less in French than in English on account of the very useful impersonal pronoun **on**. A French person wishing to say *my car has been stolen* will more readily say *on m'a volé ma voiture* than *ma voiture a été volée*, although in some cases, the **on** use is rather more informal. There are, however, many cases when the passive is used in English when it cannot be used in French:

> **on savait** qu'il était parti à l'étranger   *he **was known** to have gone abroad*
> **on ne sait pas** où elle est   *her whereabouts **are not known***

Forming compound tenses

A compound tense is a tense in which the verb consists of more than one word. *Claire **has forgotten** her keys* is an example in English. In French there are four compound tenses: the perfect, the pluperfect, the future perfect, and the past conditional. The latter three correspond to the English **had gone**, **will have gone**, and **would have gone**. In current French, the perfect is used to express both the English **has gone** and **went**. The equivalent to the English simple past, grammatically called the preterite, as in **I went** is the past historic, but this is now used almost exclusively in literary French.

In English the other verb, usually called the **auxiliary verb**, used to form compound past tenses is always **have**. This is not the case in French. Although almost all verbs do form compound tenses with **avoir** *to have*, a few verbs, many of them very important ones, do this with **être** instead. All except **rester** express movement or the fundamental change of state of being born or dying. Those in frequent use are:

aller   *to go*
arriver   *to arrive*
décéder   *to die*
descendre◇   *to go/come/take down*
entrer   *to enter*

monter◇   *to go/come/take up*
mourir   *to die*
naître   *to be born*
partir   *to leave*
rentrer◇   *to go/come/back/take in*
rester   *to stay*
retourner   *to return*
sortir◇   *to go/come/take out*
tomber◇   *to fall/cut down*
venir   *to come*

◇when these verbs have a direct object, they form compound tenses with **avoir**

> elle **est** montée dans sa chambre   *she went/has gone up to her room*
> elle **a** monté ses valises dans sa chambre   *she took/has taken her suitcases up to her room*

◇see also *Agreement of the past participle* below

All reflexive uses of verbs also form compound tenses with **être**:

> elle s'**est** déjà levée   *she **has** already got up*
> elle s'**est** cassé la jambe   *she **has** broken her leg*

◇see also *Agreement of the past participle* below

Agreement of past participles

In compound tenses, the past participle takes a gender agreement in certain cases. This means that it can have an added **-e**, **-s**, or **-es**. This happens in the following cases:

Verbs which form compound tenses with être

The past participle agrees with the subject of the verb:

> **il** est all**é** au bureau   *he has gone to the office*
> **elle** est all**ée** au bureau   *she has gone to the office*
> **ils** sont all**és** au bureau◇   *they have gone to the office*
> **elles** sont all**ées** au bureau◇   *they have gone to the office*

◇**ils** referring to plural masculine nouns or a mixture of masculine and feminine, **elles** to feminine nouns

Reflexive verbs

When the reflexive pronoun is the direct object of the verb, the participle agrees in gender and number with the subject:

elles se sont lav**ées**   *they have washed*

The past participle does not agree when the verb has an object:

ils se sont lav**é** les mains   *they have washed their hands*
elle s'est cass**é** la jambe   *she has broken her leg*

Preceding direct objects

This refers to the situation where a pronoun is used in its usual place before the verb to refer to something that has already been mentioned. When this happens in one of the compound past tenses, the past participle agrees in gender and number with the pronoun:

'Où sont mes clés?' - 'Je te **les** ai donn**ées**'   *'Where are my keys?' - 'I've already given them to you'*

Where there is a relative pronoun referring back to something that has already been mentioned, the past participle agrees in gender and number with the noun referred to:

la robe **que** j'ai fait**e**   *the dress that I made*
les livres **que** je t'ai donné**s**   *the books that I gave you*

Forming questions

When the subject is a pronoun, questions can be formed by inverting the subject and the pronoun and putting a hyphen between the two:

aimez-vous le vin blanc?   *do you **like** white wine?*

The **est-ce que?** question form can be used with both noun and pronoun subjects:

est-ce que ton fils veut des fraises?   *does your son want some strawberries?*
est-ce que vous aimez le vin blanc?   *do you like white wine?*
est-ce que vous voulez des fraises?   *do you want some strawberries?*

Forming the negative

When used with verbs, the negative has two parts in French, **ne** going before the verb and **pas** going after it; **ne** becomes **n'** before a verb beginning with a vowel or an unsounded **h**:

je **ne** veux **pas** venir avec vous   *I do not want to come with you*
elle **n'**aime **pas** les chats   *she does not like cats*

In compound tenses, the negative is applied to the auxiliary verb, as in English:

elle **n'a pas** fini son travail   *she has not finished her work*

In questions using the inverted form, the two parts of the negative surround the verb and the pronoun:

ne souhaitez-vous **pas** vous asseoir?   *do you not wish to sit down?*

Glossary of grammatical terms

Active A verb form which expresses that the subject is performing or is responsible for the action of the verb: he *is making* an omelette il *fait une omelette*

Adverb A word that describes or modifies the meaning of a verb, an adjective, or another adverb: she speaks *quickly* elle parle *vite*

Auxiliary verb A verb which is used with another verb in order to form a tense of that verb: she *has* forgotten elle *a* oublié

Conditional tense A verb tense that expresses what might happen if something else occurred or was the case: I *would buy* a car j'*achèterais une voiture*

Conjugate The way in which the form of verbs changes according to their tense and the subject of the verb within the tense: I *am* je *suis*; he *was* il *était*

Conjugation One of the three groups of verbs in French; these are identified by their infinitives and present participles; the first two, -er and -ir verbs, are regular; most verbs in the third group are irregular

Consonant A letter representing a sound that can only be used together with a vowel, thus all the letters of the alphabet, with the exception of **a, e, i, o, u**

Definite article In English *the*, in French *le* or *la* for a singular noun, according to the gender of the noun, and *les* for a plural noun: *the* dog le *chien*; *the* table la *table*; *the* houses les *maisons*

Direct object The noun or pronoun directly affected by the verb: he likes *dogs* il aime *les chiens*

Ending The letters added to the stem of a verb, according to the tense and the person and number (singular or plural) of the subject

Feminine see Gender

Future perfect tense The tense that expresses what will have happened by a certain time; the verb has two parts, an auxiliary verb, usually *avoir* but in some cases *être*, in the future tense, followed by the past participle of the verb: they *will have eaten* ils *auront mangé*

Future tense The tense of a verb that expresses something that will happen in the future: she *will leave* tomorrow elle *partira demain*

Gender There are two genders for nouns in French: masculine and feminine; these are most clearly indicated by the article used with the noun; adjectives and pronouns also carry gender information

Imperative A verb form that is used to express a command: *bring* your passport *apportez* votre passeport

Imperfect tense A verb form which expresses a continuous or habitual action in the past: I *was reading* the newspaper je *lisais* le journal

Indefinite article In English *a* or *an*, in French *un* or *une*, according to the gender of the noun: *a* man *un* homme; *a* woman *une* femme

Indicative A verb form that is used when stating a fact: Sophie *lived* in Paris Sophie *habitait* Paris

Indirect object The noun or pronoun indirectly affected by the verb and at which the direct object is aimed: I gave *her* the flowers je *lui* ai donné les fleurs

Infinitive The basic part of a verb and the one that you generally look up in a dictionary or verb book: *aimer* and *finir* are infinitives

Irregular verb A verb which does not fall into one of the two groups of regular verbs

Masculine see Gender

Part of speech A grammatical term for the function of a word: *verb*, *noun*, and *adjective* are examples of parts of speech

Passive A verb form which expresses something being done to the subject of the verb, rather than the subject performing the action of the verb: he *was killed* il *a été tué*

Past historic The tense of a verb nowadays used almost exclusively in literary French to describe something that happened or was completed in the past; it has been replaced in spoken and much written French by the perfect tense

Past participle The part of the verb that is used with an auxiliary verb to form certain past tenses; many also function as adjectives: I have *ironed* my shirt **j'ai repassé ma chemise**; an *ironed* shirt **une chemise *repassée***

Perfect conditional tense A verb tense that expresses what might have happened if something else had occurred or been the case; the verb has two parts, an auxiliary verb, usually *avoir* but in some cases *être*, in the conditional tense, followed by the past participle: I *would have bought* a car **j'*aurais acheté* une voiture**

Perfect tense The tense most commonly used in French to express something that happened in the past; the verb has two parts, an auxiliary verb, usually *avoir* but in some cases *être*, in the present tense, followed by the past participle: she *saw/has seen* the film **elle *a vu* le film**

Person One of six possible types of verb subject, in English, I, you, and he/she/it/ one in the singular, and we, you (more than one person), and they in the plural; these are usually called the first, second and third person singular and the first, second, and third person plural; the verb changes its form within a tense according to the person

Pluperfect tense The tense of a verb that expresses something that had happened before something else; the verb has two parts, an auxiliary verb, usually *avoir*, but in some cases *être*, in the imperfect tense, followed by the past participle of the verb: she *had forgotten* **elle *avait oublié***

Plural referring to more than one: *we, you* (more than one person), and *they* are plural subjects of a verb; in French these are *nous, vous*, and *ils/elles*; *vous* is also used to address someone in the singular whom one does not know well

Preposition A word that stands before a noun, pronoun, or verb relating it to the rest of the sentence; verbs in French are very often followed by either *à* or *de* when they are followed by another verb in the infinitive: I learned to do it **j'ai**

appris *à* le faire; I refused to do it **j'ai refusé *de* le faire**

Present participle The part of the verb which is used to describe a continuous activity: while *dancing* **en *dansant***

Present tense The tense of a verb that expresses something that is happening or is the case now: I *like* strawberries **j'*aime* les fraises**

Pronoun A word that stands instead of a noun: she **elle**

Reflexive pronoun The pronoun which is the object of a reflexive verb: she is washing *herself* **elle *se* lave**

Reflexive verb A verb whose object is the same as its subject: I washed *myself* **je *me* suis lavé**

Regular verb Regular verbs fall into two groups; these are identified by their infinitives and present participles as *-er* and *-ir* verbs; apart from some minor variations to do with pronunciation, the stem of regular verbs does not change; most other verbs are irregular

Singular referring to just one, so *I, you* (only one person), *he/she/one* are singular subjects of a verb; in French, these are *je, tu*, and *il/elle/on*

Stem For regular verbs, this is the part of the infinitive before the *-er* or *-ir*, ending: **fin-*ir***; most irregular verbs also have an identifiable stem in the infinitive: **fall-*oir***

Subject The noun or pronoun that is responsible for the action of the verb: *birds* fly **les oiseaux volent**; *she* writes novels **elle écrit des romans**

Subjunctive A verb form that is used to express a desire, doubt, or unlikelihood: I want her to come **je veux *qu'elle vienne***

Tense The form of a verb that indicates when the action takes place

Verb A word or phrase that expresses what is being done, what is happening, or what is the case: she *was sleeping* **elle *dormait***

Vowel A letter representing a sound that can be spoken by itself; the vowels are: **a, e, i, o, u**

Verb Patterns

1 acheter to buy

irregular verb
conjugates with **avoir** *in compound tenses*

Imperative	Present participle	Past participle
achète (tu)	achetant	acheté
achetons (nous)		
achetez (vous)		

Present
j'achète
tu achètes
il/elle achète
nous achetons
vous achetez
ils/elles achètent

Past Historic
j'achetai
tu achetas
il/elle acheta
nous achetâmes
vous achetâtes
ils/elles achetèrent

Future
j'achèterai
tu achèteras
il/elle achètera
nous achèterons
vous achèterez
ils/elles achèteront

Conditional
j'achèterais
tu achèterais
il/elle achèterait
nous achèterions
vous achèteriez
ils/elles achèteraient

Imperfect
j'achetais
tu achetais
il/elle achetait
nous achetions
vous achetiez
ils/elles achetaient

Present subjunctive
(que) j'achète
(que) tu achètes
(qu') il/elle achète
(que) nous achetions
(que) vous achetiez
(qu') ils/elles achètent

Perfect
j'ai acheté
tu as acheté
il/elle a acheté
nous avons acheté
vous avez acheté
ils/elles ont acheté

Imperfect subjunctive
(que) j'achetasse
(que) tu achetasses
(qu') il/elle achetât
(que) nous achetassions
(que) vous achetassiez
(qu') ils/elles achetassent

Some common verbs that follow the same pattern

crocheter	*to crochet*	haleter	*to pant*
fileter	*to fillet*	racheter	*to buy*

How the verb works

j'achète tous mes légumes au marché	*I buy all my vegetables on the market*
elle n'a rien acheté	*she didn't buy/hasn't bought anything*
nous achèterons les cadeaux ensemble	*we'll buy the presents together*
il faut que j'achète du beurre	*I have to buy butter*
je l'ai acheté au supermarché	*I bought it in the supermarket*
elle l'a acheté chez Durand	*she bought it in Durand's*
je vais acheter un livre à ma copine	*I'm going to buy my friend a book/I'm going to buy a book from my friend*
elle lui a acheté des fleurs	*she (has) bought him/her some flowers*
je t'achèterai une montre	*I'll buy you a watch*
on va s'acheter un nouveau canapé	*we're going to buy ourselves a new sofa*
tu devrais t'acheter un ordinateur	*you should buy yourself a computer*

Language in use

elle a acheté pour cinquante francs de fraises	*she bought fifty francs' worth of strawberries*
je l'ai acheté trente francs	*I bought it for thirty francs*
nous essayons d'acheter français	*we try to buy French products*
cela s'achète où?	*where can you get it?*
cela s'achète en pharmacie	*you can buy it in the chemist's*
cela ne s'achète pas	*it's something money can't buy*
je dois racheter du vin	*I need to buy some more wine*
je n'aime plus ces rideaux, je vais en racheter	*I don't like these curtains any more, I'm going to buy some new ones*
il m'a racheté ma voiture	*he bought my car off me*

2 acquérir to acquire

irregular verb
conjugates with **avoir** *in compound tenses*

Imperative	Present participle	Past participle
acquiers (tu)	acquér**ant**	acquis
acquér**ons** (nous)		
acquér**ez** (vous)		

Present
j'acquiers
tu acquiers
il/elle acquiert
nous acquér**ons**
vous acquér**ez**
ils/elles acquièrent

Past Historic
j'acquis
tu acquis
il/elle acquit
nous acquîmes
vous acquîtes
ils/elles acquirent

Future
j'acquerrai
tu acquerras
il/elle acquerra
nous acquerrons
vous acquerrez
ils/elles acquerront

Conditional
j'acquerrais
tu acquerrais
il/elle acquerrait
nous acquerrions
vous acquerriez
ils/elles acquerraient

Imperfect
j'acquér**ais**
tu acquér**ais**
il/elle acquér**ait**
nous acquér**ions**
vous acquér**iez**
ils/elles acquér**aient**

Present subjunctive
(que) j'acquière
(que) tu acquières
(qu') il/elle acquière
(que) nous acquér**ions**
(que) vous acquér**iez**
(qu') ils/elles acquièrent

Perfect
j'**ai** acquis
tu **as** acquis
il/elle **a** acquis
nous **avons** acquis
vous **avez** acquis
ils/elles **ont** acquis

Imperfect subjunctive
(que) j'acquisse
(que) tu acquisses
(qu') il/elle acquît
(que) nous acquissions
(que) vous acquissiez
(qu') ils/elles acquissent

Some common verbs that follow the same pattern

conquérir	*to conquer*	requérir	*to ask for/*
s'enquérir de	*to inquire about*		*require*

How the verb works

ils ont acquis un manuscrit rare	*they've acquired a rare manuscript*
la municipalité cherche à acquérir le terrain	*the local council is seeking to purchase the land*
elle a acquis une certaine notoriété dans le milieu artistique	*she has acquired a certain notoriety in artistic circles*

mon cousin a acquis par héritage une grande maison à la campagne	*my cousin has inherited a big house in the country*
leur maison a acquis de la valeur	*their house has gained in value*
il est maintenant acquis que nous devons agir	*it is now accepted that we must act*
il est acquis à notre cause	*we have his support*
l'expérience s'acquiert avec l'âge	*experience comes with age*
le pays a été conquis par les Romains	*the country was conquered by the Romans*
leur nouveau produit a vite conquis le marché	*their new product rapidly conquered the market*
leur talent a conquis Paris	*their talent captivated Paris*
elle se croit en pays conquis	*she lords it over everyone*
il s'est enquis de ma mère	*he enquired after my mother*
les refugiés requièrent la protection de l'ONU	*the refugees are asking for UN protection*
c'est une situation qui requiert des compétences spécifiques	*it is a situation which requires specific skills*

3 **aimer** to love/like

regular **-er** *verb*
conjugates with **avoir** *in compound tenses*

Imperative	**Present participle**	**Past participle**
aime (tu)	aimant	aimé
aimons (nous)		
aimez (vous)		

Present
j'aime
tu aimes
il/elle aime
nous aimons
vous aimez
ils/elles aiment

Past historic
j'aimai
tu aimas
il/elle aima
nous aimâmes
vous aimâtes
ils/elles aimèrent

Future
j'aimerai
tu aimeras
il/elle aimera
nous aimerons
vous aimerez
ils/elles aimeront

Conditional
j'aimerais
tu aimerais
il/elle aimerait
nous aimerions
vous aimeriez
ils/elles aimeraient

Imperfect
j'aimais
tu aimais
il/elle aimait
nous aimions
vous aimiez
ils/elles aimaient

Present subjunctive
(que) j'aime
(que) tu aimes
(qu') il/elle aime
(que) nous aimions
(que) vous aimiez
(qu') ils/elles aiment

Perfect
j'ai aimé
tu as aimé
il/elle a aimé
nous avons aimé
vous avez aimé
ils/elles ont aimé

Imperfect subjunctive
(que) j'aimasse
(que) tu aimasses
(qu') il/elle aimât
(que) nous aimassions
(que) vous aimassiez
(qu') ils/elles aimassent

Some common verbs that follow the same pattern

aider	to help	entrer	to go/come in
allumer	to light		
amuser	to amuse	fermer	to close
apporter	to bring	inviter	to invite
arrêter	to stop; to arrest	jouer	to play
		louer	to rent/let
attraper	to catch	marcher	to walk
chanter	to sing	monter	to go/take up
chercher	to look for	montrer	to show
danser	to dance	parler	to speak
décider	to decide	penser	to think
déjeuner	to have lunch	pleurer	to cry, weep
demander	to ask (for)	porter	to carry/wear
dîner	to have dinner/supper	pousser	to push
		prêter	to lend
		regarder	to look at/watch
donner	to give		
écouter	to listen	tirer	to pull
		trouver	to find

✧this is a small selection of the regular verbs whose infinitive ends in **-er**; this is by far the largest group of French verbs and new verbs which are created in the language always conjugate like this

How the verb works

elle aime les chats mais elle n'aime pas les chiens	she likes cats but she doesn't like dogs
j'aime bien ta jupe	I like your skirt
il aime se promener dans les bois	he likes walking in the woods
j'aimerais la revoir un jour	I'd like to see her again one day
aimeriez-vous un peu de thé?	would you like some tea?
j'aimerais que tu me dises la vérité	I'd like you to tell me the truth

---

Language in use

elles s'aiment bien	they're very fond of each other
elle aime mieux nager que courir	she prefers swimming to running
j'aimerais mieux y aller demain	I'd rather go tomorrow
j'aimerais mieux que tu ne le lui dises pas	I'd rather you didn't tell him

4 aller to go

irregular verb
conjugates with être *in compound tenses*

Imperative	Present participle	Past participle
va (tu)	allant	allé/-e(s)
allons (nous)		
allez (vous)		

Present
je vais
tu vas
il/elle va
nous allons
vous allez
ils/elles vont

Past Historic
j'allai
tu allas
il/elle alla
nous allâmes
vous allâtes
ils/elles allèrent

Future
j'irai
tu iras
il/elle ira
nous irons
vous irez
ils/elles iront

Conditional
j'irais
tu irais
il/elle irait
nous irions
vous iriez
ils/elles iraient

Imperfect
j'allais
tu allais
il/elle allait
nous allions
vous alliez
ils/elles allaient

Present subjunctive
(que) j'aille
(que) tu ailles
(qu') il/elle aille
(que) nous allions
(que) vous alliez
(qu') ils/elles aillent

Perfect
je suis allé/-e
tu es allé/-e
il/elle est allé/-ée
nous sommes allés/-ées
vous êtes allé/-e(s)
ils/elles sont allés/-ées

Imperfect subjunctive
(que) j'allasse
(que) tu allasses
(qu') il/elle allât
(que) nous allassions
(que) vous allassiez
(qu') ils/elles allassent

How the verb works

nous allons au cinéma ce soir	*we're going to the cinema this evening*
je vais en France tous les étés	*I go to France every summer*
ils sont allés en ville	*they've gone into town*
elle va chez le dentiste	*she's going to the dentist's*
je m'en vais à six heures	*I'm leaving at six*

● *used with another verb in the infinitive*

elle va nous appeler ce soir	*she's going to ring us this evening*
je vais partir à cinq heures	*I'm leaving at five*
tu vas te faire mal!	*you'll hurt yourself!*
va demander à ton frère de t'aider	*go and ask your brother to help you*
qu'est-ce qu'on va faire?	*what are we going to do?*
ah te voilà, j'allais partir justement	*oh there you are, I was just about to leave*

● *talking about how people or things are*

comment vas-tu?/comment ça va?/ça va?	*how are you?*
ça va (bien)	*I'm fine*
comment vont tes parents?	*how are your parents?*

Language in use

est-ce que tu es déjà allé à Paris?	*have you ever been to Paris?*
nous y sommes allés à pied	*we walked there*
elle va au travail en vélo/en voiture	*she cycles/drives to work*
je m'en vais!	*I'm off!*
va savoir!	*who knows?*
si tout va bien	*if all goes well*
qu'est-ce qui ne va pas?	*what's the matter?*
ça va comme ça?	*is that okay?*
ça va comme ça	*that's fine (like that)*
ça te va?	*is that okay with you?*
ça ne va pas du tout	*that's no good at all*
ça va de soi	*it goes without saying*
ça va pas la tête?*	*are you crazy?*
cette robe te va très bien	*that dress really suits you*

5 appeler to call

irregular verb
conjugates with **avoir** *in compound tenses*

Imperative	Present participle	Past participle
appelle (tu)	appelant	appelé
appelons (nous)		
appelez (vous)		

Present
j'appelle
tu appelles
il/elle appelle
nous appelons
vous appelez
ils/elles appellent

Past Historic
j'appelai
tu appelas
il/elle appela
nous appelâmes
vous appelâtes
ils/elles appelèrent

Future
j'appellerai
tu appelleras
il/elle appellera
nous appellerons
vous appellerez
ils/elles appelleront

Conditional
j'appellerais
tu appellerais
il/elle appellerait
nous appellerions
vous appelleriez
ils/elles appelleraient

Imperfect
j'appelais
tu appelais
il/elle appelait
nous appelions
vous appeliez
ils/elles appelaient

Present subjunctive
(que) j'appelle
(que) tu appelles
(qu') il/elle appelle
(que) nous appelions
(que) vous appeliez
(qu') ils/elles appellent

Perfect
j'ai appelé
tu as appelé
il/elle a appelé
nous avons appelé
vous avez appelé
ils/elles ont appelé

Imperfect subjunctive
(que) j'appelasse
(que) tu appelasses
(qu') il/elle appelât
(que) nous appelassions
(que) vous appelassiez
(qu') ils/elles appelassent

Some common verbs that follow the same pattern

amonceler	to pile up	harceler	to pester
atteler	to harness	jumeler	to twin
chanceler	to stagger	museler	to muzzle
dételer	to unharness	niveler	to level
ficeler	to tie up	rappeler	to remind/ call back
grommeler	to grumble	renouveler	to renew

How the verb works

appelle les enfants pour manger	call the children to come and eat
si elle ne va pas mieux demain, j'appellerai le médecin	if she isn't better tomorrow, I'll call the doctor
appelez-moi un taxi, s'il vous plaît	call me a taxi please
ton frère a appelé trois fois ce matin	your brother rang/called three times this morning
on s'appelle tous les soirs	we ring/call each other every evening
comment ont-ils appelé leur fille?	what have they called their daughter?
ils l'ont appelée Marie	they've called her Marie
tu t'appelles comment?	what's your name?
elle s'appelle Cécile	her name is Cécile/she's called Cécile
comment s'appelle cette fleur en français?	what's this flower called in French?

Language in use

les syndicats ont appelé à la grève	the unions have called for strike action
je leur ai rappelé qu'il est interdit de fumer dans les couloirs	I reminded them that it's forbidden to smoke in the corridors
rappelez-moi votre nom	remind me what your name is
je ne me rappelle plus	I can't remember
je me rappelle l'avoir vu il y a dix ans à Nice	I remember seeing him ten years ago in Nice
demande-lui de rappeler tout à l'heure	ask him to call back later

6 assaillir to attack

irregular verb
conjugates with **avoir** *in compound tenses*

Imperative	Present participle	Past participle
assaille (tu)	assaillant	assailli
assaillons (nous)		
assaillez (vous)		

Present
j'assaille
tu assailles
il/elle assaille
nous assaillons
vous assaillez
ils/elles assaillent

Past Historic
j'assaillis
tu assaillis
il/elle assaillit
nous assaillîmes
vous assaillîtes
ils/elles assaillirent

Future
j'assaillirai
tu assailliras
il/elle assaillira
nous assaillirons
vous assaillirez
ils/elles assailliront

Conditional
j'assaillirais
tu assaillirais
il/elle assaillirait
nous assaillirions
vous assailliriez
ils/elles assailliraient

Imperfect
j'assaillais
tu assaillais
il/elle assaillait
nous assaillions
vous assailliez
ils/elles assaillaient

Present subjunctive
(que) j'assaille
(que) tu assailles
(qu') il/elle assaille
(que) nous assaillions
(que) vous assailliez
(qu') ils/elles assaillent

Perfect
j'ai assailli
tu as assailli
il/elle a assailli
nous avons assailli
vous avez assailli
ils/elles ont assailli

Imperfect subjunctive
(que) j'assaillisse
(que) tu assaillisses
(qu') il/elle assaillît
(que) nous assaillissions
(que) vous assaillissiez
(qu') ils/elles assaillissent

How the verb works

la ville a été assaillie par les rebelles	*the town was attacked by the rebels*
ils ont été assaillis par les médias à la sortie de la réunion	*they were set upon by the media when they came out of the meeting*
ils m'ont assailli de questions	*they bombarded me with questions*
être assailli par le doute	*to be assailed by doubts*

7 s'asseoir to sit

irregular verb
conjugates with **être** *in compound tenses*

Imperative	Present participle	Past participle
assieds-toi	s'asseyant	assis/-e(s)
asseyons-nous		
asseyez-vous		

Present
je m'assieds
tu t'assieds
il/elle s'assied
nous nous asseyons
vous vous asseyez
ils/elles s'asseyent

Past Historic
je m'assis
tu t'assis
il/elle s'assit
nous nous assîmes
vous vous assîtes
ils/elles s'assirent

Future
je m'assiérai
tu t'assiéras
il/elle s'assiéra
nous nous assiérons
vous vous assiérez
ils/elles s'assiéront

Conditional
je m'assiérais
tu t'assiérais
il/elle s'assiérait
nous nous assiérions
vous vous assiériez
ils/elles s'assiéraient

Imperfect
je m'asseyais
tu t'asseyais
il/elle s'asseyait
nous nous asseyions
vous vous asseyiez
ils/elles s'asseyaient

Present subjunctive
(que) je m'asseye
(que) tu t'asseyes
(qu') il/elle s'asseye
(que) nous nous asseyions
(que) vous vous asseyiez
(qu') ils/elles s'asseyent

Perfect
je me suis assis/-e
tu t'es assis/-e
il/elle s'est assis/-e
nous nous sommes assis/-es
vous vous êtes assis/-e(s)
ils/elles se sont assis(es)

Imperfect subjunctive
(que) je m'assisse
(que) tu t'assisses
(qu') il/elle s'assît
(que) nous nous assissions
(que) vous vous assissiez
(qu') ils/elles s'assissent

Following the same pattern

se rasseoir   *to sit down again*

How the verb works

je vais asseoir mon père à votre droite	*I'll sit my father on your right*
il a assis l'enfant sur ses genoux	*he sat the child on his knee*
elle m'a fait asseoir près de la cheminée	*she offered me a seat by the fire*
je me suis assise sur une chaise à côté de la fenêtre	*I sat down on a chair by the window*
assieds-toi dans le fauteuil vert	*sit down in the green armchair*
asseyez-vous	*do sit down*
voulez-vous vous asseoir?	*would you like to sit down?*
les invités se sont assis autour de la table	*the guests sat down at the table*

Language in use

je me suis assis dessus	*I sat on it*
il n'y a rien pour s'asseoir	*there's nothing to sit on*
ça m'a assise!*	*I was staggered!*
le président s'est rassis	*the president sat down again*

8 assiéger to besiege

irregular verb
conjugates with **avoir** *in compound tenses*

Imperative	Present participle	Past participle
assiège (tu)	assiégeant	assiégé
assiégeons (nous)		
assiégez (vous)		

Present
j'assiège
tu assièges
il/elle assiège
nous assiégeons
vous assiégez
ils/elles assiègent

Past Historic
j'assiégeai
tu assiégeas
il/elle assiégea
nous assiégeâmes
vous assiégeâtes
ils/elles assiégèrent

Future
j'assiégerai
tu assiégeras
il/elle assiégera
nous assiégerons
vous assiégerez
ils/elles assiégeront

Conditional
j'assiégerais
tu assiégerais
il/elle assiégerait
nous assiégerions
vous assiégeriez
ils/elles assiégeraient

Imperfect
j'assiégeais
tu assiégeais
il/elle assiégeait
nous assiégions
vous assiégiez
ils/elles assiégeaient

Present subjunctive
(que) j'assiège
(que) tu assièges
(qu') il/elle assiège
(que) nous assiégions
(que) vous assiégiez
(qu') ils/elles assiègent

Perfect
j'**ai** assiégé
tu **as** assiégé
il/elle **a** assiégé
nous **avons** assiégé
vous **avez** assiégé
ils/elles **ont** assiégé

Imperfect subjunctive
(que) j'assiégeasse
(que) tu assiégeasses
(qu') il/elle assiégeât
(que) nous assiégeassions
(que) vous assiégeassiez
(qu') ils/elles assiégeassent

Some common verbs that follow the same pattern

alléger	*to lighten*	piéger	*to trap*
désagréger	*to disintegrate*	protéger	*to protect*
		siéger	*to sit*

How the verb works

la ville assiégée	*the besieged town*
la ville a été assiégée pendant six mois	*the town was under siege for six months*
le centre d'information a été assiégé par des touristes pendant toute la journée	*the information centre was besieged by tourists all day*
hier matin une foule de journalistes a assiégé la maison du chanteur	*yesterday morning a crowd of journalists laid siege to the singer's house*

Language in use

je vais enlever des livres pour alléger mon sac	*I'll take out some books so as to lighten my bag*
le gouvernement a promis d'alléger les impôts	*the government has promised tax cuts*
la sculpture s'est désagrégée sous la pluie	*the sculpture has disintegrated in the rain*
le voleur s'est fait piéger par la police	*the thief was trapped by the police*
hier soir trois soldats ont été tués par une voiture piégée	*last night three soldiers were killed by a booby-trapped car*
le gouvernement a lancé une campagne pour protéger l'environnement	*the government has launched a campaign to protect the environment*
elle a vite appris à se protéger contre les critiques	*she quickly learned to protect herself against critical comments*
ta terrasse est bien protégée du vent	*your terrace is well protected from the wind*
elle siège à plusieurs conseils d'administration	*she sits on several boards of directors*
l'organisation siège à Paris	*the organization has its headquarters in Paris*

9 avoir to have

irregular verb
conjugates with **avoir** *in compound tenses*

Imperative	Present participle	Past participle
aie (tu)	ayant	eu
ayons (nous)		
ayez (vous)		

Present
j'ai
tu as
il/elle a
nous av**ons**
vous av**ez**
ils/elles ont

Past Historic
j'eus
tu eus
il/elle eut
nous eûmes
vous eûtes
ils/elles eurent

Future
j'aurai
tu auras
il/elle aura
nous aurons
vous aurez
ils/elles auront

Conditional
j'aurais
tu aurais
il/elle aurait
nous aurions
vous auriez
ils/elles auraient

Imperfect
j'av**ais**
tu av**ais**
il/elle av**ait**
nous av**ions**
vous av**iez**
ils/elles av**aient**

Present subjunctive
(que) j'aie
(que) tu aies
(qu') il/elle ait
(que) nous ayons
(que) vous ayez
(qu') ils/elles aient

Perfect
j'**ai** eu
tu **as** eu
il/elle **a** eu
nous **avons** eu
vous **avez** eu
ils/elles **ont** eu

Imperfect subjunctive
(que) j'eusse
(que) tu eusses
(qu') il/elle eût
(que) nous eussions
(que) vous eussiez
(qu') ils/elles eussent

How the verb works

● *expressing possession or availability*

elle a beaucoup de livres	*she has/she's got lots of books*
nous n'avons pas assez de temps	*we don't have/haven't got enough time*
il a les yeux bleus	*he has blue eyes*

● *expressing age*

elle a cinq ans	*she's five (years old)*
il aura vingt ans cette année	*he'll be twenty this year*

● *expressing certain sensations*

j'ai froid/chaud/peur	*I'm cold/hot/afraid*
j'ai faim/soif	*I'm hungry/thirsty*
j'ai mal à la tête	*I have a headache*
qu'est-ce qu'elle a?	*what's wrong with her?*

● *as auxiliary used in forming the perfect, pluperfect, and future perfect tenses of most verbs*

j'ai vu Sophie hier	*I saw Sophie yesterday*
qu'est-ce qu'il a dit?	*what did he say?*
je te l'ai déjà dit	*I've already told you*
elle avait oublié mon nom	*she had forgotten my name*

● *expressions with 'n'avoir qu'à'*

tu n'as qu'à m'écrire	*you only have to write to me*
tu n'avais qu'à me le dire	*you should have told me*

● *'il y a' is used to mean 'there is/are'*

il y a un verre sur la table	*there's a glass on the table*
il n'y a pas de tasses	*there are no cups*
il n'y a plus de riz	*there's no rice left*
il y avait trois chats sur le canapé	*there were three cats on the sofa*
combien de couteaux y a-t-il?	*how many knives are there?*
qu'est-ce qu'il y a dans le frigo?	*what is there in the fridge?*
qu'est-ce qu'il y a?	*what's the matter?/what's going on?*

● *'il y a' in time expressions*

elle est venue ici il y a cinq ans	*she came here five years ago*

10 **battre** to hit

irregular verb
conjugates with **avoir** *in compound tenses*

Imperative	Present participle	Past participle
bats (tu)	battant	battu
battons (nous)		
battez (vous)		

Present
je bats
tu bats
il/elle bat
nous battons
vous battez
ils/elles battent

Past Historic
je battis
tu battis
il/elle battit
nous battîmes
vous battîtes
ils/elles battirent

Future
je battrai
tu battras
il/elle battra
nous battrons
vous battrez
ils/elles battront

Conditional
je battrais
tu battrais
il/elle battrait
nous battrions
vous battriez
ils/elles battraient

Imperfect
je battais
tu battais
il/elle battait
nous battions
vous battiez
ils/elles battaient

Present subjunctive
(que) je batte
(que) tu battes
(qu') il/elle batte
(que) nous battions
(que) vous battiez
(qu') ils/elles battent

Perfect
j'ai battu
tu as battu
il/elle a battu
nous avons battu
vous avez battu
ils/elles ont battu

Imperfect subjunctive
(que) je battisse
(que) tu battisses
(qu') il/elle battît
(que) nous battissions
(que) vous battissiez
(qu') ils/elles battissent

Some common verbs that follow the same pattern

abattre	to slaughter/ shoot down	s'ébattre	to frolic about
combattre	to fight	rabattre	to pull down etc.
débattre	to debate		

How the verb works

elle l'a battu aux échecs	she beat him at chess
il bat son chien	he beats his dog
son cœur battait plus vite	his/her heart beat faster
la porte battait dans le vent	the door was banging in the wind
le vent fait battre les volets	the wind is banging the shutters
ils se battaient entre eux	they were fighting
il s'est battu avec son frère	he had a fight with his brother
leurs enfants n'arrêtent pas de se battre	their children are always fighting
elle s'est battue contre la corruption	she fought against corruption

on s'est fait battre par quatre à deux	we lost four-two
il l'a battue à coups de poing	he punched her repeatedly
la victime avait été battue à mort	the victim had been beaten to death
la pluie battait les vitres	the rain was lashing against the windows
battre les œufs en neige	beat the egg whites until stiff
la soirée bat son plein	the party's in full swing
il a été abattu par un terroriste	he was shot down by a terrorist
ne te laisse pas abattre	keep your spirits up
une campagne pour combattre la délinquance informatique	a campaign to fight computer crime

11 **boire** to drink

irregular verb
conjugates with **avoir** *in compound tenses*

Imperative	**Present participle**	**Past participle**
bois (tu)	buvant	bu
buvons (nous)		
buvez (vous)		

Present
je bois
tu bois
il/elle boit
nous buvons
vous buvez
ils/elles boivent

Past Historic
je bus
tu bus
il/elle but
nous bûmes
vous bûtes
ils/elles burent

Future
je boirai
tu boiras
il/elle boira
nous boirons
vous boirez
ils/elles boiront

Conditional
je boirais
tu boirais
il/elle boirait
nous boirions
vous boiriez
ils/elles boiraient

Imperfect
je buvais
tu buvais
il/elle buvait
nous buvions
vous buviez
ils/elles buvaient

Present subjunctive
(que) je boive
(que) tu boives
(qu') il/elle boive
(que) nous buvions
(que) vous buviez
(qu') ils/elles boivent

Perfect
j'ai bu
tu as bu
il/elle a bu
nous avons bu
vous avez bu
ils/elles ont bu

Imperfect subjunctive
(que) je busse
(que) tu busses
(qu') il/elle bût
(que) nous bussions
(que) vous bussiez
(qu') ils/elles bussent

How the verb works

elle a bu un verre d'eau	*she drank a glass of water*
il ne boit pas	*he doesn't drink*
elle ne boit que de l'eau	*she only drinks water*
qu'est-ce que vous voulez boire?	*what would you like to drink?*
tu n'as pas bu ton café	*you haven't drunk your coffee*
nous buvions du champagne	*we were drinking champagne*
je bois toujours mon café dans un bol	*I always drink my coffee out of a bowl*
ce vin se boit frais	*this wine should be drunk chilled*

Language in use

son mari m'a versé à boire	*her husband poured me a drink*
il a fait boire le chien	*he gave the dog a drink*
nous avons bu à la santé de mon père	*we drank to my father's health*
buvons à la réussite de votre fille	*let us drink to your daughter's success*
ce vin n'est pas encore bon à boire	*this wine isn't ready to drink yet*
le vin rosé est à boire frais	*rosé should be drunk chilled*
allons boire un verre	*let's go for a drink*
si on allait boire un coup?*	*how about going for a drink?*
il a bu un coup de trop*	*he's had one too many*
elle s'est mise à boire	*she's taken to drink*
c'est un vin qui se boit bien	*it's a very drinkable wine*

12 **bouillir** to boil

irregular verb
conjugates with **avoir** *in compound tenses*

Imperative	Present participle	Past participle
bous (tu)	bouillant	bouilli
bouillons (nous)		
bouillez (vous)		

Present
je bous
tu bous
il/elle bout
nous bouillons
vous bouillez
ils/elles bouillent

Past Historic
je bouillis
tu bouillis
il/elle bouillit
nous bouillîmes
vous bouillîtes
ils/elles bouillirent

Future
je bouillirai
tu bouilliras
il/elle bouillira
nous bouillirons
vous bouillirez
ils/elles bouilliront

Conditional
je bouillirais
tu bouillirais
il/elle bouillirait
nous bouillirions
vous bouilliriez
ils/elles bouilliraient

Imperfect
je bouillais
tu bouillais
il/elle bouillait
nous bouillions
vous bouilliez
ils/elles bouillaient

Present subjunctive
(que) je bouille
(que) tu bouilles
(qu') il/elle bouille
(que) nous bouillions
(que) vous bouilliez
(qu') ils/elles bouillent

Perfect
j'ai bouilli
tu as bouilli
il/elle a bouilli
nous avons bouilli
vous avez bouilli
ils/elles ont bouilli

Imperfect subjunctive
(que) je bouillisse
(que) tu bouillisses
(qu') il/elle bouillît
(que) nous bouillissions
(que) vous bouillissiez
(qu') ils/elles bouillissent

How the verb works

l'eau bout	*the water is boiling*
je vais faire bouillir de l'eau	*I'm going to boil some water*
il faut faire bouillir l'eau avant de mettre les légumes	*you must bring the water to the boil before you put the vegetables in*
faire bouillir pendant dix minutes	*boil for ten minutes*
du lait bouilli	*boiled milk*
je vais mettre ces draps à bouillir	*I'm going to boil these sheets*

Language in use

je bouillais intérieurement	*I was seething inside*
il bouillait de rage	*he was seething with rage*

13 **céder** to give up

irregular verb
conjugates with **avoir** *in compound tenses*

Imperative	**Present participle**	**Past participle**
cède (tu)	cédant	cédé
cédons (nous)		
cédez (vous)		

Present
je cède
tu cèdes
il/elle cède
nous cédons
vous cédez
ils/elles cèdent

Past Historic
je cédai
tu cédas
il/elle céda
nous cédâmes
vous cédâtes
ils/elles cédèrent

Future
je céderai
tu céderas
il/elle cédera
nous céderons
vous céderez
ils/elles céderont

Conditional
je céderais
tu céderais
il/elle céderait
nous céderions
vous céderiez
ils/elles céderaient

Imperfect
je cédais
tu cédais
il/elle cédait
nous cédions
vous cédiez
ils/elles cédaient

Present subjunctive
(que) je cède
(que) tu cèdes
(qu') il/elle cède
(que) nous cédions
(que) vous cédiez
(qu') ils/elles cèdent

Perfect
j'ai cédé
tu as cédé
il/elle a cédé
nous avons cédé
vous avez cédé
ils/elles ont cédé

Imperfect subjunctive
(que) je cédasse
(que) tu cédasses
(qu') il/elle cédât
(que) nous cédassions
(que) vous cédassiez
(qu') ils/elles cédassent

Some common verbs that follow the same pattern

accélérer	to accelerate	obséder	to obsess
célébrer	to celebrate	opérer	to operate
compléter	to complete	pénétrer	to penetrate
considérer	to consider	persévérer	to persevere
coopérer	to cooperate	posséder	to possess
désespérer	to despair	précéder	to precede
désintégrer	to disintegrate	préférer	to prefer
dessécher	to dry out	procéder	to proceed
différer	to differ	refléter	to reflect
digérer	to digest	répéter	to repeat/
espérer	to hope		rehearse
exagérer	to exaggerate	révéler	to reveal
inquiéter	to worry	rouspéter	to grumble
insérer	to insert	sécher	to dry
lécher	to lick	suggérer	to suggest
libérer	to free	tolérer	to tolerate
modérer	to moderate	transférer	to transfer

How the verb works

je cède la parole a mon collègue	I'll hand you over to my colleague
il m'a cédé sa place	he let me have his seat
elle a fini par céder	she ended up by giving in
la branche a cédé	the branch gave way

'cédez le passage'	'give way' (on road sign)
il n'a pas cédé un pouce de terrain	he didn't yield an inch
elle célèbre son anniversaire samedi prochain	she's celebrating her birthday next week
je le considère comme un ami	I consider him to be a friend
ils désespèrent de le retrouver	they've given up hope of finding him
elle espère le voir demain	she's hoping to see him tomorrow
j'espère qu'ils n'ont pas oublié	I hope they haven't forgotten
ça m'inquiète un peu	it's a bit worrying
on va l'opérer du genou demain	he/she's having a knee operation tomorrow
j'aurais préféré la voir moi-même	I would rather have seen her myself
je suggère qu'on s'en aille	I suggest we leave

14 clore to enclose/close (down)

irregular defective verb
conjugates with avoir in compound tenses

Imperative	Present participle	Past participle
clos (tu)	closant	clos

Present
je clos
tu clos
il/elle clôt
nous closons
vous closez
ils/elles closent

Future
je clorai
tu cloras
il/elle clora
nous clorons
vous clorez
ils/elles cloront

Conditional
je clorais
tu clorais
il/elle clorait
nous clorions
vous cloriez
ils/elles cloraient

Present subjunctive
(que) je close
(que) tu closes
(qu') il/elle close
(que) nous closions
(que) vous closiez
(qu') ils/elles closent

Following the same pattern

éclore✧   to hatch/
                     open

✧except that the 3rd person singular of the present tense is
éclot with no circumflex on the **o**

How the verb works

nous allons clore la séance par un débat	*we are going to close the session with a debate*
l'exercice clos le 31 décembre	*the tax year which ended on 31 December*
le festival se clôt par un récital de piano	*the festival ends with a piano recital*

un dîner a clos le congrès	*the conference ended with a dinner*
l'auteur clôt son livre avec un poème	*the author ends his book with a poem*
les œufs éclosent quinze jours plus tard	*the eggs hatch two weeks later*
les fleurs éclosent début mai	*the flowers open at the beginning of May*
ensuite, nous faisons éclore les œufs	*next, we incubate the eggs*

15 conclure to conclude

irregular verb
conjugates with **avoir** *in compound tenses*

Imperative
conclus (tu)
concluons (nous)
concluez (vous)

Present participle
concluant

Past participle
conclu

Present
je conclus
tu conclus
il/elle conclut
nous concluons
vous concluez
ils/elles concluent

Past Historic
je conclus
tu conclus
il/elle conclut
nous conclûmes
vous conclûtes
ils/elles conclurent

Future
je conclurai
tu concluras
il/elle conclura
nous conclurons
vous conclurez
ils/elles concluront

Conditional
je conclurais
tu conclurais
il/elle conclurait
nous conclurions
vous concluriez
ils/elles concluraient

Imperfect
je concluais
tu concluais
il/elle concluait
nous concluions
vous concluiez
ils/elles concluaient

Present subjunctive
(que) je conclue
(que) tu conclues
(qu') il/elle conclue
(que) nous concluions
(que) vous concluiez
(qu') ils/elles concluent

Perfect
j'ai conclu
tu as conclu
il/elle a conclu
nous avons conclu
vous avez conclu
ils/elles ont conclu

Imperfect subjunctive
(que) je conclusse
(que) tu conclusses
(qu') il/elle conclût
(que) nous conclussions
(que) vous conclussiez
(qu') ils/elles conclussent

Following the same pattern

exclure   *to exclude*   inclure✧   *to include*

✧but the past participle of **inclure** is **inclus**

How the verb works

j'ai conclu qu'il ne voulait pas le faire	*I concluded that he didn't want to do it*
que concluez-vous de ces résultats?	*what conclusion do you draw from these results?*
nous avons conclu à la nécessité d'un nouveau système	*we concluded that a new system was needed*
ce concert se conclut par une dernière chanson de Jo et Rachel	*this concert ends with a last song from Jo and Rachel*

Language in use
---

il ne faut pas se hâter d'en conclure que c'était elle	*we mustn't jump to the conclusion that it was her*
les deux pays ont conclu des accords	*the two countries have concluded agreements*
'la situation est donc loin d'être désespérée,' dit-elle pour conclure	*'so the situation is far from hopeless,' she concluded*
ils ont conclu la soirée par quelques chansons	*they finished off the evening with a few songs*
ils ont fini par conclure un marché	*they eventually struck a deal*
marché conclu!	*it's a deal!*
nous n'excluons pas l'éventualité d'un suicide	*we are not ruling out the possibility of suicide*
il a été définitivement exclu de l'école	*he has been expelled from the school*
il est totalement exclu qu'elle vienne ici	*it's absolutely out of the question that she should come here*
il n'est pas exclu qu'il se soit simplement trompé	*it's not impossible that he simply made a mistake*
nous vous incluons sur la liste	*we are including you on the list*
nous serons trente personnes, enfants inclus	*there will be thirty of us, including children*
jusqu'à mardi inclus	*up to and including Tuesday*

16 conduire to drive

irregular verb
conjugates with **avoir** *in compound tenses*

Imperative	Present participle	Past participle
conduis (tu)	conduisant	conduit
conduisons		
(nous)		
conduisez (vous)		

Present
je conduis
tu conduis
il/elle conduit
nous conduisons
vous conduisez
ils/elles conduisent

Past Historic
je conduisis
tu conduisis
il/elle conduisit
nous conduisîmes
vous conduisîtes
ils/elles conduisirent

Future
je conduirai
tu conduiras
il/elle conduira
nous conduirons
vous conduirez
ils/elles conduiront

Conditional
je conduirais
tu conduirais
il/elle conduirait
nous conduirions
vous conduiriez
ils/elles conduiraient

Imperfect
je conduisais
tu conduisais
il/elle conduisait
nous conduisions
vous conduisiez
ils/elles conduisaient

Present subjunctive
(que) je conduise
(que) tu conduises
(qu') il/elle conduise
(que) nous conduisions
(que) vous conduisiez
(qu') ils/elles conduisent

Perfect
j'**ai** conduit
tu **as** conduit
il/elle **a** conduit
nous **avons** conduit
vous **avez** conduit
ils/elles **ont** conduit

Imperfect subjunctive
(que) je conduisisse
(que) tu conduisisses
(qu') il/elle conduisît
(que) nous conduisissions
(que) vous conduisissiez
(qu') ils/elles conduisissent

Following the same pattern

reconduire   *to see out*

How the verb works

je te conduirai à la gare	*I'll take/drive you to the station*
est-ce que tu sais conduire?	*can you drive?*
je n'aimerais pas conduire un camion	*I wouldn't like to drive a lorry*
ma mère n'aime pas conduire la nuit	*my mother doesn't like driving at night*
qui va conduire?	*who's going to drive?*
le car vous conduira à l'hôtel	*the coach will take you to the hotel*
il m'a conduit dans son bureau	*he led me into his office*
elle se conduit mal	*she behaves badly*

> **Language in use**

à gauche il y a un chemin qui conduit à l'église	*on the left there is a path that leads to the church*
c'est la route qui conduit à Ménerbes	*it's the road that goes to Ménerbes*
la grève a conduit à la fermeture de l'usine	*the strike led to the closing of the factory*
leur recherche a conduit à améliorer le vaccin	*their research led to improvements in the vaccine*
ses problèmes financiers l'ont conduit au suicide	*his financial problems drove him to suicide*
il a conduit la nation pendant la guerre	*he led the nation during the war*
il ne sait pas se conduire en société	*he doesn't know how to behave in company*
elle s'est mal conduite envers son mari	*she behaved badly towards her husband*
il s'est conduit comme un imbécile	*he behaved like an idiot*
ma secrétaire vous reconduira	*my secretary will see you out*
je te reconduis chez toi?	*shall I take/walk you home?*
elle m'a reconduit à la gare	*she took/drove me to the station*

17 connaître to know

irregular verb
conjugates with avoir in compound tenses

Imperative	Present participle	Past participle
connais (tu)	connaissant	connu
connaissons		
(nous)		
connaissez (vous)		

Present
je connais
tu connais
il/elle connaît
nous connaissons
vous connaissez
ils/elles connaissent

Past Historic
je connus
tu connus
il/elle connut
nous connûmes
vous connûtes
ils/elles connurent

Future
je connaîtrai
tu connaîtras
il/elle connaîtra
nous connaîtrons
vous connaîtrez
ils/elles connaîtront

Conditional
je connaîtrais
tu connaîtrais
il/elle connaîtrait
nous connaîtrions
vous connaîtriez
ils/elles connaîtraient

Imperfect
je connaissais
tu connaissais
il/elle connaissait
nous connaissions
vous connaissiez
ils/elles connaissaient

Present subjunctive
(que) je connaisse
(que) tu connaisses
(qu') il/elle connaisse
(que) nous connaissions
(que) vous connaissiez
(qu') ils/elles connaissent

Perfect
j'ai connu
tu as connu
il/elle a connu
nous avons connu
vous avez connu
ils/elles ont connu

Imperfect subjunctive
(que) je connusse
(que) tu connusses
(qu') il/elle connût
(que) nous connussions
(que) vous connussiez
(qu') ils/elles connussent

Following the same pattern

méconnaître *to misunderstand* reconnaître *to recognize*

How the verb works

je connais son frère	*I know his/her brother*
je ne connais pas son nom	*I don't know his/her name*
est-ce que tu connais leur adresse?	*do you know their address?*
je le connais depuis longtemps	*I've known him for a long time*
je la connais de vue	*I know her by sight*
c'est un écrivain que je ne connais pas du tout	*he's a writer I don't know at all*
ils ont connu la pauvreté	*they have known poverty*
elle est très connue	*she's very well-known*

Language in use
---

il nous a fait connaître son avis	*he made his opinion known to us*
elle n'arrête pas de se disputer avec son mari, c'est bien connu	*it's common knowledge that she's always fighting with her husband*
tu connais l'histoire du médecin qui...	*you know the one about the doctor who...*
c'est elle qui m'a fait connaître la musique de Clam	*it was she who introduced me to Clam's music*
je connais l'histoire par cœur	*I know the story by heart*
le roman a connu un certain succès	*the novel has enjoyed a certain amount of success*
il a connu la prison	*he's been in prison*
elle a méconnu le problème	*she misunderstood the problem*
j'ai méconnu les difficultés	*I underestimated the difficulties*
je l'ai reconnue tout de suite	*I recognized her at once*
je ne l'aurais pas reconnu	*I wouldn't have recognized him*
je reconnais que je me suis trompé	*I admit I was mistaken*

18 coudre to sew

irregular verb
conjugates with **avoir** *in compound tenses*

Imperative	Present participle	Past participle
couds (tu)	cousant	cousu
cousons (nous)		
cousez (vous)		

Present
je couds
tu couds
il/elle coud
nous cousons
vous cousez
ils/elles cousent

Past Historic
je cousis
tu cousis
il/elle cousit
nous cousîmes
vous cousîtes
ils/elles cousirent

Future
je coudrai
tu coudras
il/elle coudra
nous coudrons
vous coudrez
ils/elles coudront

Conditional
je coudrais
tu coudrais
il/elle coudrait
nous coudrions
vous coudriez
ils/elles coudraient

Imperfect
je cousais
tu cousais
il/elle cousait
nous cousions
vous cousiez
ils/elles cousaient

Present subjunctive
(que) je couse
(que) tu couses
(qu') il/elle couse
(que) nous cousions
(que) vous cousiez
(qu') ils/elles cousent

Perfect
j'**ai** cousu
tu **as** cousu
il/elle **a** cousu
nous **avons** cousu
vous **avez** cousu
ils/elles **ont** cousu

Imperfect subjunctive
(que) je cousisse
(que) tu cousisses
(qu') il/elle cousît
(que) nous cousissions
(que) vous cousissiez
(qu') ils/elles cousissent

Following the same pattern

découdre — *to unstitch* · recoudre — *to sew up (again)*

How the verb works

elle sait très bien coudre	*she's very good at sewing*
elle était en train de coudre	*she was sewing*
je couds l'ourlet	*I'm sewing (up) the hem*
il ne me reste qu'à coudre les boutons	*I've only got the buttons to sew on now*
il faut coudre les deux morceaux de tissu ensemble	*you have to sew the two pieces of material together*

Language in use

je le coudrai à la machine	*I'll sew/stitch it on the machine*
la robe est cousue à la main	*the dress is hand-sewn*
est-ce que tu as une machine à coudre?	*do you have a sewing machine?*
je vais découdre l'ourlet	*I'm going to unpick the hem*
elle a décousu les boutons	*she took the buttons off*
l'ourlet s'est décousu	*the hem has come unstitched*
le bouton s'est décousu	*the button has come off*
ta chemise est décousue au col	*your shirt has come unstitched at the collar*
je vais recoudre ton bouton	*I'll sew the button on again for you*

19 courir to run

irregular verb
conjugates with **avoir** *in compound tenses*

Imperative	Present participle	Past participle
cours (tu)	courant	couru
courons (nous)		
courez (vous)		

Present
je cours
tu cours
il/elle court
nous courons
vous courez
ils/elles courent

Past Historic
je courus
tu courus
il/elle courut
nous courûmes
vous courûtes
ils/elles coururent

Future
je courrai
tu courras
il/elle courra
nous courrons
vous courrez
ils/elles courront

Conditional
je courrais
tu courrais
il/elle courrait
nous courrions
vous courriez
ils/elles courraient

Imperfect
je courais
tu courais
il/elle courait
nous courions
vous couriez
ils/elles couraient

Present subjunctive
(que) je coure
(que) tu coures
(qu') il/elle coure
(que) nous courions
(que) vous couriez
(qu') ils/elles courent

Perfect
j'ai couru
tu as couru
il/elle a couru
nous avons couru
vous avez couru
ils/elles ont couru

Imperfect subjunctive
(que) je courusse
(que) tu courusses
(qu') il/elle courût
(que) nous courussions
(que) vous courussiez
(qu') ils/elles courussent

Some common verbs that follow the same pattern

accourir✧	*to rush*	parcourir	*to go through*
concourir	*to compete*	recourir à	*to use/resort to*
discourir	*to hold forth*		
		secourir	*to rescue*

✧conjugates with **être** in perfect, pluperfect, and future perfect tenses

How the verb works

il est interdit de courir dans les couloirs	*it's forbidden to run in the corridors*
elle court vite	*she's a fast runner*
ils courent tous les soirs	*they go running every evening*
il est sorti en courant	*he ran out*
elle s'est mise à courir	*she started running*
l'enfant courait vers moi	*the child was running towards me*
cours chercher de l'aide	*run and fetch help*

Language in use

tout le monde court voir sa nouvelle pièce	*everyone is rushing to see his/her new play*
j'ai couru toute la journée	*I've been rushing around all day*
elle court sans arrêt	*she's always on the go*
il a couru après le voleur	*he chased the thief*
ton chien m'a couru après	*your dog chased me*
j'ai couru toute la ville pour trouver ce tissu	*I went all over town to find this fabric*
il y a un bruit qui court	*there's a rumour going around*
je ne veux courir aucun risque	*I don't want to run any risks*
tu peux toujours courir!*	*you can go whistle for it!*
j'ai parcouru la ville à la recherche d'un cadeau pour ma femme	*I went all over town in search of a present for my wife*

20 couvrir to cover

irregular verb
*conjugates with **avoir** in compound tenses*

Imperative	Present participle	Past participle
couvre (tu)	couvrant	couvert
couvrons (nous)		
couvrez (vous)		

Present
je couvre
tu couvres
il/elle couvre
nous couvrons
vous couvrez
ils/elles couvrent

Past Historic
je couvris
tu couvris
il/elle couvrit
nous couvrîmes
vous couvrîtes
ils/elles couvrirent

Future
je couvrirai
tu couvriras
il/elle couvrira
nous couvrirons
vous couvrirez
ils/elles couvriront

Conditional
je couvrirais
tu couvrirais
il/elle couvrirait
nous couvririons
vous couvririez
ils/elles couvriraient

Imperfect
je couvrais
tu couvrais
il/elle couvrait
nous couvrions
vous couvriez
ils/elles couvraient

Present subjunctive
(que) je couvre
(que) tu couvres
(qu') il/elle couvre
(que) nous couvrions
(que) vous couvriez
(qu') ils/elles couvrent

Perfect
j'**ai** couvert
tu **as** couvert
il/elle **a** couvert
nous **avons** couvert
vous **avez** couvert
ils/elles **ont** couvert

Imperfect subjunctive
(que) je couvrisse
(que) tu couvrisses
(qu') il/elle couvrît
(que) nous couvrissions
(que) vous couvrissiez
(qu') ils/elles couvrissent

Some common verbs that follow the same pattern

découvrir	to discover	recouvrir	to cover
ouvrir	to open	rouvrir	to open (again)

How the verb works

ils ont couvert les murs de tableaux	they've covered the walls with pictures
tout mon corps était couvert de boutons	my body was covered in spots
mon bureau est couvert de papiers	my desk is covered in papers
un paysage couvert de neige	a snow-covered landscape
tous les quotidiens ont couvert les émeutes	all the daily papers covered the riots
le film couvre les événements de mai '68	the film covers the events of May '68

Language in use

ils n'ont pas encore couvert la maison	they haven't roofed the house yet
ils vont couvrir le toit de tuiles	they're going to tile the roof
il vaut mieux acheter une peinture qui couvre bien	it's best to buy paint that gives good coverage
il fait froid dehors, couvre-toi bien	it's cold outside, wrap up warmly
ils m'ont couvert de compliments	they showered me with compliments
le temps se couvrira en cours d'après-midi	it will cloud over in the course of the afternoon
les chercheurs ont découvert un nouveau remède	scientists have discovered a new cure
c'est un artiste qui a été découvert dans les années soixante	he's an artist who was discovered in the sixties
elle m'a fait découvrir l'opéra	she introduced me to opera
j'ouvrirai la fenêtre	I'll open the window
la porte s'est ouverte	the door opened
les magasins ouvrent le dimanche matin	the shops open on Sunday mornings
elle n'a pas ouvert la bouche	she didn't say a word

21 craindre to fear

irregular verb
*conjugates with **avoir** in compound tenses*

Imperative	Present participle	Past participle
crains (tu)	craignant	craint
craignons (nous)		
craignez (vous)		

Present
je crains
tu crains
il/elle craint
nous craignons
vous craignez
ils/elles craignent

Past Historic
je craignis
tu craignis
il/elle craignit
nous craignîmes
vous craignîtes
ils/elles craignirent

Future
je craindrai
tu craindras
il/elle craindra
nous craindrons
vous craindrez
ils/elles craindront

Conditional
je craindrais
tu craindrais
il/elle craindrait
nous craindrions
vous craindriez
ils/elles craindraient

Imperfect
je craignais
tu craignais
il/elle craignait
nous craignions
vous craigniez
ils/elles craignaient

Present subjunctive
(que) je craigne
(que) tu craignes
(qu') il/elle craigne
(que) nous craignions
(que) vous craigniez
(qu') ils/elles craignent

Perfect
j'**ai** craint
tu **as** craint
il/elle **a** craint
nous **avons** craint
vous **avez** craint
ils/elles **ont** craint

Imperfect subjunctive
(que) je craignisse
(que) tu craignisses
(qu') il/elle craignît
(que) nous craignissions
(que) vous craignissiez
(qu') ils/elles craignissent

How the verb works

elle craint les chiens	*she's afraid of dogs*
ne craignez rien	*don't be afraid*
je crains pour sa réputation	*I fear for his/her reputation*
elle craignait d'être attaquée	*she was afraid of being attacked*

Language in use

à mon avis tu as tout à craindre de lui	*in my opinion you have every reason to be afraid of him*
tu n'as rien à craindre du chien	*you have nothing to fear from the dog*
nous craignons le pire	*we fear the worst*
il sait se faire craindre	*he knows how to make himself feared*
je crains d'avoir à le lui dire	*I'm afraid I may have to tell him/her*
je crains de ne pouvoir y aller	*I'm afraid I may not be able to go*
je crains qu'il n'ait eu un accident	*I'm afraid he may have had an accident*
je crains que vous ne fassiez erreur	*I'm afraid you are mistaken*
je crains de ne pas savoir	*I'm afraid I don't know*
je crains que non	*I'm afraid not*
elle craint le froid	*she's sensitive to the cold*
pour les peaux qui craignent le soleil	*for skin which is sensitive to the sun*
ce produit craint l'humidité	*this product must be kept in a dry place*
une explosion est à craindre	*there is some danger of an explosion*
ça craint!*	*that's bad!*

22 créer to create

irregular verb
conjugates with **avoir** *in compound tenses*

Imperative	Present participle	Past participle
crée (tu)	créant	créé
créons (nous)		
créez (vous)		

Present
je crée
tu crées
il/elle crée
nous créons
vous créez
ils/elles créent

Past Historic
je créai
tu créas
il/elle créa
nous créâmes
vous créâtes
ils/elles créèrent

Future
je créerai
tu créeras
il/elle créera
nous créerons
vous créerez
ils/elles créeront

Conditional
je créerais
tu créerais
il/elle créerait
nous créerions
vous créeriez
ils/elles créeraient

Imperfect
je créais
tu créais
il/elle créait
nous créions
vous créiez
ils/elles créaient

Present subjunctive
(que) je crée
(que) tu crées
(qu') il/elle crée
(que) nous créions
(que) vous créiez
(qu') ils/elles créent

Perfect
j'ai créé
tu as créé
il/elle a créé
nous avons créé
vous avez créé
ils/elles ont créé

Imperfect subjunctive
(que) je créasse
(que) tu créasses
(qu') il/elle créât
(que) nous créassions
(que) vous créassiez
(qu') ils/elles créassent

Some common verbs that follow the same pattern

| agréer | to accept | procréer | to procreate |
| maugréer | to grumble | recréer | to recreate |

How the verb works

ils essaient de créer des emplois dans la région	they are trying to create jobs in the area
cela va nous créer des problèmes	this is going to create problems for us
il s'est créé des problèmes	he has created problems for himself

le plaisir de créer	the pleasure of creating something
c'est ma sœur qui a créé les costumes	my sister designed the costumes
l'équipe a créé un nouveau type de scanner	the team has invented a new type of scanner
il crée des objets en bois	he makes wood carvings
l'année dernière elle a créé une société d'exportation	last year she set up an export company
c'est lui qui a créé la pièce au festival d'Édimbourg	he directed the first performance of the play at the Edinburgh festival
elle a créé le rôle de Mélisande	she was the first person to perform the role of Mélisande
il faudra que votre demande soit agréée par la direction	your request will have to be agreed by the management
veuillez agréer, Madame/ Monsieur, mes salutations distinguées	yours faithfully/yours sincerely
un concessionnaire agréé	an authorized dealer
un médecin agréé	a registered doctor

23 **croire** to believe

irregular verb
conjugates with **avoir** *in compound tenses*

Imperative	**Present participle**	**Past participle**
crois (tu)	croyant	cru
croyons (nous)		
croyez (vous)		

Present
je crois
tu crois
il/elle croit
nous croyons
vous croyez
ils/elles croient

Past Historic
je crus
tu crus
il/elle crut
nous crûmes
vous crûtes
ils/elles crurent

Future
je croirai
tu croiras
il/elle croira
nous croirons
vous croirez
ils/elles croiront

Conditional
je croirais
tu croirais
il/elle croirait
nous croirions
vous croiriez
ils/elles croiraient

Imperfect
je croyais
tu croyais
il/elle croyait
nous croyions
vous croyiez
ils/elles croyaient

Present subjunctive
(que) je croie
(que) tu croies
(qu') il/elle croie
(que) nous croyions
(que) vous croyiez
(qu') ils/elles croient

Perfect
j'ai cru
tu as cru
il/elle a cru
nous avons cru
vous avez cru
ils/elles ont cru

Imperfect subjunctive
(que) je crusse
(que) tu crusses
(qu') il/elle crût
(que) nous crussions
(que) vous crussiez
(qu') ils/elles crussent

How the verb works

je ne crois pas son histoire	*I don't believe his story*
il n'a pas voulu me croire	*he wouldn't believe me*
est-ce que tu crois aux fantômes?	*do you believe in ghosts?*
ils ne croient pas en Dieu	*they don't believe in God*
je crois qu'il est déjà parti	*I think he's already left*
je ne crois pas qu'elle l'ait fait exprès	*I don't think she did it on purpose*
je crois n'avoir rien oublié	*I don't think I've forgotten anything*
je crois pouvoir vous aider	*I think I can help you*
il se croit malin	*he thinks he's clever*

Language in use

il faut le voir pour le croire	*it has to be seen to be believed*
il leur a fait croire à son histoire	*he made them believe his story*
tu me croiras si tu veux	*believe it or not*
je n'en ai pas cru mes yeux/oreilles	*I couldn't believe my eyes/ears*
elle croyait bien faire	*she thought she was doing the right thing*
j'ai cru mourir	*I thought I was dying*
je la croyais partie	*I thought she'd left*
je te croyais en France	*I thought you were in France*
c'est à croire qu'elle le fait exprès	*anyone would think she was doing it on purpose*
à en croire les sondages, c'est lui qui va gagner	*if the polls are anything to go by, he's going to win*
on se croirait en Inde	*you'd think we were in India*

24 croître to grow

irregular verb
conjugates with avoir in compound tenses

Imperative	Present participle	Past participle
croîs (tu)	croissant	crû
croissons (nous)		
croissez (vous)		

Present
je croîs
tu croîs
il/elle croît
nous croissons
vous croissez
ils/elles croissent

Past Historic
je crûs
tu crûs
il/elle crût
nous crûmes
vous crûtes
ils/elles crûrent

Future
je croîtrai
tu croîtras
il/elle croîtra
nous croîtrons
vous croîtrez
ils/elles croîtront

Conditional
je croîtrais
tu croîtrais
il/elle croîtrait
nous croîtrions
vous croîtriez
ils/elles croîtraient

Imperfect
je croissais
tu croissais
il/elle croissait
nous croissions
vous croissiez
ils/elles croissaient

Present subjunctive
(que) je croisse
(que) tu croisses
(qu') il/elle croisse
(que) nous croissions
(que) vous croissiez
(qu') ils/elles croissent

Perfect
j'ai crû
tu as crû
il/elle a crû
nous avons crû
vous avez crû
ils/elles ont crû

Imperfect subjunctive
(que) je crusse
(que) tu crusses
(qu') il/elle crût
(que) nous crussions
(que) vous crussiez
(qu') ils/elles crussent

Following the same pattern

accroître   *to increase*   décroître   *to decrease*

◇but **croître** has more circumflex accents than these verbs in order to distinguish it from forms of the verb **croire**

How the verb works

c'est une plante qui va croître très rapidement	*it's a plant that will grow very quickly*
cette année la production a crû de 5%	*this year production increased by 5%*
sa colère/peur allait croissant	*he became increasingly angry/frightened*
leur optimisme ne cesse de croître	*their optimism is growing all the time*

Language in use

le bruit croissait progressivement	*the noise was getting steadily louder*
les ventes croissent chaque année	*sales are going up every year*
les jours croissent	*the days are getting longer*
nous espérons vivement que les bénéfices vont s'accroître considérablement l'année prochaine	*we are very much hoping that profits will increase considerably next year*
la population continue à s'accroître de 2% par an	*the population continues to increase by 2% a year*
il éprouvait un besoin accru de sécurité	*he felt a greater need for security*
le niveau d'eau a décru d'un mètre	*the water level has gone down by a metre*
les jours décroissent	*the days are getting shorter*
la lumière décroissait	*the light was fading*

25 cueillir to gather/pick

irregular verb
conjugates with avoir in compound tenses

Imperative	Present participle	Past participle
cueille (tu)	cueillant	cueilli
cueillons (nous)		
cueillez (vous)		

Present
je cueille
tu cueilles
il/elle cueille
nous cueillons
vous cueillez
ils/elles cueillent

Past Historic
je cueillis
tu cueillis
il/elle cueillit
nous cueillîmes
vous cueillîtes
ils/elles cueillirent

Future
je cueillerai
tu cueilleras
il/elle cueillera
nous cueillerons
vous cueillerez
ils/elles cueilleront

Conditional
je cueillerais
tu cueillerais
il/elle cueillerait
nous cueillerions
vous cueilleriez
ils/elles cueilleraient

Imperfect
je cueillais
tu cueillais
il/elle cueillait
nous cueillions
vous cueilliez
ils/elles cueillaient

Present subjunctive
(que) je cueille
(que) tu cueilles
(qu') il/elle cueille
(que) nous cueillions
(que) vous cueilliez
(qu') ils/elles cueillent

Perfect
j'ai cueilli
tu as cueilli
il/elle a cueilli
nous avons cueilli
vous avez cueilli
ils/elles ont cueilli

Imperfect subjunctive
(que) je cueillisse
(que) tu cueillisses
(qu') il/elle cueillît
(que) nous cueillissions
(que) vous cueillissiez
(qu') ils/elles cueillissent

Some common verbs that follow the same pattern

accueillir   *to welcome*   recueillir   *to gather*

How the verb works

elle était en train de cueillir des fraises	*she was busy picking strawberries*
nous cueillerons des fleurs cet après-midi	*we'll pick some flowers this afternoon*
il faut que je cueille les framboises	*I must pick the raspberries*

Language in use

cueillir des lauriers	*to cover oneself in glory*
le maire a accueilli les délégués	*the mayor welcomed the delegates*
le film a été bien accueilli par les critiques	*the film was well received by the critics*
nous avons été bien accueillis	*we were given a warm welcome/we were made to feel very welcome*
nous espérons vous accueillir chez nous l'année prochaine	*we hope to welcome you to our home next year*
ils ont été accueillis par des acclamations	*they were greeted with cheers*
elle a recueilli des informations sur les restaurants de la région	*she gathered information on the restaurants in the area*
ils espèrent recueillir au moins cinq cents signatures	*they hope to collect at least five hundred signatures*
le candidat a recueilli mille cinq cents voix	*the candidate obtained one thousand five hundred votes*
ils recueillent le miel en septembre	*they collect the honey in September*
les musiciens ont recueilli des applaudissements	*the musicians were greeted with applause*

26 devoir to owe/have to

irregular verb
*conjugates with **avoir** in compound tenses*

Imperative	Present participle	Past participle
dois (tu)	devant	dû
devons (nous)		
devez (vous)		

Present
je dois
tu dois
il/elle doit
nous devons
vous devez
ils/elles doivent

Past Historic
je dus
tu dus
il/elle dut
nous dûmes
vous dûtes
ils/elles durent

Future
je devrai
tu devras
il/elle devra
nous devrons
vous devrez
ils/elles devront

Conditional
je devrais
tu devrais
il/elle devrait
nous devrions
vous devriez
ils/elles devraient

Imperfect
je devais
tu devais
il/elle devait
nous devions
vous deviez
ils/elles devaient

Present subjunctive
(que) je doive
(que) tu doives
(qu') il/elle doive
(que) nous devions
(que) vous deviez
(qu') ils/elles doivent

Perfect
j'ai dû
tu as dû
il/elle a dû
nous avons dû
vous avez dû
ils/elles ont dû

Imperfect subjunctive
(que) je dusse
(que) tu dusses
(qu') il/elle dût
(que) nous dussions
(que) vous dussiez
(qu') ils/elles dussent

How the verb works

● *as auxiliary expressing obligation*

tu dois te brosser les dents au moins deux fois par jour	*you must brush your teeth at least twice a day*
je dois aller travailler	*I must go to work*
je devais aller travailler	*I had to go to work*
il doit accepter	*he has to accept*
il a dû accepter	*he had to accept*
nous allons devoir vendre la voiture	*we will have to sell the car*
je dois dire que cela ne m'étonne pas	*I have to say I'm not surprised*
je dois avouer que j'ai hésité	*I must admit I hesitated*

● *used in the conditional to express 'should' or 'ought'*

tu devrais écrire à ton père	*you should/ought to write to your father*
elle ne devrait pas manger autant de bonbons	*she shouldn't eat so many sweets*
j'aurais dû te le dire	*I should have told you*
tu n'aurais pas dû le faire	*you shouldn't have done it*

● *expressing strong probability*

elle doit avoir au moins trente ans	*she must be at least thirty*
il doit être chez lui	*he must be at home*
elle a dû oublier	*she must have forgotten*

● *expressing something that is to happen*

ils doivent arriver à cinq heures	*they're to arrive at five o' clock*
ils devaient arriver à cinq heures	*they were to arrive at five o' clock*
à quelle heure doit-il rentrer?	*what time should he be home?*
je dois la voir demain	*I'll be seeing her tomorrow*

● *meaning 'to owe'*

je leur dois cent francs	*I owe them a hundred francs*
je te dois combien?	*how much do I owe you?*
il me doit des excuses	*he owes me an apology*

27 écrire to write

irregular verb
conjugates with **avoir** *in compound tenses*

Imperative	Present participle	Past participle
écris (tu)	écrivant	écrit
écrivons (nous)		
écrivez (vous)		

Present
j'écris
tu écris
il/elle écrit
nous écrivons
vous écrivez
ils/elles écrivent

Past Historic
j'écrivis
tu écrivis
il/elle écrivit
nous écrivîmes
vous écrivîtes
ils/elles écrivirent

Future
j'écrirai
tu écriras
il/elle écrira
nous écrirons
vous écrirez
ils/elles écriront

Conditional
j'écrirais
tu écrirais
il/elle écrirait
nous écririons
vous écririez
ils/elles écriraient

Imperfect
j'écrivais
tu écrivais
il/elle écrivait
nous écrivions
vous écriviez
ils/elles écrivaient

Present subjunctive
(que) j'écrive
(que) tu écrives
(qu') il/elle écrive
(que) nous écrivions
(que) vous écriviez
(qu') ils/elles écrivent

Perfect
j'ai écrit
tu as écrit
il/elle a écrit
nous avons écrit
vous avez écrit
ils/elles ont écrit

Imperfect subjunctive
(que) j'écrivisse
(que) tu écrivisses
(qu') il/elle écrivît
(que) nous écrivissions
(que) vous écrivissiez
(qu') ils/elles écrivissent

Some common verbs that follow the same pattern

circonscrire	*to circumscribe*	prescrire	*to prescribe*
décrire	*to describe*	réécrire	*to rewrite*
inscrire	*to enrol*	souscrire	*to subscribe*
		transcrire	*to transcribe*

How the verb works

elle était en train d'écrire une lettre	*she was writing a letter*
je lui ai écrit une lettre	*I wrote/have written him/her a letter*
il m'a écrit pour me donner des nouvelles de sa mère	*he wrote to me to give me news of his mother*
elle sait déjà écrire son nom	*she can write her name already*

Language in use

tu écris bien	*you have nice writing*
elle écrit	*she's a writer*
il vit en écrivant	*he makes a living by writing*
est-ce que tu sais comment il écrit son nom?	*do you know how he spells his name?*
ça s'écrit comment?	*how is that spelled?*
ça s'écrit avec deux b	*it's spelled with two b's*
elle m'a décrit sa nouvelle maison	*she described her new house to me*
je ne peux pas te décrire comment c'était	*I can't describe to you what it was like*
elle a inscrit ses enfants à l'école du quartier	*she's enrolled her children at the local school*
il faut t'inscrire avant la fin du mois	*you have to enrol before the end of the month*
elle s'est inscrite au club de tennis	*she joined/has joined the tennis club*
le médecin m'a prescrit des antibiotiques	*the doctor prescribed/has prescribed me antibiotics*
'ne pas dépasser la dose prescrite'	*'do not exceed stated dose'*

28 employer to employ

irregular verb
conjugates with **avoir** *in compound tenses*

Imperative	Present participle	Past participle
emploie (tu)	employ**ant**	employ**é**
employ**ons** (nous)		
employ**ez** (vous)		

Present
j'emploie
tu emploies
il/elle emploie
nous employ**ons**
vous employ**ez**
ils/elles emploient

Past Historic
j'employ**ai**
tu employ**as**
il/elle employ**a**
nous employ**âmes**
vous employ**âtes**
ils/elles employ**èrent**

Future
j'emploierai
tu emploieras
il/elle emploiera
nous emploierons
vous emploierez
ils/elles emploieront

Conditional
j'emploierais
tu emploierais
il/elle emploierait
nous emploierions
vous emploieriez
ils/elles emploieraient

Imperfect
j'employ**ais**
tu employ**ais**
il/elle employ**ait**
nous employ**ions**
vous employ**iez**
ils/elles employ**aient**

Present subjunctive
(que) j'emploie
(que) tu emploies
(qu') il/elle emploie
(que) nous employ**ions**
(que) vous employ**iez**
(qu') ils/elles emploient

Perfect
j'**ai** employ**é**
tu **as** employ**é**
il/elle **a** employ**é**
nous **avons** employ**é**
vous **avez** employ**é**
ils/elles **ont** employ**é**

Imperfect subjunctive
(que) j'employ**asse**
(que) tu employ**asses**
(qu') il/elle employ**ât**
(que) nous employ**assions**
(que) vous employ**assiez**
(qu') ils/elles employ**assent**

Some common verbs that follow the same pattern

aboyer	to bark	nettoyer	to clean
apitoyer	to move to pity	noyer	to drown
broyer	to grind/ crush	tournoyer	to swirl/twirl
choyer	to pamper	tutoyer	to address (someone) as 'tu'
côtoyer	to be next to/ mix with	vouvoyer	to address (someone) as 'vous'
foudroyer	to strike down		

How the verb works

la société emploie trois cents personnes	the company employs three hundred people
elle a été employée comme secrétaire	she's been employed as a secretary
je compte employer une secrétaire	I'm planning to take on a secretary
ils ont été obligés d'employer la force	they were obliged to use force
ce produit ne s'emploie plus	this product is no longer used

Language in use

si quelqu'un s'approche, les chiens aboieront	if anyone comes near, the dogs will bark
n'essaie pas de m'apitoyer	don't try to get my sympathy
elle aime côtoyer les artistes et les musiciens	she likes mixing with artists and musicians
elle le foudroya du regard	she looked daggers at him
il faut bien nettoyer les pinceaux	the paintbrushes must be thoroughly cleaned
je nettoierai la cuisine demain	I'll clean up the kitchen tomorrow
je tutoie toute la famille d'Isabelle, sauf sa grand-mère, qui préfère qu'on la vouvoie	I say 'tu' to everyone in Isabelle's family except her grandmother, who prefers to be addressed as 'vous'

29 envoyer to send

irregular verb
conjugates with **avoir** *in compound tenses*

Imperative	Present participle	Past participle
envoie (tu)	envoy**ant**	envoy**é**
envoy**ons** (nous)		
envoy**ez** (vous)		

Present
j'envoie
tu envoies
il/elle envoie
nous envoy**ons**
vous envoy**ez**
ils/elles envoient

Past Historic
j'envoy**ai**
tu envoy**as**
il/elle envoy**a**
nous envoy**âmes**
vous envoy**âtes**
ils/elles envoy**èrent**

Future
j'enverrai
tu enverras
il/elle enverra
nous enverrions
vous enverriez
ils/elles enverront

Conditional
j'enverrais
tu enverrais
il/elle enverrait
nous enverrions
vous enverriez
ils/elles enverraient

Imperfect
j'envoy**ais**
tu envoy**ais**
il/elle envoy**ait**
nous envoy**ions**
vous envoy**iez**
ils/elles envoy**aient**

Present subjunctive
(que) j'envoie
(que) tu envoies
(qu') il/elle envoie
(que) nous envoy**ions**
(que) vous envoy**iez**
(qu') ils/elles envoient

Perfect
j'**ai** envoyé
tu **as** envoyé
il/elle **a** envoyé
nous **avons** envoyé
vous **avez** envoyé
ils/elles **ont** envoyé

Imperfect subjunctive
(que) j'envoy**asse**
(que) tu envoy**asses**
(qu') il/elle envoy**ât**
(que) nous envoy**assions**
(que) vous envoy**assiez**
(qu') ils/elles envoy**assent**

Following the same pattern

renvoyer   *to send back*

How the verb works

Sophie a envoyé un cadeau à sa mère	*Sophie sent/has sent a present to her mother*
envoie-moi les photos	*send me the photos*
envoies-en à Sylvie	*send some to Sylvie*
nous leur enverrons une lettre de remerciement	*we'll send them a thankyou letter*
je vous envoie un technicien	*I'll send you an engineer*
Cathy t'envoie ses amitiés	*Cathy sends you her regards*
on l'a envoyé en prison	*he was sent to prison*
son père l'a envoyée acheter le journal	*her father sent/has sent her out to buy the newspaper*

<hr>

Language in use

envoie-lui le ballon	*throw him the ball*
il m'a envoyé un coup de pied	*he kicked me*
ils s'envoyaient des baisers	*they were blowing each other kisses*
nous l'avons envoyé promener*	*we sent him packing*
renvoie-moi le ballon	*throw the ball back to me*
l'eau dans le bassin renvoie la lumière	*the water in the pond reflects the light*
ma lettre a été renvoyée sans avoir été ouverte	*my letter was returned unopened*
on l'a renvoyé à l'hôpital	*he's been sent back to hospital*
on l'a renvoyée chez elle	*she was sent home*
elle travaillait dans une banque mais elle a été renvoyée	*she worked in a bank but she's been sacked*

30 essuyer to wipe/dry

irregular verb
conjugates with **avoir** *in compound tenses*

Imperative	Present participle	Past participle
essuie (tu)	essuy**ant**	essuy**é**
essuy**ons** (nous)		
essuy**ez** (vous)		

Present
j'essuie
tu essuies
il/elle essuie
nous essuyons
vous essuyez
ils/elles essuient

Past Historic
j'essuyai
tu essuyas
il/elle essuya
nous essuyâmes
vous essuyâtes
ils/elles essuyèrent

Future
j'essuierai
tu essuieras
il/elle essuiera
nous essuierons
vous essuierez
ils/elles essuieront

Conditional
j'essuierais
tu essuierais
il/elle essuierait
nous essuierions
vous essuieriez
ils/elles essuieraient

Imperfect
j'essuyais
tu essuyais
il/elle essuyait
nous essuyions
vous essuyiez
ils/elles essuyaient

Present subjunctive
(que) j'essuie
(que) tu essuies
(qu') il/elle essuie
(que) nous essuyions
(que) vous essuyiez
(qu') ils/elles essuient

Perfect
j'**ai** essuyé
tu **as** essuyé
il/elle **a** essuyé
nous **avons** essuyé
vous **avez** essuyé
ils/elles **ont** essuyé

Imperfect subjunctive
(que) j'essuyasse
(que) tu essuyasses
(qu') il/elle essuyât
(que) nous essuyassions
(que) vous essuyassiez
(qu') ils/elles essuyassent

Some common verbs that follow the same pattern

appuyer — to lean

ennuyer — to bore/ annoy

How the verb works

peux-tu essuyer les verres, s'il te plaît? — *can you dry up the glasses, please?*

j'essuierai la table — *I'll wipe the table*

il est en train d'essuyer la vaisselle — *he's busy doing the drying-up*

elle a essuyé ses larmes — *she wiped away her tears*

tu peux t'essuyer les mains avec la serviette bleue — *you can dry your hands on the blue towel*

Language in use

ils ont essuyé beaucoup de critiques — *they came in for a lot of criticism*

appuie ton vélo contre le mur — *lean your bike against the wall*

appuyez sur la sonnette — *press the bell*

elle s'appuyait contre le mur — *she was leaning against the wall*

mon travail m'ennuie — *my work bores me*

lire m'ennuie — *I find reading boring*

il m'ennuie à mourir — *he bores me to death*

excusez-moi de vous ennuyer — *I'm sorry to disturb you*

est-ce que ca vous ennuierait si j'ouvrais la fenêtre? — *would you mind if I opened the window?*

si ça ne vous ennuie pas trop — *if you don't mind*

ça m'ennuie de la déranger — *I don't want to disturb her*

arrête de m'ennuyer! — *stop hassling me!*

je m'ennuie à la campagne — *I get bored in the country*

tu as l'air de t'ennuyer — *you look bored*

nous nous sommes ennuyés mortellement — *we were bored stiff*

31 être to be

irregular verb
conjugates with avoid in compound tenses

Imperative	Present participle	Past participle
sois (tu)	étant	été
soyons (nous)		
soyez (vous)		

Present
je suis
tu es
il/elle est
nous sommes
vous êtes
ils/elles sont

Past Historic
je fus
tu fus
il/elle fut
nous fûmes
vous fûtes
ils/elles furent

Future
je serai
tu seras
il/elle sera
nous serons
vous serez
ils/elles seront

Conditional
je serais
tu serais
il/elle serait
nous serions
vous seriez
ils/elles seraient

Imperfect
j'étais
tu étais
il/elle était
nous étions
vous étiez
ils/elles étaient

Present subjunctive
(que) je sois
(que) tu sois
(qu') il/elle soit
(que) nous soyons
(que) vous soyez
(qu') ils/elles soient

Perfect
j'**ai** été
tu **as** été
il/elle **a** été
nous **avons** été
vous **avez** été
ils/elles **ont** été

Imperfect subjunctive
(que) je fusse
(que) tu fusses
(qu') il/elle fût
(que) nous fussions
(que) vous fussiez
(qu') ils/elles fussent

How the verb works

- *meaning* **to be** *expressing location or describing state*

les verres sont sur la table	*the glasses are on the table*
j'étais dans la cuisine	*I was in the kitchen*
l'eau est froide	*the water is cold*
sa mère est malade	*his/her mother is ill*

- *giving profession or status: note that a/an is not translated*

leur père est médecin	*their father is a doctor*
ma fille est étudiante	*my daughter's a student*
quand j'étais enfant	*when I was a child*

- *using c'est/ce sont*

c'est une araignée	*it's a spider*
qui est-ce?	*who's that?/who is it?*
c'est moi	*it's me*
ce sont mes enfants	*these/they are my children*
c'est facile	*it's easy*

- *est-ce que/qu'est-ce que etc. beginning a question*

est-ce que tu le connais?	*do you know him?*
est-ce qu'elle est arrivée?	*has she arrived?*
qu'est-ce que c'est?	*what is it?*
qu'est-ce qu'il y a?	*what's the matter?*

- *using être à*

ces livres sont à Paul	*these books are Paul's*

- *as auxiliary forming the perfect, pluperfect, and future perfect of certain verbs*

elle est allée chez le médecin	*she's gone/she went to the doctor's*
j'étais déjà monté dans ma chambre	*I had already gone up to my room*
je me suis lavé les mains	*I've washed/I washed my hands*

- *forming the passive of all verbs*

les draps ont été lavés	*the sheets have been washed*

32 faire to make / to do

irregular verb
conjugates with **avoir** *in compound tenses*

Imperative	Present participle	Past participle
fais (tu)	faisant	fait
faisons (nous)		
faites (vous)		

Present
je fais
tu fais
il/elle fait
nous faisons
vous faites
ils/elles font

Past Historic
je fis
tu fis
il/elle fit
nous fîmes
vous fîtes
ils/elles firent

Future
je ferai
tu feras
il/elle fera
nous ferons
vous ferez
ils/elles feront

Conditional
je ferais
tu ferais
il/elle ferait
nous ferions
vous feriez
ils/elles feraient

Imperfect
je faisais
tu faisais
il/elle faisait
nous faisions
vous faisiez
ils/elles faisaient

Present subjunctive
(que) je fasse
(que) tu fasses
(qu') il/elle fasse
(que) nous fassions
(que) vous fassiez
(qu') ils/elles fassent

Perfect
j'ai fait
tu as fait
il/elle a fait
nous avons fait
vous avez fait
ils/elles ont fait

Imperfect subjunctive
(que) je fisse
(que) tu fisses
(qu') il/elle fît
(que) nous fissions
(que) vous fissiez
(qu') ils/elles fissent

How the verb works

● *meaning 'to do'*

qu'est-ce que tu fais?	*what are you doing?*
qu'est-ce que tu as fait hier?	*what did you do yesterday?*
faire le ménage/la vaisselle	*to do the housework/washing-up*
faire la cuisine	*to do the cooking*
elle fait ses devoirs	*she's doing her homework*
j'ai des choses à faire	*I have things to do*
qu'est-ce que tu as fait du couteau?	*what have you done with the knife?*
fais comme tu veux	*do as you like*

● *meaning 'to make'*

j'ai fait les rideaux moi-même	*I made the curtains myself*
il m'a fait une omelette	*he made me an omelette*
je vais faire à manger	*I'm going to make something to eat*
je me suis fait un café	*I made myself a coffee*
as-tu fait ton lit?	*have you made your bed?*
j'ai fait une faute	*I made/I've made a mistake*
deux et deux font quatre	*two and two make four*

● *expressing force or persuasion*

ça m'a fait rire	*it made me laugh*
il m'a fait attendre	*he kept me waiting*
ça me fait penser...	*that reminds me...*

● *expressing having something done*

elle s'est fait couper les cheveux	*she's had her hair cut*

● *talking about the weather and temperature*

il fait froid/chaud aujourd'hui	*it's cold/hot today*
il fait trente degrés	*it's thirty degrees*

● *expressing an effect*

tu m'as fait peur	*you frightened me*
ça va lui faire plaisir	*he'll/she'll be pleased*

● *with cooking verbs*

faire bouillir de l'eau	*to boil water*
faire cuire/mijoter la viande	*to cook/simmer the meat*

33 falloir to have to/must

impersonal irregular verb
conjugates with avoir in compound tenses

Past participle
fall**u**

Present il faut	**Past Historic** il fall**ut**
Future il faudra	**Conditional** il faudrait
Imperfect il fall**ait**	**Present subjunctive** (qu') il faille
Perfect il **a** fallu	**Imperfect subjunctive** (qu') il fall**ût**

How the verb works

il faut encore trois chaises	*we need three more chairs*
il faudrait trois voitures	*we would need three cars*
ce qu'il faut	*what is needed*
il faut trois jours	*it will take three days*
il faut de la patience pour apprendre une langue	*you need patience to learn a language*
il leur faut deux voitures	*they need two cars*
il te faut combien?	*how much/many do you need?*
il faut fermer les volets	*we/you/etc. must close the shutters*
il faut manger des fruits	*you should eat fruit*
il faut faire quelque chose	*something must be done*
il ne faut pas le déranger	*he mustn't be disturbed*
il fallait venir me voir	*you should have come to see me*
il a fallu changer les serrures	*we/they/etc. had to change the locks*
il faut que tu fasses tes devoirs avant de regarder la télé	*you must do your homework before watching telly*
il a fallu qu'on s'en aille	*we had to leave*

Language in use

il faut dire qu'elle nous a beaucoup aidés	*it must be said that she has helped us a lot*
on peut toujours racheter de la viande s'il le faut	*we can always buy more meat if necessary*
ce n'est pas l'outil qu'il faut	*that's not the tool we need*
il va falloir plusieurs personnes	*it will take several people*
arrête de faire des bêtises et mange comme il faut!	*stop messing about and eat properly!*
fallait le dire plus tôt!*	*why didn't you say so before?*
il faut ce qu'il faut!	*there's no point in skimping!*

34 finir to finish

regular -ir verb
conjugates with avoir in compound tenses

Imperative	Present participle	Past participle
finis (tu)	finissant	fini
finissons (nous)		
finissez (vous)		

Present
je finis
tu finis
il/elle finit
nous finissons
vous finissez
ils/elles finissent

Past historic
je finis
tu finis
il/elle finit
nous finîmes
vous finîtes
ils/elles finirent

Future
je finirai
tu finiras
il/elle finira
nous finirons
vous finirez
ils/elles finiront

Conditional
je finirais
tu finirais
il/elle finirait
nous finirions
vous finiriez
ils/elles finiraient

Imperfect
je finissais
tu finissais
il/elle finissait
nous finissions
vous finissiez
ils/elles finissaient

Present subjunctive
(que) je finisse
(que) tu finisses
(qu') il/elle finisse
(que) nous finissions
(que) vous finissiez
(qu') ils/elles finissent

Perfect
j'ai fini
tu as fini
il/elle a fini
nous avons fini
vous avez fini
ils/elles ont fini

Imperfect subjunctive
(que) je finisse
(que) tu finisses
(qu') il/elle finît
(que) nous finissions
(que) vous finissiez
(qu') ils/elles finissent

Some common verbs that follow the same pattern

aboutir à	*to lead to*	s'évanouir	*to faint*
accomplir	*to accomplish*	fournir	*to supply*
affaiblir	*to weaken*	frémir	*to tremble*
agir	*to act*	garantir	*to guarantee*
applaudir	*to applaud*	grandir	*to grow (up)*
atterrir	*to land*	guérir	*to cure*
bâtir	*to build*	investir	*to invest*
bondir	*to leap*	mûrir	*to ripen*
choisir	*to choose*	obéir	*to obey*
convertir	*to convert*	punir	*to punish*
démolir	*to demolish*	ralentir	*to slow down*
désobéir	*to disobey*	réfléchir	*to think*
durcir	*to harden*	remplir	*to fill*
éblouir	*to dazzle*	réussir	*to succeed*
élargir	*to enlarge*	saisir	*to seize*
envahir	*to invade*	vomir	*to vomit*

How the verb works

le film finit à neuf heures	*the film finishes at nine o'clock*
j'ai fini le roman	*I've finished the novel*
qui veut finir la tarte?	*who wants to finish the tart?*
il faut que je finisse ma lettre	*I must finish my letter*
tu as fini avec les ciseaux?	*have you finished with the scissors?*
avez-vous fini de manger?	*have you finished eating?*
quand j'aurai fini de faire la vaisselle	*when I've finished doing the washing-up*

nous avons fini la soirée dans une boîte de nuit	*we ended the evening in a night club*
tu n'as pas fini de m'embêter?	*have you quite finished annoying me?*
le film finit bien/mal	*the film has a happy/unhappy ending*
tout est bien qui finit bien	*all's well that ends well*
il finira en prison	*he'll end up in prison*
elle a fini par accepter	*she eventually accepted*
tu vas finir par te faire mal!	*you'll end up hurting yourself!*
il faut en finir avec cette situation	*we must put an end to this situation*
nous avons des problèmes à n'en plus finir	*we have endless problems*

35 fuir to flee

irregular verb
conjugates with **avoir** *in compound tenses*

Imperative	Present participle	Past participle
fuis (tu)	fuyant	fui
fuyons (nous)		
fuyez (vous)		

Present
je fuis
tu fuis
il/elle fuit
nous fuyons
vous fuyez
ils/elles fuient

Past Historic
je fuis
tu fuis
il/elle fuit
nous fuîmes
vous fuîtes
ils/elles fuirent

Future
je fuirai
tu fuiras
il/elle fuira
nous fuirons
vous fuirez
ils/elles fuiront

Conditional
je fuirais
tu fuirais
il/elle fuirait
nous fuirions
vous fuiriez
ils/elles fuiraient

Imperfect
je fuyais
tu fuyais
il/elle fuyait
nous fuyions
vous fuyiez
ils/elles fuyaient

Present subjunctive
(que) je fuie
(que) tu fuies
(qu') il/elle fuie
(que) nous fuyions
(que) vous fuyiez
(qu') ils/elles fuient

Perfect
j'ai fui
tu as fui
il/elle a fui
nous avons fui
vous avez fui
ils/elles ont fui

Imperfect subjunctive
(que) je fuisse
(que) tu fuisses
(qu') il/elle fuît
(que) nous fuissions
(que) vous fuissiez
(qu') ils/elles fuissent

Following the same pattern

s'enfuir   *to run away*

How the verb works

la plupart des habitants ont été obligés de fuir la ville	*most of the inhabitants have been forced to flee the town*
ils ont fui à l'étranger	*they fled abroad*
nous fuyons l'hiver en partant pour l'Australie	*we're escaping the winter by going to Australia*
elle se débrouille toujours pour fuir ses responsabilités	*she always manages to avoid responsibility*
c'est un écrivain qui fuit les journalistes	*he's a writer who steers clear of journalists*
elle fuit les médias	*she shuns publicity*
les deux familles se fuient	*the two families avoid each other*

Language in use

quand l'alarme a sonné ils ont fui à toute jambes	*when the alarm went off they ran for it*
les aboiements du chien ont fait fuir les voleurs	*the dog's barking scared off the thieves*
il se peut que l'instabilité économique actuelle fasse fuir les investisseurs	*the current economic instability may scare off investors*
le robinet de la cuisine fuit	*the kitchen tap is leaking*
le chat s'enfuit chaque fois que je m'approche de lui	*the cat runs away every time I go near it*
ils se sont enfuis à Paris	*they ran/have run off to Paris*
elle s'est enfuie dans sa chambre	*she rushed off to her room*
le voleur s'est enfui par les toits	*the thief escaped over the rooftops*
nous nous sommes enfuis à toutes jambes	*we ran away as fast as our legs could carry us*
le temps s'enfuit	*time flies*

36 **geler** to freeze

irregular verb
conjugates with **avoir** *in compound tenses*

Imperative	Present participle	Past participle
gèle (tu)	gelant	gelé
gelons (nous)		
gelez (vous)		

Present
je gèle
tu gèles
il/elle gèle
nous gelons
vous gelez
ils/elles gèlent

Past Historic
je gelai
tu gelas
il/elle gela
nous gelâmes
vous gelâtes
ils/elles gelèrent

Future
je gèlerai
tu gèleras
il/elle gèlera
nous gèlerons
vous gèlerez
ils/elles gèleront

Conditional
je gèlerais
tu gèlerais
il/elle gèlerait
nous gèlerions
vous gèleriez
ils/elles gèleraient

Imperfect
je gelais
tu gelais
il/elle gelait
nous gelions
vous geliez
ils/elles gelaient

Present subjunctive
(que) je gèle
(que) tu gèles
(qu') il/elle gèle
(que) nous gelions
(que) vous geliez
(qu') ils/elles gèlent

Perfect
j'ai gelé
tu as gelé
il/elle a gelé
nous avons gelé
vous avez gelé
ils/elles ont gelé

Imperfect subjunctive
(que) je gelasse
(que) tu gelasses
(qu') il/elle gelât
(que) nous gelassions
(que) vous gelassiez
(qu') ils/elles gelassent

Some common verbs that follow the same pattern

ciseler	*to chisel*	écarteler	*to tear apart*
congeler	*to freeze*	marteler	*to beat/ hammer*
décongeler	*to defrost*		
dégeler	*to thaw*	modeler	*to model*
déceler	*to detect*	peler	*to peel*
démanteler	*to dismantle*	receler	*to conceal*

How the verb works

le lac gèle en hiver	*the lake freezes in winter*
le vent froid me gelait les doigts	*the cold wind froze my fingers*
les géraniums ont gelé	*the geraniums have got frosted*
tu es gelé!	*you're freezing!*

Language in use

nous avons congelé des framboises	*we froze some raspberries*
les haricots se congèlent bien	*green beans freeze well*
il faut que je décongèle le frigo	*I must defrost the fridge*
laissez décongeler la viande avant de la faire cuire	*let the meat thaw before cooking it*
le soleil a fait dégeler les flaques	*the sun thawed the puddles*
ça dégèle aujourd'hui	*it's thawing today*
l'analyse a permis de déceler des traces de poison	*the analysis revealed traces of poison*
c'est un artiste qui modèle des formes abstraites dans l'argile	*he's an artist who models abstract forms out of clay*

37 **haïr** to hate

irregular verb
conjugates with **avoir** *in compound tenses*

Imperative	**Present participle**	**Past participle**
haïs (tu)	haïssant	haï
haïssons (nous)		
haïssez (vous)		

Present
je hais
tu hais
il/elle hait
nous haïssons
vous haïssez
ils/elles haïssent

Past historic
je haïs
tu haïs
il/elle haït
nous haïmes
vous haïtes
ils/elles haïrent

Future
je haïrai
tu haïras
il/elle haïra
nous haïrons
vous haïrez
ils/elles haïront

Conditional
je haïrais
tu haïrais
il/elle haïrait
nous haïrions
vous haïriez
ils/elles haïraient

Imperfect
je haïssais
tu haïssais
il/elle haïssait
nous haïssions
vous haïssiez
ils/elles haïssaient

Present subjunctive
(que) je haïsse
(que) tu haïsses
(qu') il/elle haïsse
(que) nous haïssions
(que) vous haïssiez
(qu') ils/elles haïssent

Perfect
j'ai haï
tu as haï
il/elle a haï
nous avons haï
vous avez haï
ils/elles ont haï

Imperfect subjunctive
(que) je haïsse
(que) tu haïsses
(qu') il/elle haït
(que) nous haïssions
(que) vous haïssiez
(qu') ils/elles haïssent

How the verb works

je hais les dimanches	*I hate Sundays*
il hait le mensonge	*he hates lies*
il hait son père	*he hates his father*
elle s'est fait haïr de ses élèves	*she made herself hated by her students*
il la hait de l'avoir quitté	*he hates her for leaving him*
elle hait qu'on se moque d'elle	*she hates it when people make fun of her*
je haïrais qu'on me traite en esclave	*I'd hate to be treated as a slave*

38 jeter to throw

irregular verb
conjugates with **avoir** *in compound tenses*

Imperative	Present participle	Past participle
jette (tu)	jetant	jeté
jetons (nous)		
jettez (vous)		

Present
je jette
tu jettes
il/elle jette
nous jetons
vous jetez
ils/elles jettent

Past Historic
je jetai
tu jetas
il/elle jeta
nous jetâmes
vous jetâtes
ils/elles jetèrent

Future
je jetterai
tu jetteras
il/elle jettera
nous jetterons
vous jetterez
ils/elles jetteront

Conditional
je jetterais
tu jetterais
il/elle jetterait
nous jetterions
vous jetteriez
ils/elles jetteraient

Imperfect
je jetais
tu jetais
il/elle jetait
nous jetions
vous jetiez
ils/elles jetaient

Present subjunctive
(que) je jette
(que) tu jettes
(qu') il/elle jette
(que) nous jetions
(que) vous jetiez
(qu') ils/elles jettent

Perfect
j'ai jeté
tu as jeté
il/elle a jeté
nous avons jeté
vous avez jeté
ils/elles ont jeté

Imperfect subjunctive
(que) je jetasse
(que) tu jetasses
(qu') il/elle jetât
(que) nous jetassions
(que) vous jetassiez
(qu') ils/elles jetassent

Some common verbs that follow the same pattern

becqueter	*to peck at*	feuilleter	*to leaf through*
déchiqueter	*to tear to shreds*	projeter	*to project/ plan*
étiqueter	*to label*	rejeter	*to reject*

How the verb works

arrête de jeter des pierres à ton frère!
stop throwing stones at your brother!

jette-moi une serviette, s'il te plaît
throw me a towel please

il jette toujours ses vêtements par terre
he always throws his clothes on the floor

elle a jeté quelques couteaux sur la table
she threw some knives down on the table

elle s'est jetée du haut d'un pont
she threw herself off a bridge

Language in use

tu devrais jeter ces chaussures à la poubelle
you should throw these shoes in the bin/throw out these shoes

je vais jeter tous mes vieux pulls
I'm going to throw out all my old sweaters

c'est jeter l'argent par les fenêtres
it's throwing money away

il s'est fait jeter du bar*
he got thrown out of the bar

le choc l'a projetée par terre
the shock threw her to the ground

je projette de passer un an en Inde
I'm planning to spend a year in India

il était en train de feuilleter un livre de cuisine
he was leafing through a cookbook

elle a toujours été rejetée par la famille de son mari
she has always been rejected by her husband's family

votre candidature a été rejetée
your application has been turned down

39 **joindre** to join

irregular verb
*conjugates with **avoir** in compound tenses*

Imperative	Present participle	Past participle
joins (tu)	joignant	joint
joignons (nous)		
joignez (vous)		

Present
je joins
tu joins
il/elle joint
nous joignons
vous joignez
ils/elles joignent

Past Historic
je joignis
tu joignis
il/elle joignit
nous joignîmes
vous joignîtes
ils/elles joignirent

Future
je joindrai
tu joindras
il/elle joindra
nous joindrons
vous joindrez
ils/elles joindront

Conditional
je joindrais
tu joindrais
il/elle joindrait
nous joindrions
vous joindriez
ils/elles joindraient

Imperfect
je joignais
tu joignais
il/elle joignait
nous joignions
vous joigniez
ils/elles joignaient

Present subjunctive
(que) je joigne
(que) tu joignes
(qu') il/elle joigne
(que) nous joignions
(que) vous joigniez
(qu') ils/elles joignent

Perfect
j'ai joint
tu as joint
il/elle a joint
nous avons joint
vous avez joint
ils/elles ont joint

Imperfect subjunctive
(que) je joignisse
(que) tu joignisses
(qu') il/elle joignît
(que) nous joignissions
(que) vous joignissiez
(qu') ils/elles joignisssent

Following the same pattern

adjoindre   *to attach*   rejoindre   *to meet up*
                                                          with

How the verb works

je n'ai pas réussi à la joindre   *I didn't manage to get hold of*
                                   her

je cherche à joindre Marie   *I'm trying to get hold of Marie*
  Perrier   *Perrier*

tu peux essayer de la joindre   *you could try to get in touch*
  par téléphone   *with her by telephone*

je joins les documents à mon   *I am sending the documents as*
  envoi   *well*

Language in use

prière de trouver ci-jointe la   *please find enclosed a*
  photocopie du contrat   *photocopy of the contract*

toute la famille se joint à moi   *all the family join me in*
  pour vous souhaiter une *wishing you a happy New*
  bonne année   *Year*

voulez-vous vous joindre à   *would you like to join us to*
  nous pour fêter l'anniversaire *celebrate Valentin's birthday?*
  de Valentin?

joindre les deux bouts*   *to make ends meet*

on se rejoint devant le   *shall we meet up outside the*
  cinéma?   *cinema?*

le sentier rejoint la route juste *the path joins the road just*
  après l'église   *after the church*

vos idées rejoignent les   *your ideas are similar to mine*
  miennes

cela rejoint ce qu'elle a dit   *it ties in with what she said*

40 **lever** to raise

irregular verb
conjugates with **avoir** *in compound tenses*

Imperative	Present participle	Past participle
lève (tu)	levant	levé
levons (nous)		
levez (vous)		

Present
je lève
tu lèves
il/elle lève
nous levons
vous levez
ils/elles lèvent

Past Historic
je levai
tu levas
il/elle leva
nous levâmes
vous levâtes
ils/elles levèrent

Future
je lèverai
tu lèveras
il/elle lèvera
nous lèverons
vous lèverez
ils/elles lèveront

Conditional
je lèverais
tu lèverais
il/elle lèverait
nous lèverions
vous lèveriez
ils/elles lèveraient

Imperfect
je levais
tu levais
il/elle levait
nous levions
vous leviez
ils/elles levaient

Present subjunctive
(que) je lève
(que) tu lèves
(qu') il/elle lève
(que) nous levions
(que) vous leviez
(qu') ils/elles lèvent

Perfect
j'ai levé
tu as levé
il/elle a levé
nous avons levé
vous avez levé
ils/elles ont levé

Imperfect subjunctive
(que) je levasse
(que) tu levasses
(qu') il/elle levât
(que) nous levassions
(que) vous levassiez
(qu') ils/elles levassent

Some common verbs that follow the same pattern

achever	to finish	mener	to lead
amener	to take/bring	peser	to weigh
crever	to burst/*die	promener	to walk
élever	to bring up	ramener	to bring/take back
emmener	to take away		
enlever	to take away/remove	semer	to sow

How the verb works

levez la main tous ceux qui veulent des glaces	those who want ice creams put up their hands
levons nos verres au succès du projet	let's raise our glasses to the success of the project
je me lève à huit heures du matin	I get up at eight in the morning
elle s'est levée pour poser une question	she stood up to ask a question

Language in use

il a répondu sans lever les yeux	he answered without looking up
le soleil va se lever	the sun is about to rise
le jour se lève	it's getting light
j'amène ma fille chez le dentiste	I'm taking my daughter to the dentist's
tu peux amener tes amis	you can bring your friends
je crève de faim!*	I'm starving!
il a été élevé par ses grand-parents	he was brought up by his grandparents
la température va s'élever de dix degrés	the temperature will rise by ten degrees
elle est partie emmener les enfants à l'école	she's left to take the children to school
il a enlevé sa veste	he took off his jacket
il faut d'abord peser les fruits	first you must weigh the fruit
je pèse soixante kilos	I weigh sixty kilos
elle promène son chien tous les soirs	she takes her dog for a walk every evening
j'aime bien me promener dans les bois	I like walking in the woods
je te ramènerai à la maison	I'll take you home

41 lire to read

irregular verb
conjugates with **avoir** *in compound tenses*

Imperative	Present participle	Past participle
lis (tu)	lisant	lu
lisons (nous)		
lisez (vous)		

Present
je lis
tu lis
il/elle lit
nous lisons
vous lisez
ils/elles lisent

Past Historic
je lus
tu lus
il/elle lut
nous lûmes
vous lûtes
ils/elles lurent

Future
je lirai
tu liras
il/elle lira
nous lirons
vous lirez
ils/elles liront

Conditional
je lirais
tu lirais
il/elle lirait
nous lirions
vous liriez
ils/elles liraient

Imperfect
je lisais
tu lisais
il/elle lisait
nous lisions
vous lisiez
ils/elles lisaient

Present subjunctive
(que) je lise
(que) tu lises
(qu') il/elle lise
(que) nous lisions
(que) vous lisiez
(qu') ils/elles lisent

Perfect
j'ai lu
tu as lu
il/elle a lu
nous avons lu
vous avez lu
ils/elles ont lu

Imperfect subjunctive
(que) je lusse
(que) tu lusses
(qu') il/elle lût
(que) nous lussions
(que) vous lussiez
(qu') ils/elles lussent

Following the same pattern

élire	*to elect*	relire	*to reread*

How the verb works

c'est un livre pour les enfants qui apprennent à lire	*it's a book for children who are learning to read*
il sait déjà lire et écrire	*he can already read and write*
elle lisait une histoire à son fils	*she was reading her son a story*
peux-tu me lire sa lettre?	*can you read me her letter?*
il a lu le poème à voix haute	*he read the poem aloud*

Language in use

c'est un livre à lire	*it's a book worth reading*
elle a lu mes remarques comme une critique	*she interpreted my remarks as a criticism*
c'est un magazine qui est très lu	*it's a widely read magazine*
'lu et approuvé'	*'read and approved'*
dans l'espoir de vous lire bientôt...	*hoping to hear from you soon...*
il m'a lu les lignes de la main	*he read my palm*
elle a lu la tristesse dans ses yeux	*she saw sadness written in his/her eyes*
je veux relire sa lettre avant de répondre	*I want to reread his/her letter before replying*
il faut prendre le temps de relire tes copies d'examen	*you must leave yourself the time to read through your exam papers*
mon travail consiste à relire des articles de recherche	*my work consists in proofreading research articles*
elle a été élue à l'unanimité	*she was elected unanimously*
elle a été élue maire	*she was elected mayor*

42 manger to eat

irregular verb
conjugates with **avoir** *in compound tenses*

Imperative	Present participle	Past participle
mange (tu)	mangeant	mangé
mangeons (nous)		
mangez (vous)		

Present
je mange
tu manges
il/elle mange
nous mangeons
vous mangez
ils/elles mangent

Past Historic
je mangeai
tu mangeas
il/elle mangea
nous mangeâmes
vous mangeâtes
ils/elles mangèrent

Future
je mangerai
tu mangeras
il/elle mangera
nous mangerons
vous mangerez
ils/elles mangeront

Conditional
je mangerais
tu mangerais
il/elle mangerait
nous mangerions
vous mangeriez
ils/elles mangeraient

Imperfect
je mangeais
tu mangeais
il/elle mangeait
nous mangions
vous mangiez
ils/elles mangeaient

Present subjunctive
(que) je mange
(que) tu manges
(qu') il/elle mange
(que) nous mangions
(que) vous mangiez
(qu') ils/elles mangent

Perfect
j'ai mangé
tu as mangé
il/elle a mangé
nous avons mangé
vous avez mangé
ils/elles ont mangé

Imperfect subjunctive
(que) je mangeasse
(que) tu mangeasses
(qu') il/elle mangeât
(que) nous mangeassions
(que) vous mangeassiez
(qu') ils/elles mangeassent

Some common verbs that follow the same pattern

affliger	to afflict	déménager	to move house
aménager	to convert/ develop/ equip	déranger	to disturb
		diriger	to be in charge of/ direct
arranger	to arrange		
avantager	to favour		
changer	to change	échanger	to exchange
charger	to load	émerger	to emerge
corriger	to correct	encourager	to encourage
décharger	to unload	engager	to engage
décourager	to discourage	envisager	to plan/ envisage
dégager	to clear		
		infliger	to inflict

◇according to French pronunciation rules, **g** when followed by **a** or **o** would be pronounced as in the English word **go**; to prevent this happening, an **e** is added after the **g** where an **a** or an **o** follows

How the verb works

elle ne mange pas de viande	she doesn't eat meat
nous mangeons à sept heures	we eat at seven
il mangeait une pomme	he was eating an apple
tu devrais manger plus de légumes	you should eat more vegetables
il n'y a rien à manger	there's nothing to eat
venez manger!	come and eat!

Language in use

où est-ce qu'on mange?	where shall we eat?
nous allons manger au restaurant ce soir	we're going out for a meal this evening
c'est un plat qui se mange chaud ou froid	it's a dish which can be served hot or cold
elle a changé d'emploi	she's got a new job
j'ai changé d'avis	I've changed my mind
il a été découragé par son échec	he was discouraged by his failure
je déteste qu'on me dérange quand je travaille	I hate being disturbed when I'm working

43 maudire to curse

irregular verb
conjugates with **avoir** *in compound tenses*

Imperative	Present participle	Past participle
maudis (tu)	maudissant	maudit
maudissons		
(nous)		
maudissez (vous)		

Present
je maudis
tu maudis
il/elle maudit
nous maudissons
vous maudissez
ils/elles maudissent

Past Historic
je maudis
tu maudis
il/elle maudit
nous maudîmes
vous maudîtes
ils/elles maudirent

Future
je maudirai
tu maudiras
il/elle maudira
nous maudirons
vous maudirez
ils/elles maudiront

Conditional
je maudirais
tu maudirais
il/elle maudirait
nous maudirions
vous maudiriez
ils/elles maudiraient

Imperfect
je maudissais
tu maudissais
il/elle maudissait
nous maudissions
vous maudissiez
ils/elles maudissaient

Present subjunctive
(que) je maudisse
(que) tu maudisses
(qu') il/elle maudisse
(que) nous maudissions
(que) vous maudissiez
(qu') ils/elles maudissent

Perfect
j'ai maudit
tu as maudit
il/elle a maudit
nous avons maudit
vous avez maudit
ils/elles ont maudit

Imperfect subjunctive
(que) je maudisse
(que) tu maudisses
(qu') il/elle maudît
(que) nous maudissions
(que) vous maudissiez
(qu') ils/elles maudissent

How the verb works

il maudit toutes les inventions modernes
he curses all modern inventions

elle maudissait le mauvais temps qui avait détruit sa récolte
she cursed the bad weather which had destroyed her harvest

les réformes ont été maudites par les paysans
the reforms were cursed by the peasants

Language in use

je maudis le jour où j'ai acheté cette voiture!
I curse the day I bought that car!

cette maudite voiture ne veut toujours pas démarrer!*
that blasted car still won't start!

le héros maudit de la pièce de Shakespeare
the ill-starred hero of Shakespeare's play

44 médire to malign

irregular verb
*conjugates with **avoir** in compound tenses*

Imperative	Present participle	Past participle
médis (tu)	médisant	médit
médisons (nous)		
médisez (vous)		

Present
je médis
tu médis
il/elle médit
nous médisons
vous médisez
ils/elles médisent

Past Historic
je médis
tu médis
il/elle médit
nous médîmes
vous médîtes
ils/elles médirent

Future
je médirai
tu médiras
il/elle médira
nous médirons
vous médirez
ils/elles médiront

Conditional
je médirais
tu médirais
il/elle médirait
nous médirions
vous médiriez
ils/elles médiraient

Imperfect
je médisais
tu médisais
il/elle médisait
nous médisions
vous médisiez
ils/elles médisaient

Present subjunctive
(que) je médise
(que) tu médises
(qu') il/elle médise
(que) nous médisions
(que) vous médisiez
(qu') ils/elles médisent

Perfect
j'ai médit
tu as médit
il/elle a médit
nous avons médit
vous avez médit
ils/elles ont médit

Imperfect subjunctive
(que) je médisse
(que) tu médisses
(qu') il/elle médît
(que) nous médissions
(que) vous médissiez
(qu') ils/elles médissent

Following the same pattern

dire◇	to say	interdire	to forbid
redire◇	to say again	prédire	to predict

◇except the second person plural of the present tense: **dites** and **redites**

How the verb works

j'essaie de ne pas médire des gens	*I try not to speak ill of people*
les médias ont beaucoup médit du premier ministre récemment	*the prime minister has been much maligned by the press recently*

qu'est-ce qu'il t'a dit?	*what did he say to you ?*
elle m'a dit que tu allais partir en vacances	*she told me you were going on holiday*
'entrez' dit-elle	*'come in,' she said*
dis-moi ce qui s'est passé	*tell me what happened*
dis-le à ton frère	*tell your brother*
c'est le moins qu'on puisse dire	*that's the least one can say*
comment dirais-je?	*how shall I put it?*
ça ne se dit pas	*you can't say that*
je leur ai dit de ne plus revenir	*I told them not to come back again*
elle leur a interdit de fumer à l'intérieur de la maison	*she forbade them to smoke inside the house*
'il est interdit de fumer'	*'no smoking'*
le film a été interdit en Italie	*the film has been banned in Italy*
la discrétion m'interdit d'en dire plus	*discretion prevents me from saying any more*
personne n'aurait pu prédire la catastrophe	*no-one could have predicted the disaster*
je prédis qu'il va démissionner avant la fin de l'année	*I predict that he will resign before the end of the year*

45 **mettre** to put

irregular verb
conjugates with **avoir** *in compound tenses*

Imperative	**Present participle**	**Past participle**
mets (tu)	mett**ant**	mis
mett**ons** (nous)		
mett**ez** (vous)		

Present
je mets
tu mets
il/elle met
nous mett**ons**
vous mett**ez**
ils/elles mett**ent**

Past Historic
je mis
tu mis
il/elle mit
nous mîmes
vous mîtes
ils/elles mirent

Future
je mett**rai**
tu mett**ras**
il/elle mett**ra**
nous mett**rons**
vous mett**rez**
ils/elles mett**ront**

Conditional
je mett**rais**
tu mett**rais**
il/elle mett**rait**
nous mett**rions**
vous mett**riez**
ils/elles mett**raient**

Imperfect
je mett**ais**
tu mett**ais**
il/elle mett**ait**
nous mett**ions**
vous mett**iez**
ils/elles mett**aient**

Present subjunctive
(que) je mette
(que) tu mett**es**
(qu') il/elle mette
(que) nous mett**ions**
(que) vous mett**iez**
(qu') ils/elles mett**ent**

Perfect
j'**ai** mis
tu **as** mis
il/elle **a** mis
nous **avons** mis
vous **avez** mis
ils/elles **ont** mis

Imperfect subjunctive
(que) je misse
(que) tu misses
(qu') il/elle mît
(que) nous missions
(que) vous missiez
(qu') ils/elles missent

Some common verbs that follow the same pattern

admettre	to admit	omettre	to omit
commettre	to commit	remettre	to put back
émettre	to emit	transmettre	to transmit

How the verb works

mets la viande au frigo	*put the meat in the fridge*
je mettrai ton manteau dans la chambre	*I'll put your coat in the bedroom*
où est-ce que tu as mis les ciseaux?	*where have you/did you put the scissors?*
mets les pommes de terre à cuire	*put the potatoes on to cook*
elle avait mis sa robe jaune	*she'd put on her yellow dress*
je vais mettre le chauffage/la radio	*I'll put on the heating/the radio*
est-ce que tu as mis les verres?	*have you put out the glasses?*
on va mettre une nappe propre	*we'll put on a clean tablecloth*

Language in use

qui va mettre la table?	*who's going to set the table?*
ils ont fait mettre du carrelage	*they've had tiles laid*
tu as mis de la confiture partout!	*you've got jam all over everything!*
j'ai mis une heure pour trouver le numéro	*it took me an hour to find the number*
je vous mets un peu de riz?	*would you like some rice?*
où est-ce que ça se met?	*where does this go?*
elle s'est mise devant la fenêtre	*she went and stood/sat in front of the window*
tout le monde s'est mis debout	*everyone stood up*
elle s'est mise au lit	*she went to/has gone to bed*
tout d'un coup il s'est mis à chanter	*all of a sudden he started to sing*
il se met à faire froid	*it's starting to get cold*
elle s'est mise en colère	*she got angry*

46 moudre to grind

irregular verb
conjugates with **avoir** *in compound tenses*

Imperative	Present participle	Past participle
mouds (tu)	moulant	moulu
moulons (nous)		
moulez (vous)		

Present
je mouds
tu mouds
il/elle moud
nous moulons
vous moulez
ils/elles moulent

Past Historic
je moulus
tu moulus
il/elle moulut
nous moulûmes
vous moulûtes
ils/elles moulurent

Future
je moudrai
tu moudras
il/elle moudra
nous moudrons
vous moudrez
ils/elles moudront

Conditional
je moudrais
tu moudrais
il/elle moudrait
nous moudrions
vous moudriez
ils/elles moudraient

Imperfect
je moulais
tu moulais
il/elle moulait
nous moulions
vous mouliez
ils/elles moulaient

Present subjunctive
(que) je moule
(que) tu moules
(qu') il/elle moule
(que) nous moulions
(que) vous mouliez
(qu') ils/elles moulent

Perfect
j'ai moulu
tu as moulu
il/elle a moulu
nous avons moulu
vous avez moulu
ils/elles ont moulu

Imperfect subjunctive
(que) je moulusse
(que) tu moulusses
(qu') il/elle moulût
(que) nous moulussions
(que) vous moulussiez
(qu') ils/elles moulussent

How the verb works

elle moud le café	*she is grinding the coffee*
quand tu auras fini de moudre les épices, tu pourras les rajouter à la sauce	*when you've finished grinding the spices, you can add them to the sauce*
j'achète toujours du café moulu	*I always buy ground coffee*

47 mourir to die

irregular verb
conjugates with **être** *in compound tenses*

Imperative	Present participle	Past participle
meurs (tu)	mourant	mort/-e(s)
mourons (nous)		
mourez (vous)		

Present
je meurs
tu meurs
il/elle meurt
nous mourons
vous mourez
ils/elles meurent

Past Historic
je mourus
tu mourus
il/elle mourut
nous mourûmes
vous mourûtes
ils/elles moururent

Future
je mourrai
tu mourras
il/elle mourra
nous mourrons
vous mourrez
ils/elles mourront

Conditional
je mourrais
tu mourrais
il/elle mourrait
nous mourrions
vous mourriez
ils/elles mourraient

Imperfect
je mourais
tu mourais
il/elle mourait
nous mourions
vous mouriez
ils/elles mouraient

Present subjunctive
(que) je meure
(que) tu meures
(qu') il/elle meure
(que) nous mourions
(que) vous mouriez
(qu') ils/elles meurent

Perfect
je **suis** mort/-e
tu **es** mort/-e
il/elle **est** mort/-e
nous **sommes** morts/-tes
vous **êtes** mort/-e(s)
ils/elles **sont** morts/-tes

Imperfect subjunctive
(que) je mourusse
(que) tu mourusses
(qu') il/elle mourût
(que) nous mourussions
(que) vous mourussiez
(qu') ils/elles mourussent

How the verb works

tes plantes vont mourir si tu ne les arroses pas plus souvent	*your plants are going to die if you don't water them more often*
elle est morte la semaine dernière	*she died last week*
elle est morte d'un cancer	*she died of cancer*
Schubert est mort jeune	*Schubert died young*
des centaines de refugiés sont morts de faim	*hundreds of refugees have died of hunger*

Language in use

on dit qu'elle est morte de chagrin	*people say she died of a broken heart*
il est mort assassiné	*he was murdered*
il s'est laissé mourir après la mort de sa femme	*he gave up and died after his wife's death*
tu mourras centenaire!	*you'll live to be a hundred!*
je meurs de faim!	*I'm starving!*
nous mourons de soif!	*we're dying of thirst!*
elle mourait de sommeil	*she was dropping with tiredness*
c'était à mourir de rire!	*it was hilarious!*
plutôt mourir que de leur demander une faveur	*I'd rather die than ask them a favour*
on n'en meurt pas!	*it won't kill you!*
plus paresseux que lui, tu meurs!*	*they don't come any lazier!*

48 mouvoir to move

irregular verb
conjugates with **avoir** *in compound tenses*

Imperative	Present participle	Past participle
meus (tu)	mouvant	mû
mouvons (nous)		
mouvez (vous)		

Present
je meus
tu meus
il/elle meut
nous mouvons
vous mouvez
ils/elles meuvent

Past Historic
je mus
tu mus
il/elle mut
nous mûmes
vous mûtes
ils/elles murent

Future
je mouvrai
tu mouvras
il/elle mouvra
nous mouvrons
vous mouvrez
ils/elles mouvront

Conditional
je mouvrais
tu mouvrais
il/elle mouvrait
nous mouvrions
vous mouvriez
ils/elles mouvraient

Imperfect
je mouvais
tu mouvais
il/elle mouvait
nous mouvions
vous mouviez
ils/elles mouvaient

Present subjunctive
(que) je meuve
(que) tu meuves
(qu') il/elle meuve
(que) nous mouvions
(que) vous mouviez
(qu') ils/elles meuvent

Perfect
j'ai mû
tu as mû
il/elle a mû
nous avons mû
vous avez mû
ils/elles ont mû

Imperfect subjunctive
(que) je musse
(que) tu musses
(qu') il/elle mût
(que) nous mussions
(que) vous mussiez
(qu') ils/elles mussent

Following the same pattern

émouvoir   *to move*   promouvoir   *to promote*

How the verb works

la machine est mue par l'électricité	*the machine is driven by electricity*
elle était mue par l'ambition	*she was driven by ambition*
mes jambes ne peuvent plus se mouvoir	*I can't move my legs any more*

Language in use

son courage m'émeut	*I find his/her courage moving*
votre sympathie m'émeut	*I am touched by your sympathy*
son discours m'a ému jusqu'aux larmes	*his/her speech moved me to tears*
leur nouveau film a ému l'opinion	*their new film has caused a stir*
elle s'émeut à peine de la maladie de sa fille	*she is not deeply concerned about her daughter's illness*
il ne s'émeut nullement de leur retard	*he's not the least bit worried by the fact that they're late*
elle ne s'est pas émue de mes remarques	*my remarks didn't bother her*
il n'y a pas de quoi s'émouvoir	*there's nothing to get excited about*
le premier ministre a répondu à toutes les questions sans s'émouvoir	*the prime minister answered all the questions calmly*
elle a été promue l'année dernière	*she was promoted last year*
il a été promu chef de service	*he's been promoted to head of department*
une campagne pour promouvoir le recyclage	*a campaign to promote recycling*

49 naître to be born

irregular verb
conjugates with **être** *in compound tenses*

Imperative	Present participle	Past participle
nais (tu)	naissant	né/-e(s)
naissons (nous)		
naissez (vous)		

Present
je nais
tu nais
il/elle naît
nous naissons
vous naissez
ils/elles naissent

Past Historic
je naquis
tu naquis
il/elle naquit
nous naquîmes
vous naquîtes
ils/elles naquirent

Future
je naîtrai
tu naîtras
il/elle naîtra
nous naîtrons
vous naîtrez
ils/elles naîtront

Conditional
je naîtrais
tu naîtrais
il/elle naîtrait
nous naîtrions
vous naîtriez
ils/elles naîtraient

Imperfect
je naissais
tu naissais
il/elle naissait
nous naissions
vous naissiez
ils/elles naissaient

Present subjunctive
(que) je naisse
(que) tu naisses
(qu') il/elle naisse
(que) nous naissions
(que) vous naissiez
(qu') ils/elles naissent

Perfect
je **suis** né/-e
tu **es** né/-e
il/elle **est** né/-e
nous **sommes** nés/-ées
vous **êtes** né/-ée(s)
ils/elles **sont** nés/-ées

Imperfect subjunctive
(que) je naquisse
(que) tu naquisses
(qu') il/elle naquît
(que) nous naquissions
(que) vous naquissiez
(qu') ils/elles naquissent

Following the same pattern

renaître   *to be reborn*

How the verb works

elle est née en Afrique	*she was born in Africa*
il est né le 24 juin	*he was born on the 24th of June*

Language in use

leur bébé doit naître la semaine prochaine	*their baby is due next week*
les bébés qui viennent de naître	*newborn babies*
je l'ai vu naître	*I've known him since he was born*
elle est née pour enseigner	*she was born to teach*
il est né paresseux	*he was born lazy*
une amitié est née entre eux	*a friendship sprang up between them*
l'année 1993 a vu naître un nouveau journal	*the year 1993 saw the birth of a new newspaper*
le cinéma du quartier renaît cette année grâce aux efforts d'un groupe de jeunes	*the local cinema is coming back to life this year thanks to the efforts of a group of young people*
l'amélioration des routes a fait renaître la région	*road improvements have revitalized the region*

50 offrir to offer

irregular verb
conjugates with **avoir** *in compound tenses*

Imperative	Present participle	Past participle
offre (tu)	offrant	offert
offrons (nous)		
offrez (vous)		

Present
j'offre
tu offres
il/elle offre
nous offrons
vous offrez
ils/elles offrent

Past historic
j'offris
tu offris
il/elle offrit
nous offrîmes
vous offrîtes
ils/elles offrirent

Future
j'offrirai
tu offriras
il/elle offrira
nous offrirons
vous offrirez
ils/elles offriront

Conditional
j'offrirais
tu offrirais
il/elle offrirait
nous offririons
vous offririez
ils/elles offriraient

Imperfect
j'offrais
tu offrais
il/elle offrait
nous offrions
vous offriez
ils/elles offraient

Present subjunctive
(que) j'offre
(que) tu offres
(qu') il/elle offre
(que) nous offrions
(que) vous offriez
(qu') ils/elles offrent

Perfect
j'ai offert
tu as offert
il/elle a offert
nous avons offert
vous avez offert
ils/elles ont offert

Imperfect subjunctive
(que) j'offrisse
(que) tu offrisses
(qu') il/elle offrît
(que) nous offrissions
(que) vous offrissiez
(qu') ils/elles offrissent

Following the same pattern

souffrir   *to suffer*

How the verb works

je lui ai offert une montre pour son anniversaire	*I gave him/her a watch for his/her birthday*
elle a offert une cravate à son père	*she gave her father a tie*
on lui a offert le rôle de Hamlet	*he was offered the part of Hamlet*
elle nous a offert à manger	*she offered us something to eat*
ils ont offert de nous aider	*they offered to help us*
il m'a offert de repeindre la cuisine	*he offered to paint the kitchen for me*
tu m'offres combien?	*how much are you offering?*
je t'en offre 200 francs	*I'll give you 200 francs for it*
je n'ai rien à offrir	*I have nothing to offer*

Language in use

c'est pour offrir?	*would you like it gift-wrapped?*
si tu aimes cette robe, je te l'offre	*if you like that dress, I'll buy it for you*
je vais m'offrir des fleurs	*I'm going to buy myself some flowers*
je t'offre un verre?	*can I buy you a drink?*
il m'a offert le restaurant	*he took me out for a meal*
c'est moi qui offre	*it's my treat*
cela offre plusieurs avantages	*there are several advantages*
ils ne peuvent pas s'offrir une secrétaire	*they can't afford a secretary*
il s'est offert comme chauffeur	*he offered to drive*
il a beaucoup souffert	*he's suffered a great deal*
elle souffre de rhumatismes	*she suffers from rheumatism*
elle ne peut plus le souffrir	*she can't stand him any more*

51 partir to leave

irregular verb
*conjugates with **être** in compound tenses*

Imperative	Present participle	Past participle
pars (tu)	partant	parti/-e(s)
partons (nous)		
partez (vous)		

Present
je pars
tu pars
il/elle part
nous partons
vous partez
ils/elles part

Past Historic
je partis
tu partis
il/elle partit
nous partîmes
vous partîtes
ils/elles partirent

Future
je partirai
tu partiras
il/elle partira
nous partirons
vous partirez
ils/elles partiront

Conditional
je partirais
tu partirais
il/elle partirait
nous partirions
vous partiriez
ils/elles partiraient

Imperfect
je partais
tu partais
il/elle partait
nous partions
vous partiez
ils/elles partaient

Present subjunctive
(que) je parte
(que) tu partes
(qu') il/elle parte
(que) nous partions
(que) vous partiez
(qu') ils/elles partent

Perfect
je suis parti/-e
tu es parti/-e
il/elle est parti/-e
nous sommes partis/-ies
vous êtes parti/-ie(s)
ils/elles sont partis/-ies

Imperfect subjunctive
(que) je partisse
(que) tu partisses
(qu') il/elle partît
(que) nous partissions
(que) vous partissiez
(qu') ils/elles partissent

Some common verbs that follow the same pattern

départir	*to allot*	repartir	*to leave (again)*

How the verb works

nous partons demain matin	*we're leaving tomorrow morning*
ils viennent de partir pour Paris	*they've just left for Paris*
elle est partie en voiture	*she left by car*
de quelle gare pars-tu?	*which station are you leaving from?*
je suis parti de chez moi à huit heures	*I left the house at eight o'clock*
il est parti chercher des chaises	*he's gone to fetch some chairs*

Language in use

je pars à Londres demain	*I'm going to London tomorrow*
tu pars pour combien de temps?	*how long are you going away for?*
le train à destination de Nantes va partir	*the train for Nantes is about to depart*
elle est partie en vacances	*she's away on holiday*
il est parti au travail	*he's gone to work*
la rue qui part de l'église	*the street which goes from the church*
le sentier part d'ici	*the path starts here*
c'est mal parti*	*things don't look too good*
une tache qui ne part pas	*a stain which won't come out*
à partir de seize heures	*from four p.m. onwards*
à partir de maintenant	*from now on*
tu repars déjà?	*are you leaving already?*
il est reparti chez lui	*he's gone back home*
il va falloir repartir à zéro	*we'll have to start all over again*

52 payer to pay

irregular verb
conjugates with **avoir** *in compound tenses*

Imperative	Present participle	Past participle
paie (tu)	payant	payé
payons (nous)		
payez (vous)		

Present
je paie/paye
tu paies/payes
il/elle paie/paye
nous payons
vous payez
ils/elles paient/payent

Past Historic
je payai
tu payas
il/elle paya
nous payâmes
vous payâtes
ils/elles payèrent

Future
je paierai/payerai
tu paieras/payeras
il/elle paiera/payera
nous paierons/payerons
vous paierez/payerez
ils/elles paieront/payeront

Conditional
je paierais/payerais
tu paierais/payerais
il/elle paierait/payerait
nous paierions/payerions
vous paieriez/payeriez
ils/elles paieraient/payeraient

Imperfect
je payais
tu payais
il/elle payait
nous payions
vous payiez
ils/elles payaient

Present subjunctive
(que) je paie/paye
(que) tu paies/payes
(qu') il/elle paie/paye
(que) nous payions
(que) vous payiez
(qu') ils/elles paient/payent

Perfect
j'ai payé
tu as payé
il/elle a payé
nous avons payé
vous avez payé
ils/elles ont payé

Imperfect subjunctive
(que) je payasse
(que) tu payasses
(qu') il/elle payât
(que) nous payassions
(que) vous payassiez
(qu') ils/elles payassent

Some common verbs that follow the same pattern

déblayer	to clear	égayer	to cheer up/
délayer	to dilute		brighten
effrayer	to frighten	essayer	to try
		frayer	to clear

How the verb works

j'ai payé la note	I've paid the bill
j'ai payé le serveur	I've paid the waiter
combien as-tu payé ces chaussures?	how much did you pay for these shoes?
il faut que je paie le téléphone	I must pay the telephone bill
elle paie 4000 francs de loyer	she pays 4000 francs in rent
je vais payer par chèque/par carte de crédit	I'm going to pay by cheque/ credit card
elle a payé son fils pour repeindre la cuisine	she paid her son to paint the kitchen
il est payé à l'heure	he's paid by the hour

Language in use

je ne suis pas payé pour ça!	that's not what I'm paid for!
elle est payée pour ne rien faire	she's paid for doing nothing
ils sont trop payés	they're overpaid
elles sont trop peu payées	they're underpaid
c'est un métier qui paie bien/mal	it's a well paid/badly paid job
je te paierai un verre*	I'll buy you a drink
mon frère va nous payer le restaurant dimanche*	my brother's taking us out for a meal on Sunday
je vais me payer des vacances au soleil*	I'm going to treat myself to a holiday in the sun
tu me le paieras cher!	I'll make you pay for this!
il a payé de sa personne	it cost him dear
la quantité de travail m'effraie	the amount of work scares me
nous allons essayer le nouveau restaurant ce soir	we're going to try the new restaurant this evening
est-ce que je peux essayer ces jupes?	can I try these skirts on?
j'ai tout essayé	I've tried everything
il a essayé de la convaincre	he tried to convince her

53 peindre to paint

irregular verb
conjugates with **avoir** *in compound tenses*

Imperative	Present participle	Past participle
peins (tu)	peignant	peint
peignons (nous)		
peignez (vous)		

Present
je peins
tu peins
il/elle peint
nous peignons
vous peignez
ils/elles peignent

Past Historic
je peignis
tu peignis
il/elle peignit
nous peignîmes
vous peignîtes
ils/elles peignirent

Future
je peindrai
tu peindras
il/elle peindra
nous peindrons
vous peindrez
ils/elles peindront

Conditional
je peindrais
tu peindrais
il/elle peindrait
nous peindrions
vous peindriez
ils/elles peindraient

Imperfect
je peignais
tu peignais
il/elle peignait
nous peignions
vous peigniez
ils/elles peignaient

Present subjunctive
(que) je peigne
(que) tu peignes
(qu') il/elle peigne
(que) nous peignions
(que) vous peigniez
(qu') ils/elles peignent

Perfect
j'**ai** peint
tu **as** peint
il/elle **a** peint
nous **avons** peint
vous **avez** peint
ils/elles **ont** peint

Imperfect subjunctive
(que) je peignisse
(que) tu peignisses
(qu') il/elle peignît
(que) nous peignissions
(que) vous peignissiez
(qu') ils/elles peignissent

Some common verbs that follow the same pattern

astreindre	to force	feindre	to feign
atteindre	to reach/ affect	geindre	to moan
		repeindre	to repaint
enfreindre	to infringe	restreindre	to restrict
éteindre	to put out	teindre	to dye

How the verb works

il était en train de peindre les murs en jaune	he was busy painting the walls yellow
mon frère peint des paysages	my brother paints landscapes
j'apprends à peindre sur soie	I'm learning to paint on silk

Language in use

il va falloir qu'on repeigne la cuisine	we're going to have to repaint the kitchen
il a maintenant atteint l'âge de quatre-vingts ans	he has now reached the age of eighty
la température pourrait atteindre trente-cinq degrés	the temperature may reach thirty-five degrees
plusieurs centaines de personnes ont été atteintes par l'épidémie	several hundred people have been hit by the epidemic
leurs critiques ne m'atteignent pas	I'm impervious to their criticism
elle a tendance à feindre la timidité	she has a tendency to pretend she's shy
il feignait de ne rien savoir	he pretended to know nothing about it
il faut éteindre ta cigarette	you must put out your cigarette
nous éteindrons les bougies avant de partir	we'll blow out the candles before we leave
est-ce que tu peux éteindre avant de te coucher?	can you turn the lights off before you go to bed?
il a éteint ses phares	he switched off his headlights

54 placer to put

irregular verb
conjugates with **avoir** *in compound tenses*

Imperative	Present participle	Past participle
place (tu)	plaçant	placé
plaçons (nous)		
placez (vous)		

Present
je place
tu places
il/elle place
nous plaçons
vous placez
ils/elles placent

Past Historic
je plaçai
tu plaças
il/elle plaça
nous plaçâmes
vous plaçâtes
ils/elles placèrent

Future
je placerai
tu placeras
il/elle placera
nous placerons
vous placerez
ils/elles placeront

Conditional
je placerais
tu placerais
il/elle placerait
nous placerions
vous placeriez
ils/elles placeraient

Imperfect
je plaçais
tu plaçais
il/elle plaçait
nous placions
vous placiez
ils/elles plaçaient

Present subjunctive
(que) je place
(que) tu places
(qu') il/elle place
(que) nous placions
(que) vous placiez
(qu') ils/elles placent

Perfect
j'ai placé
tu as placé
il/elle a placé
nous avons placé
vous avez placé
ils/elles ont placé

Imperfect subjunctive
(que) je plaçasse
(que) tu plaçasses
(qu') il/elle plaçât
(que) nous plaçassions
(que) vous plaçassiez
(qu') ils/elles plaçassent

Some common verbs that conjugate in the same way

agacer	*to annoy*	divorcer	*to divorce*
annoncer	*to announce*	effacer	*to erase*
avancer	*to advance*	s'efforcer	*to try hard*
coincer	*to wedge/ jam*	influencer	*to influence*
		lancer	*to throw*
commencer	*to begin*	menacer	*to threaten*
concurrencer	*to compete with*	prononcer	*to pronounce*
		sucer	*to suck*
déplacer	*to move*	tracer	*to draw*

◇note that with these verbs the **c** becomes **ç** when followed by **a** or **o** in order to prevent it being sounded like a **k** in accordance with French pronunciation rules

How the verb works

elle a placé un vase de fleurs au milieu de la table	*she put a vase of flowers in the middle of the table*
en général, nous plaçons les enfants devant	*we usually seat the children in front*
il s'est placé devant la porte	*he positioned himself in front of the door*
va te placer à côté d'Amélie	*go and sit/stand next to Amélie*
où se placent les verres?	*where do the glasses go?*

Language in use

le directeur l'a placée à la tête du service informatique	*the manager put/has put her in charge of the IT department*
je n'arrive pas à en placer une avec elle!	*I can't get a word in edgeways with her!*
tu commences à m'agacer!	*you're getting on my nerves!*
il commence à pleuvoir	*it's starting to rain*
on va commencer par une chanson	*we're going to start with a song*
il a divorcé d'avec sa femme	*he divorced/has divorced his wife*
ils ont divorcé l'année dernière	*they divorced last year*

55 plaire to please

irregular verb
conjugates with **avoir** *in compound tenses*

Imperative	Present participle	Past participle
plais (tu)	plaisant	plu
plaisons (nous)		
plaisez (vous)		

Present
je plais
tu plais
il/elle plaît
nous plaisons
vous plaisez
ils/elles plaisent

Past Historic
je plus
tu plus
il/elle plut
nous plûmes
vous plûtes
ils/elles plurent

Future
je plairai
tu plairas
il/elle plaira
nous plairons
vous plairez
ils/elles plairont

Conditional
je plairais
tu plairais
il/elle plairait
nous plairions
vous plairiez
ils/elles plairaient

Imperfect
je plaisais
tu plaisais
il/elle plaisait
nous plaisions
vous plaisiez
ils/elles plaisaient

Present subjunctive
(que) je plaise
(que) tu plaises
(qu') il/elle plaise
(que) nous plaisions
(que) vous plaisiez
(qu') ils/elles plaisent

Perfect
j'ai plu
tu as plu
il/elle a plu
nous avons plu
vous avez plu
ils/elles ont plu

Imperfect subjunctive
(que) je plusse
(que) tu plusses
(qu') il/elle plût
(que) nous plussions
(que) vous plussiez
(qu') ils/elles plussent

Following the same pattern

se complaire à   *to take*   déplaire   *to displease*
pleasure in

How the verb works

mon nouveau travail me plaît	*I like my new job*
est-ce que la maison te plaît?	*do you like the house?*
j'essaie de trouver un cadeau qui plaira à mon mari	*I'm trying to find a present that my husband will like*
le film leur a beaucoup plu	*they liked the film a lot*
il m'a plu tout de suite	*I liked him straight away*
elle ne m'a jamais plu	*I've never liked her*
est-ce que tu te plais ici?	*do you like it here?*
elle se plaît à dire non à tout	*she likes saying no to everything*

Language in use

c'est un produit qui plaît beaucoup	*it's a very popular product*
ça te plairait de venir manger avec nous ce soir?	*would you like to come and eat with us this evening?*
passe-moi le sel, s'il te plaît	*pass me the salt please*
je voudrais deux kilos de pommes, s'il vous plaît	*I'd like two kilos of apples please*
il se complaît à critiquer tout le monde	*he takes pleasure in criticizing everyone*
cela m'a déplu	*I didn't like it*
il me déplaît	*I don't like him*
le film m'a profondément déplu	*I didn't like the film at all*
je ne me déplais pas ici	*I rather like it here*

56 pleuvoir to rain

irregular impersonal verb (apart from figurative use: see opposite)

conjugates with avoir in compound tenses

Present participle
pleuvant

Past participle
plu

Present
il pleut
ils/elles pleuvent

Past Historic
il plut
ils/elles plurent

Future
il pleuvra
ils/elles pleuvront

Conditional
il pleuvrait
ils/elles pleuvraient

Imperfect
il pleuvait
ils/elles pleuvaient

Present subjunctive
(qu') il pleuve
(qu') ils/elles pleuvent

Perfect
il a plu
ils/elles ont plu

Imperfect subjunctive
(qu') il plût
(qu') ils/elles plussent

How the verb works

il pleut	*it's raining*
il va pleuvoir ce soir	*it's going to rain tonight*
il pleut beaucoup en hiver	*it rains a lot in winter*
il a beaucoup plu la semaine dernière	*it rained a lot last week*

Language in use

il pleut à torrents	*it's pouring with rain*
il pleut à seaux	*it's bucketing down*
il pleut des cordes	*it's chucking it down*
les candidatures pleuvaient	*applications poured in*
les compliments pleuvaient	*compliments were being handed out left, right, and centre*
les mauvaises nouvelles pleuvent	*bad news is coming in thick and fast*
il y avait des gâteaux comme s'il en pleuvait*	*there were loads of cakes*

57 plier to fold

regular -er verb
conjugates with avoir in compound tenses

Imperative	Present participle	Past participle
plie (tu)	pliant	plié
plions (nous)		
pliez (vous)		

Present
je plie
tu plies
il/elle plie
nous plions
vous pliez
ils/elles plient

Past historic
je pliai
tu plias
il/elle plia
nous pliâmes
vous pliâtes
ils/elles plièrent

Future
je plierai
tu plieras
il/elle pliera
nous plierons
vous plierez
ils/elles plieront

Conditional
je plierais
tu plierais
il/elle plierait
nous plierions
vous plieriez
ils/elles plieraient

Imperfect
je pliais
tu pliais
il/elle pliait
nous pliions
vous pliiez
ils/elles pliaient

Present subjunctive
(que) je plie
(que) tu plies
(qu') il/elle plie
(que) nous pliions
(que) vous pliiez
(qu') ils/elles plient

Perfect
j'ai plié
tu as plié
il/elle a plié
nous avons plié
vous avez plié
ils/elles ont plié

Imperfect subjunctive
(que) je pliasse
(que) tu pliasses
(qu') il/elle pliât
(que) nous pliassions
(que) vous pliassiez
(qu') ils/elles pliassent

Some common verbs that follow the same pattern

apprécier	*to appreciate*	injurier	*to swear at*
associer	*to bring together/combine*	justifier	*to justify*
		se marier	*to get married*
bénéficier	*to benefit*	se méfier	*to distrust/be careful*
certifier	*to certify*		
clarifier	*to clarify*	mendier	*to beg*
classifier	*to classify*	modifier	*to modify*
contrarier	*to upset, annoy*	négocier	*to negotiate*
copier	*to copy*	nier	*to deny*
crier	*to shout*	oublier	*to forget*
diversifier	*to diversify*	planifier	*to plan*
expédier	*to send*	prier	*to ask/pray*
se fier à	*to trust*	privilégier	*to favour*
fortifier	*to fortify/strengthen*	publier	*to publish*
		remercier	*to thank*
horrifier	*to horrify*	signifier	*to mean*
humilier	*to humiliate*	simplifier	*to simplify*
identifier	*to identify*	terrifier	*to terrify*
		varier	*to vary*

How the verb works

je suis en train de plier mes vêtements	*I'm just folding my clothes*
il faudra qu'on plie tous ces draps	*we'll have to fold all these sheets*
il a plié le papier en deux	*he folded the paper in two*
nous pouvons plier les chaises maintenant	*we can fold up the chairs now*
la table se plie facilement	*the table folds up easily*
la branche a plié	*the branch bent*
je n'arrive pas à plier le bras	*I can't bend my arm*
elle doit se plier au règlement	*she must submit to the rules*

Language in use

nous allons plier bagage	*we're going to pack our things and go*
elles étaient pliées en quatre	*they were doubled up with laughter/pain*

58 pourvoir to fill

irregular verb
conjugates with **avoir** *in compound tenses*

Imperative	**Present participle**	**Past participle**
pourvois (tu)	pourvoyant	pourvu
pourvoyons (nous)		
pourvoyez (vous)		

Present
je pourvois
tu pourvois
il/elle pourvoit
nous pourvoyons
vous pourvoyez
ils/elles pourvoient

Past Historic
je pourvus
tu pourvus
il/elle pourvut
nous pourvûmes
vous pourvûtes
ils/elles pourvurent

Future
je pourvoirai
tu pourvoiras
il/elle pourvoira
nous pourvoirons
vous pourvoirez
ils/elles pourvoiront

Conditional
je pourvoirais
tu pourvoirais
il/elle pourvoirait
nous pourvoirions
vous pourvoiriez
ils/elles pourvoiraient

Imperfect
je pourvoyais
tu pourvoyais
il/elle pourvoyait
nous pourvoyions
vous pourvoyiez
ils/elles pourvoyaient

Present subjunctive
(que) je pourvoie
(que) tu pourvoies
(qu') il/elle pourvoie
(que) nous pourvoyions
(que) vous pourvoyiez
(qu') ils/elles pourvoient

Perfect
j'ai pourvu
tu as pourvu
il/elle a pourvu
nous avons pourvu
vous avez pourvu
ils/elles ont pourvu

Imperfect subjunctive
(que) je pourvusse
(que) tu pourvusses
(qu') il/elle pourvût
(que) nous pourvussions
(que) vous pourvussiez
(qu') ils/elles pourvussent

How the verb works

il y a plusieurs postes à pourvoir	*there are several positions available*
être pourvu des qualités requises	*to have the necessary qualities*
nous essayons de pourvoir à leurs besoins	*we try to provide for their needs*
je m'étais pourvu de mon passeport et de mon billet d'avion	*I had armed myself with my passport and my plane ticket*
il va falloir vous pourvoir de chaussures de marche et de sacs à dos	*you will have to equip yourselves with walking shoes and rucksacks*

Language in use

Dieu y pourvoira	*God will provide*

59 pouvoir to be able/can

irregular verb
conjugates with **avoir** *in compound tenses*

Present participle **Past participle**
pouv**ant** pu

Present
je peux (puis-je?)
tu peux
il/elle peut
nous pouv**ons**
vous pouv**ez**
ils/elles peuvent

Past Historic
je pus
tu pus
il/elle put
nous pûmes
vous pûtes
ils/elles purent

Future
je pourrai
tu pourras
il/elle pourra
nous pourrons
vous pourrez
ils/elles pourront

Conditional
je pourrais
tu pourrais
il/elle pourrait
nous pourrions
vous pourriez
ils/elles pourraient

Imperfect
je pouv**ais**
tu pouv**ais**
il/elle pouv**ait**
nous pouv**ions**
vous pouv**iez**
ils/elles pouv**aient**

Present subjunctive
(que) je puisse
(que) tu puisses
(qu') il/elle puisse
(que) nous puissions
(que) vous puissiez
(qu') ils/elles puissent

Perfect
j'**ai** pu
tu **as** pu
il/elle **a** pu
nous **avons** pu
vous **avez** pu
ils/elles **ont** pu

Imperfect subjunctive
(que) je pusse
(que) tu pusses
(qu') il/elle pût
(que) nous pussions
(que) vous pussiez
(qu') ils/elles pussent

How the verb works

je ne peux pas ouvrir la porte	*I can't open the door*
il ne pouvait pas fermer le tiroir	*he couldn't close the drawer*
j'espère pouvoir partir samedi	*I hope to be able to leave on Saturday*
si tu peux	*if you can*
il ne pourra pas venir cette semaine	*he won't be able to come this week*
est-ce que je peux fumer ici?	*can I smoke here?*
est-ce que je peux emprunter ton vélo?	*can I borrow your bike?*
pourriez-vous appeler un taxi, s'il vous plaît?	*could you call a taxi, please?*
il se peut qu'elle ait oublié	*she might have forgotten*

Language in use

dès que je pourrai	*as soon as I can*
elle aurait pu me le dire!	*she could have told me!*
je n'en peux plus!	*I've had it!*
cela pourrait arriver à n'importe qui	*it could happen to anyone*
que peut-elle bien faire?	*what on earth can she be doing?*
tout le monde peut se tromper	*anyone can make a mistake*
je n'y peux rien	*there's nothing I can do about it*
tout peut arriver!	*anything could happen!*
il peut faire très froid la nuit	*it can get very cold at night*
qu'est-ce qu'il peut y avoir comme monde!	*what a crowd there is!*
que puis-je pour vous?	*what can I do for you?*

60 prendre to take

irregular verb
conjugates with **avoir** *in compound tenses*

Imperative	Present participle	Past participle
prends (tu)	prenant	pris
prenons (nous)		
prenez (vous)		

Present
je prends
tu prends
il/elle prend
nous prenons
vous prenez
ils/elles prennent

Past Historic
je pris
tu pris
il/elle prit
nous prîmes
vous prîtes
ils/elles prirent

Future
je prendrai
tu prendras
il/elle prendra
nous prendrons
vous prendrez
ils/elles prendront

Conditional
je prendrais
tu prendrais
il/elle prendrait
nous prendrions
vous prendriez
ils/elles prendraient

Imperfect
je prenais
tu prenais
il/elle prenait
nous prenions
vous preniez
ils/elles prenaient

Present subjunctive
(que) je prenne
(que) tu prennes
(qu') il/elle prenne
(que) nous prenions
(que) vous preniez
(qu') ils/elles prennent

Perfect
j'ai pris
tu as pris
il/elle a pris
nous avons pris
vous avez pris
ils/elles ont pris

Imperfect subjunctive
(que) je prisse
(que) tu prisses
(qu') il/elle prît
(que) nous prissions
(que) vous prissiez
(qu') ils/elles prissent

Following the same pattern

entreprendre   *to undertake*   reprendre   *to take (again)*

How the verb works

tu devrais prendre un parapluie	*you should take an umbrella*
qui a pris mon stylo?	*who's taken my pen?*
prends un bol dans le placard	*take a bowl out of the cupboard*
il a refusé de prendre l'argent	*he refused to take the money*
le trajet me prend une heure	*the journey takes me an hour*
ils ont pris le train	*they took the train*
je prends le train de cinq heures	*I'm catching the five o'clock train*
il a pris l'avion pour aller à Paris	*he flew to Paris*

Language in use

j'ai pris l'habitude de lire le journal tous les matins	*I've got into the habit of reading the newspaper every morning*
je vais prendre de l'argent au distributeur	*I'm going to get some money from the cashpoint*
qu'est-ce que tu prends?	*what would you like (to eat/ drink)?*
je vais prendre une bière	*I'm going to have a beer*
elle prend combien de l'heure?	*how much does she charge an hour?*
n'oublie pas de prendre de l'essence	*don't forget to get petrol*
tu peux prendre du fromage en même temps	*you can get some cheese at the same time*
ce fauteuil prend trop de place	*that armchair takes up too much room*
je passe te prendre ce soir	*I'll pick you up this evening*
prenez à gauche/droite	*turn left/right*
qu'est-ce qui te prend?*	*what's the matter with you?*
elle me prend pour un imbécile	*she takes me for a fool*
elle se prend pour un génie	*she thinks she's a genius*
il se prend pour qui?	*who does he think he is?*

61 prévoir to predict

irregular verb
conjugates with **avoir** *in compound tenses*

Imperative	Present participle	Past participle
prévois (tu)	prévoyant	prévu
prévoyons (nous)		
prévoyez (vous)		

Present
je prévois
tu prévois
il/elle prévoit
nous prévoyons
vous prévoyez
ils/elles prévoient

Past Historic
je prévis
tu prévis
il/elle prévit
nous prévîmes
vous prévîtes
ils/elles prévirent

Future
je prévoirai
tu prévoiras
il/elle prévoira
nous prévoirons
vous prévoirez
ils/elles prévoiront

Conditional
je prévoirais
tu prévoirais
il/elle prévoirait
nous prévoirions
vous prévoiriez
ils/elles prévoiraient

Imperfect
je prévoyais
tu prévoyais
il/elle prévoyait
nous prévoyions
vous prévoyiez
ils/elles prévoyaient

Present subjunctive
(que) je prévoie
(que) tu prévoies
(qu') il/elle prévoie
(que) nous prévoyions
(que) vous prévoyiez
(qu') ils/elles prévoient

Perfect
j'ai prévu
tu as prévu
il/elle a prévu
nous avons prévu
vous avez prévu
ils/elles ont prévu

Imperfect subjunctive
(que) je prévisse
(que) tu prévisses
(qu') il/elle prévisse
(que) nous prévissions
(que) vous prévissiez
(qu') ils/elles prévissent

How the verb works

les journalistes prévoient plusieurs changements
journalists are predicting several changes

on prévoit de la pluie pour demain
rain is forecast for tomorrow

qui pouvait prévoir ce qui se passerait?
who could have foreseen what would happen?

il prévoit de revenir samedi prochain
he's planning to come back next Saturday

j'ai prévu de les inviter à dîner
I'm planning to invite them to dinner

est-ce que tu as prévu quelque chose pour dimanche?
do you have any plans for Sunday?

les inondations étaient moins graves que prévu
the floods were less serious than anticipated

il faut prévoir au moins deux heures
you should allow at least two hours

Language in use

c'était à prévoir!
that was to be expected!

ce n'était pas prévu!
that wasn't meant to happen!

la réunion prévue pour le 19 juin
the meeting planned for 19 June

nous nous réunirons le 12 mai comme prévu
we will meet on 12 May as arranged

nous prévoyons deux chambres d'amis
we're planning to have two spare bedrooms

rien n'est prévu pour l'année prochaine
no plans have been made for next year

vous devriez prévoir des vêtements chauds
you should make sure you take warm clothes

62 recevoir to receive

irregular verb
conjugates with **avoir** *in compound tenses*

Imperative	Present participle	Past participle
reçois (tu)	recevant	reçu
recevons (nous)		
recevez (vous)		

Present
je reçois
tu reçois
il/elle reçoit
nous recevons
vous recevez
ils/elles reçoivent

Past Historic
je reçus
tu reçus
il/elle reçut
nous reçûmes
vous reçûtes
ils/elles reçurent

Future
je recevrai
tu recevras
il/elle recevra
nous recevrons
vous recevrez
ils/elles recevront

Conditional
je recevrais
tu recevrais
il/elle recevrait
nous recevrions
vous recevriez
ils/elles recevraient

Imperfect
je recevais
tu recevais
il/elle recevait
nous recevions
vous receviez
ils/elles recevaient

Present subjunctive
(que) je reçoive
(que) tu reçoives
(qu') il/elle reçoive
(que) nous recevions
(que) vous receviez
(qu') ils/elles reçoivent

Perfect
j'ai reçu
tu as reçu
il/elle a reçu
nous avons reçu
vous avez reçu
ils/elles ont reçu

Imperfect subjunctive
(que) je reçusse
(que) tu reçusses
(qu') il/elle reçût
(que) nous reçussions
(que) vous reçussiez
(qu') ils/elles reçussent

Some common verbs that follow the same pattern

apercevoir	*to see, catch sight of*	concevoir	*to design/ conceive*
s'apercevoir de	*to notice*	décevoir	*to disappoint*

How the verb works

j'ai reçu une lettre de ton frère	*I got a letter from your brother*
quand allons-nous recevoir votre réponse?	*when will we have your reply?*
Mme. Giroud vous recevra dans son bureau	*Mme. Giroud will see you in her office*
nous avons été très bien reçus	*we were very well looked after*
ils reçoivent beaucoup	*they do a lot of entertaining*
il reçoit uniquement sur rendez-vous	*he only sees people by appointment*

Language in use

il a reçu un coup de pied	*he was kicked*
je n'ai d'ordre à recevoir de personne	*I don't take orders from anyone*
je n'ai reçu aucun encouragement de sa part	*he/she gave me no encouragement*
elle a été reçue première au concours	*she came first in the exam*
je l'ai aperçue dans la foule	*I caught a glimpse of her in the crowd*
nous ne nous sommes pas aperçus de l'erreur	*we didn't notice the mistake*
elle s'en est aperçue trop tard	*she only noticed it when it was too late to do anything about it*
les bureaux sont très mal conçus	*the offices are really badly designed*
tu me déçois	*I'm disappointed in you*
il était vraiment déçu	*he was really disappointed*
nous étions déçus d'apprendre que le concert avait été annulé	*we were disappointed to hear that the concert had been cancelled*

63 rendre to give back

regular -re verb
conjugates with avoir in compound tenses

Imperative	Present participle	Past participle
rends (tu)	rendant	rendu
rendons (nous)		
rendez (vous)		

Present
je rends
tu rends
il/elle rend
nous rendons
vous rendez
ils/elles rendent

Past Historic
je rendis
tu rendis
il/elle rendit
nous rendîmes
vous rendîtes
ils/elles rendirent

Future
je rendrai
tu rendras
il/elle rendra
nous rendrons
vous rendrez
ils/elles rendront

Conditional
je rendrais
tu rendrais
il/elle rendrait
nous rendrions
vous rendriez
ils/elles rendraient

Imperfect
je rendais
tu rendais
il/elle rendait
nous rendions
vous rendiez
ils/elles rendaient

Present subjunctive
(que) je rende
(que) tu rendes
(qu') il/elle rende
(que) nous rendions
(que) vous rendiez
(qu') ils/elles rendent

Perfect
j'ai rendu
tu as rendu
il/elle a rendu
nous avons rendu
vous avez rendu
ils/elles ont rendu

Imperfect subjunctive
(que) je rendisse
(que) tu rendisses
(qu') il/elle rendît
(que) nous rendissions
(que) vous rendissiez
(qu') ils/elles rendissent

Some common verbs that follow the same pattern

attendre	to wait	fendre	to split
confondre	to confuse	mordre	to bite
correspondre	to correspond	pendre	to hang
descendre	to go/come/ take/bring down	perdre	to lose
		répandre	to spread
		répondre	to answer
défendre	to defend	tendre	to stretch
dépendre	to depend	tondre	to shear
entendre	to hear	tordre	to twist
		vendre	to sell

How the verb works

rendre quelque chose à quelqu'un	to give something back to someone
elle leur a rendu les livres hier	she gave them back the books yesterday
si tu peux me prêter cent francs, je te les rends demain	if you can lend me a hundred francs, I'll pay you back tomorrow

Language in use

son troisième film l'a rendue célèbre	her third film made her famous
mes problèmes de santé ont rendu la situation encore plus difficile	my health problems have made the situation even more difficult
elle s'est rendue à Dijon/chez des amis	she went to Dijon/to visit friends
en me rendant à Londres	on my way to London
elle a oublié de me rendre la monnaie	she forgot to give me my change
quand est-ce qu'il faut rendre le devoir?	when do we have to hand in the homework?
malheureusement, il s'est rendu ridicule	unfortunately he made a fool of himself
je t'attends à la sortie	I'll wait for you at the exit
j'attends qu'il finisse	I'm waiting for him to finish
elle attend un bébé	she's expecting a baby
attends un instant	hang on a minute

64 résoudre to resolve

irregular verb
conjugates with **avoir** *in compound tenses*

Imperative	**Present participle**	**Past participle**
résous (tu)	résolvant	résolu
résolvons (nous)		
résolvez (vous)		

Present
je résous
tu résous
il/elle résout
nous résolvons
vous résolvez
ils/elles résolvent

Past Historic
je résolus
tu résolus
il/elle résolut
nous résolûmes
vous résolûtes
ils/elles résolurent

Future
je résoudrai
tu résoudras
il/elle résoudra
nous résoudrons
vous résoudrez
ils/elles résoudront

Conditional
je résoudrais
tu résoudrais
il/elle résoudrait
nous résoudrions
vous résoudriez
ils/elles résoudraient

Imperfect
je résolvais
tu résolvais
il/elle résolvait
nous résolvions
vous résolviez
ils/elles résolvaient

Present subjunctive
(que) je résolve
(que) tu résolves
(qu') il/elle résolve
(que) nous résolvions
(que) vous résolviez
(qu') ils/elles résolvent

Perfect
j'ai résolu
tu as résolu
il/elle a résolu
nous avons résolu
vous avez résolu
ils/elles ont résolu

Imperfect subjunctive
(que) je résolusse
(que) tu résolusses
(qu') il/elle résolût
(que) nous résolussions
(que) vous résolussiez
(qu') ils/elles résolussent

Following the same pattern

dissoudre◇   *to dissolve*   absoudre◇   *to resolve*

◇past participles **absous, -oute** and **dissous, -oute**

How the verb works

le gouvernement prend des mesures pour résoudre la crise	*the government is taking steps to resolve the crisis*
nous essayons de résoudre le problème	*we are trying to solve the problem*
cela ne résoudra rien	*that won't solve anything*

Language in use

il résolut d'attendre	*he resolved to wait*
il s'est résolu à démissionner	*he made up his mind to resign*
elle ne s'est toujours pas résolue à lui en parler	*she still hasn't made up her mind to talk to him about it*
je ne peux pas me résoudre à la renvoyer	*I can't bring myself to dismiss her*
nous sommes résolus à attendre	*we're resigned to waiting*
seul le président a le pouvoir de dissoudre l'assemblée	*only the president has the power to dissolve the assembly*
le mouvement dissous	*the disbanded movement*
le parti s'est dissous	*the party has disbanded*
il faut le faire dissoudre dans l'eau	*you must dissolve it in water*
c'est une substance qui se dissout dans l'eau	*it's a substance which dissolves in water*

65 rire to laugh

irregular verb
conjugates with **avoir** *in compound tenses*

Imperative	Present participle	Past participle
ris (tu)	riant	ri
rions (nous)		
riez (vous)		

Present
je ris
tu ris
il/elle rit
nous rions
vous riez
ils/elles rient

Past Historic
je ris
tu ris
il/elle rit
nous rîmes
vous rîtes
ils/elles rirent

Future
je rirai
tu riras
il/elle rira
nous rirons
vous rirez
ils/elles riront

Conditional
je rirais
tu rirais
il/elle rirait
nous ririons
vous ririez
ils/elles riraient

Imperfect
je riais
tu riais
il/elle riait
nous riions
vous riiez
ils/elles riaient

Present subjunctive
(que) je rie
(que) tu ries
(qu') il/elle rie
(que) nous riions
(que) vous riiez
(qu') ils/elles rient

Perfect
j'ai ri
tu as ri
il/elle a ri
nous avons ri
vous avez ri
ils/elles ont ri

Imperfect subjunctive
(que) je rissse
(que) tu risses
(qu') il/elle rît
(que) nous rissions
(que) vous rissiez
(qu') ils/elles rissent

Following the same pattern

sourire   *to smile*

How the verb works

pourquoi tu ris?	*why are you laughing?*
elle s'est mise à rire	*she burst out laughing*
il me fait rire	*he makes me laugh*
il n'y a pas de quoi rire	*it's not funny/it's no laughing matter*
elle ne rit jamais de mes plaisanteries	*she never laughs at my jokes*
ne ris pas de mon chapeau	*don't laugh at my hat*

"tu es impossible," dit-elle en riant	*"you're impossible," she said, laughing*
on en a beaucoup ri	*we laughed about it a lot*
on a ri un bon coup*	*we had a good laugh*
il m'a ri au nez	*he laughed in my face*
ils ne pensent qu'à rire	*all they care about is having fun*
il faut bien rire un peu	*you need a bit of fun now and again*
on va bien rire	*we're going to have a lot of fun*
j'ai dit ça pour rire	*I was only joking*
tu veux rire!	*you must be joking!*
sans rire, qu'est-ce que tu en penses?	*seriously, what do you think?*
laisse-moi rire!	*don't make me laugh!*
on rit de lui	*everyone's laughing at him*
on était mort de rire*	*we were doubled up with laughter*
rira bien qui rira le dernier	*he who laughs last laughs longest*
il souriait timidement	*he smiled shyly*
elle souriait jusqu'aux oreilles	*she was grinning from ear to ear*

66 **rompre** to break

irregular verb
conjugates with **avoir** *in compound tenses*

Imperative	Present participle	Past participle
romps (tu)	rompant	rompu
rompons (nous)		
rompez (vous)		

Present
je romps
tu romps
il/elle rompt
nous rompons
vous rompez
ils/elles rompent

Past Historic
je rompis
tu rompis
il/elle rompit
nous rompîmes
vous rompîtes
ils/elles rompirent

Future
je romprai
tu rompras
il/elle rompra
nous romprons
vous romprez
ils/elles rompront

Conditional
je romprais
tu romprais
il/elle romprait
nous romprions
vous rompriez
ils/elles rompraient

Imperfect
je rompais
tu rompais
il/elle rompait
nous rompions
vous rompiez
ils/elles rompaient

Present subjunctive
(que) je rompe
(que) tu rompes
(qu') il/elle rompe
(que) nous rompions
(que) vous rompiez
(qu') ils/elles rompent

Perfect
j'ai rompu
tu as rompu
il/elle a rompu
nous avons rompu
vous avez rompu
ils/elles ont rompu

Imperfect subjunctive
(que) je rompisse
(que) tu rompisses
(qu') il/elle rompît
(que) nous rompissions
(que) vous rompissiez
(qu') ils/elles rompissent

Following the same pattern

interrompre   *to interrupt*

How the verb works

elle ne voulait pas rompre le silence	*she didn't want to break the silence*
on l'accuse d'avoir rompu son contrat	*he's accused of having broken his contract*
ils ont rompu les négociations	*they've broken off negotiations*
ils ont décidé de rompre avec les vieilles traditions	*they've decided to break with the old traditions*
elle a rompu avec son copain	*she's broken up with her boyfriend*

Language in use

ils ont rompu	*they've broken up*
la branche s'est rompue	*the branch broke*
arrête de m'interrompre!	*stop interrupting me!*
ils ont interrompu l'émission pour annoncer la nouvelle	*they interrupted the programme to announce the news*
elle a interrompu son repas pour répondre au téléphone	*she stopped eating to answer the phone*
il a interrompu son discours	*he broke off in the middle of his speech*
sa maladie a interrompu sa carrière	*his/her illness put an end to his/her career*

67 savoir to know

irregular verb
conjugates with **avoir** *in compound tenses*

Imperative	Present participle	Past participle
sache (tu)	sachant	su
sachons (nous)		
sachez (vous)		

Present
je sais
tu sais
il/elle sait
nous savons
vous savez
ils/elles savent

Past Historic
je sus
tu sus
il/elle sut
nous sûmes
vous sûtes
ils/elles surent

Future
je saurai
tu sauras
il/elle saura
nous saurons
vous saurez
ils/elles sauront

Conditional
je saurais
tu saurais
il/elle saurait
nous saurions
vous sauriez
ils/elles sauraient

Imperfect
je savais
tu savais
il/elle savait
nous savions
vous saviez
ils/elles savaient

Present subjunctive
(que) je sache
(que) tu saches
(qu') il/elle sache
(que) nous sachions
(que) vous sachiez
(qu') ils/elles sachent

Perfect
j'ai su
tu as su
il/elle a su
nous avons su
vous avez su
ils/elles ont su

Imperfect subjunctive
(que) je susse
(que) tu susses
(qu') il/elle sût
(que) nous sussions
(que) vous sussiez
(qu') ils/elles sussent

How the verb works

je sais	I know
je ne sais pas	I don't know
je ne le savais pas	I didn't know
on le saura demain	we'll know tomorrow
elle n'a jamais su où il habitait	she never knew where he lived
elle sait que nous sommes là	she knows we're here
est-ce que tu sais quand ils vont arriver?	do you know when they're arriving?
je ne sais pas pourquoi il a fait ça	I don't know why he did that
il sait ce qu'il veut	he knows what he wants

● *followed by infinitive*

est-ce que tu sais faire une omelette?	do you know how to make an omelette?
elle ne sait pas lire	she can't read

Language in use

c'est vrai, tu sais	it's true, you know
va savoir!	who knows!
on ne sait jamais	you never know
pour autant que je sache	as far as I know
pas que je sache	not as far as I know
elle sait très bien que je suis malade	she knows very well that I'm ill
je n'en sais rien	I don't know
je ne sais rien de ce qui se passe	I know nothing about what's going on
ils savent les paroles par cœur	they know the words by heart
elle ne sait plus ce qu'elle dit	she doesn't know what she's saying
il ne sait rien de moi	he doesn't know anything about me
fais-moi savoir si tu as besoin d'aide	let me know if you need help
elle a je ne sais combien de chats	she's got goodness knows how many cats
il ne sait pas dire non	he can't say no
dans trois jours, à savoir jeudi	in three days, that's to say on Thursday

68 suffire to be enough

irregular verb
conjugates with **avoir** *in compound tenses*

Imperative	Present participle	Past participle
suffis (tu)	suffisant	suffi
suffisons (nous)		
suffisez (vous)		

Present
je sufis
tu suffis
il/elle suffit
nous suffisons
vous suffisez
ils/elles suffisent

Past Historic
je suffis
tu suffis
il/elle suffit
nous suffîmes
vous suffîtes
ils/elles suffirent

Future
je suffirai
tu suffiras
il/elle suffira
nous suffirons
vous suffirez
ils/elles suffiront

Conditional
je suffirais
tu suffirais
il/elle suffirait
nous suffirions
vous suffiriez
ils/elles suffiraient

Imperfect
je suffisais
tu suffisais
il/elle suffisait
nous suffisions
vous suffisiez
ils/elles suffisaient

Present subjunctive
(que) je suffise
(que) tu suffises
(qu') il/elle suffise
(que) nous suffisions
(que) vous suffisiez
(qu') ils/elles suffisent

Perfect
j'ai suffi
tu as suffi
il/elle a suffi
nous avons suffi
vous avez suffi
ils/elles ont suffi

Imperfect subjunctive
(que) je suffisse
(que) tu suffisses
(qu') il/elle suffît
(que) nous suffissions
(que) vous suffissiez
(qu') ils/elles suffissent

Following the same pattern

frire   *to fry*   circoncire   *to circumcise*

How the verb works

quelques gouttes suffisent	*a few drops are enough*
cinquante francs suffiront	*fifty francs will be enough*
le salaire est modeste mais il suffit à mes besoins	*the salary is modest but it is enough to cover my needs*
deux heures suffisent largement pour faire le trajet	*two hours is easily enough for the journey*

Language in use

je l'ai rencontrée une fois et ça m'a suffi!	*I met her once and that was enough!*
un rien suffit à la mettre en colère	*the slightest thing makes her lose her temper*
il suffit de mettre la table et on peut manger	*all we need to do is set the table and then we can eat*
il suffit d'un coup de téléphone pour s'abonner	*it only takes a phone call to subscribe*
il suffit qu'elle y aille	*she only has to go there*
il suffit d'une seconde d'inattention pour qu'un accident se produise	*it only takes a second's carelessness for an accident to happen*
il suffit qu'elle ouvre la bouche pour dire une bêtise	*every time she opens her mouth she says something stupid*
ça suffit (comme ça)!	*that's enough!*
je vais faire frire le poisson	*I'm going to deep-fry the fish*
nous avons mangé du poisson frit	*we had fried fish*

69 suivre to follow

irregular verb
conjugates with **avoir** *in compound tenses*

Imperative	Present participle	Past participle
suis (tu)	suivant	suivi
suivons (nous)		
suivez (vous)		

Present
je suis
tu suis
il/elle suit
nous suivons
vous suivez
ils/elles suivent

Past Historic
je suivis
tu suivis
il/elle suivit
nous suivîmes
vous suivîtes
ils/elles suivirent

Future
je suivrai
tu suivras
il/elle suivra
nous suivrons
vous suivrez
ils/elles suivront

Conditional
je suivrais
tu suivrais
il/elle suivrait
nous suivrions
vous suivriez
ils/elles suivraient

Imperfect
je suivais
tu suivais
il/elle suivait
nous suivions
vous suiviez
ils/elles suivaient

Present subjunctive
(que) je suive
(que) tu suives
(qu') il/elle suive
(que) nous suivions
(que) vous suiviez
(qu') ils/elles suivent

Perfect
j'ai suivi
tu as suivi
il/elle a suivi
nous avons suivi
vous avez suivi
ils/elles ont suivi

Imperfect subjunctive
(que) je suivisse
(que) tu suivisses
(qu') il/elle suivît
(que) nous suivissions
(que) vous suivissiez
(qu') ils/elles suivissent

Following the same pattern

s'ensuivre   *to ensue*   poursuivre   *to chase*

How the verb works

suivez-moi, s'il vous plaît — *follow me please*

elle m'a suivi dans mon bureau — *she followed me into my office*

il est entré, suivi de son fils — *he came in followed by his son*

le repas sera suivi d'un concert — *the meal will be followed by a concert*

suivez le sentier jusqu'à l'église — *follow the path as far as the church*

j'ai décidé de suivre leurs conseils — *I decided/have decided to follow their advice*

Language in use

partez sans moi, je vous suis — *don't wait for me, I'll follow*

il la suivait des yeux — *he followed her with his eyes*

le jour qui suivit — *the following day*

'à suivre' — *'to be continued'*

elle ne suit pas son régime — *she doesn't keep to her diet*

j'essaie de suivre l'actualité — *I try to keep up with the news*

il suit un stage de formation — *he's on a training course*

je ne te suis pas très bien — *I'm not quite with you*

les prix augmentent mais les salaires ne suivent pas — *prices are rising but wages are not keeping pace*

(prière de) faire suivre — *please forward*

les pages ne se suivent pas — *the pages are not in order*

les policiers ont poursuivi la voiture — *the police chased the car*

les négociations se poursuivent — *negotiations are continuing*

70 **traire** to milk

irregular verb
conjugates with **avoir** *in compound tenses*

Imperative	Present participle	Past participle
trais (tu)	trayant	trait
trayons (nous)		
trayez (vous)		

Present
je trais
tu trais
il/elle trait
nous trayons
vous trayez
ils/elles traient

Future
je trairai
tu trairas
il/elle traira
nous trairons
vous trairez
ils/elles trairont

Imperfect
je trayais
tu trayais
il/elle trayait
nous trayions
vous trayiez
ils/elles trayaient

Perfect
j'ai trait
tu as trait
il/elle a trait
nous avons trait
vous avez trait
ils/elles ont trait

Past Historic
obsolete

Conditional
je trairais
tu trairais
il/elle trairait
nous trairions
vous trairiez
ils/elles trairaient

Present subjunctive
(que) je traie
(que) tu traies
(qu') il/elle traie
nous trayions
(que) vous trayiez
(qu') ils/elles traient

Imperfect subjunctive
obsolete

Some common verbs that follow the same pattern

abstraire	*to abstract*	distraire	*to distract*
braire	*to bray*	soustraire	*to subtract*

How the verb works

nous trayons les vaches deux fois par jour	*we milk the cows twice a day*
il est en train de traire	*he's busy milking*
ils vont acheter une machine à traire	*they're going to buy a milking machine*

Language in use

cela l'a distraite un moment	*that kept her amused for a while*
tu devrais aller voir un film pour te distraire de tes problèmes	*you should go and see a film to take your mind off your problems*
votre fils distrait les autres élèves	*your son distracts the other pupils*
le bruit de la circulation me distrait	*I find the traffic noise distracting*
il faisait tout pour distraire son attention	*he was doing everything he could to distract her attention*
je me suis laissé distraire	*I allowed myself to be distracted*
il faut se distraire de temps en temps	*one has to enjoy oneself from time to time*
j'ai besoin de me distraire	*I need to take my mind off things*
que fais-tu pour te distraire?	*what do you do for entertainment?*

71 vaincre to defeat

irregular verb
conjugates with **avoir** *in compound tenses*

Imperative	Present participle	Past participle
vaincs (tu)	vainquant	vaincu
vainquons (nous)		
vainquez (vous)		

Present
je vaincs
tu vaincs
il/elle vainc
nous vainquons
vous vainquez
ils/elles vainquent

Past Historic
je vainquis
tu vainquis
il/elle vainquit
nous vainquîmes
vous vainquîtes
ils/elles vainquirent

Future
je vaincrai
tu vaincras
il/elle vaincra
nous vaincrons
vous vaincrez
ils/elles vaincront

Conditional
je vaincrais
tu vaincrais
il/elle vaincrait
nous vaincrions
vous vaincriez
ils/elles vaincraient

Imperfect
je vainquais
tu vainquais
il/elle vainquait
nous vainquions
vous vainquiez
ils/elles vainquaient

Present subjunctive
(que) je vainque
(que) tu vainques
(qu') il/elle vainque
(que) nous vainquions
(que) vous vainquiez
(qu') ils/elles vainquent

Perfect
j'ai vaincu
tu as vaincu
il/elle a vaincu
nous avons vaincu
vous avez vaincu
ils/elles ont vaincu

Imperfect subjunctive
(que) je vainquisse
(que) tu vainquisses
(qu') il/elle vainquît
(que) nous vainquissions
(que) vous vainquissiez
(qu') ils/elles vainquissent

Following the same pattern

convaincre   *to convince*

How the verb works

l'équipe a été vaincue trois fois cette année	*the team has been beaten three times this year*
il fait des efforts pour vaincre sa dépression	*he is struggling to overcome his depression*
il faut faire des efforts pour vaincre nos préjugés	*we must make an effort to overcome our prejudices*
le gouvernement s'efforce de vaincre le chomage	*the government is trying hard to conquer unemployment*

Language in use

j'essaie de le convaincre de sa bêtise	*I'm trying to convince him of his stupidity*
j'ai réussi à la convaincre qu'il fallait partir	*I managed to convince her that we had to leave*
on a fini par le convaincre de rester	*we managed to persuade him to stay*
je ne suis pas convaincu	*I'm not convinced*
au départ elle ne voulait pas du tout venir avec nous mais elle a fini par se laisser convaincre	*to start with she didn't want to come with us at all but she let herself be persuaded in the end*

72 valoir to be worth

irregular verb
conjugates with avoir in compound tenses

Imperative	Present participle	Past participle
vaux (tu)	valant	valu
valons (nous)		
valez (vous)		

Present
je vaux
tu vaux
il/elle vaut
nous valons
vous valez
ils/elles valent

Past Historic
je valus
tu valus
il/elle valut
nous valûmes
vous valûtes
ils/elles valurent

Future
je vaudrai
tu vaudras
il/elle vaudra
nous vaudrons
vous vaudrez
ils/elles vaudront

Conditional
je vaudrais
tu vaudrais
il/elle vaudrait
nous vaudrions
vous vaudriez
ils/elles vaudraient

Imperfect
je valais
tu valais
il/elle valait
nous valions
vous valiez
ils/elles valaient

Present subjunctive
(que) je vaille
(que) tu vailles
(qu') il/elle vaille
(que) nous valions
(que) vous valiez
(qu') ils/elles vaillent

Perfect
j'ai valu
tu as valu
il/elle a valu
nous avons valu
vous avez valu
ils/elles ont valu

Imperfect subjunctive
(que) je valusse
(que) tu valusses
(qu') il/elle valût
(que) nous valussions
(que) vous valussiez
(qu') ils/elles valussent

Following the same pattern

équivaloir   *to be equivalent to*   prévaloir   *to prevail*

How the verb works

ça vaut combien?	*how much is it worth?*
ça vaut cher	*it's worth a lot of money*
ça vaut bien cinquante francs	*it's easily worth fifty francs*
ça ne vaut pas grand-chose	*it's not worth much*

mon assistante vaut de l'or	*my assistant is worth her weight in gold*
que vaut-il en tant que rédacteur?	*how good an editor is he?*
le film ne vaut pas grand-chose	*the film isn't up to much*
ce tissu ne vaut rien	*this fabric's rubbish*
il ne vaut rien comme cuisinier	*he's a useless cook*
elle valait mieux que cela!	*she deserved better than that!*
ton travail vaut largement le leur	*your work is every bit as good as theirs*
rien ne vaut la soie	*there's nothing like silk*
la nouvelle galerie vaut le déplacement	*the new gallery is worth a visit*
ça ne vaut pas la peine d'y aller	*it's not worth going*
ça vaudrait la peine que tu y ailles	*it would be worth your while going*
ça vaut le coup d'œil*	*it's worth seeing*
il vaut mieux que tu sois là	*it's better that you be there*
les deux candidats se valent	*there's nothing to choose between the two candidates*
cela ne m'a valu que des ennuis	*it brought me nothing but trouble*
cela lui a valu d'être exclu du parti	*it got him expelled from the party*
cela équivaut à un refus	*it's tantamount to a refusal*

73 **venir** to come

irregular verb
*conjugates with **être** in compound tenses*

Imperative	**Present participle**	**Past participle**
viens (tu)	venant	venu/-e(s)
venons (nous)		
venez (vous)		

Present
je viens
tu viens
il/elle vient
nous venons
vous venez
ils/elles viennent

Past Historic
je vins
tu vins
il/elle vint
nous vînmes
vous vîntes
ils/elles vinrent

Future
je viendrai
tu viendras
il/elle viendra
nous viendrons
vous viendrez
ils/elles viendront

Conditional
je viendrais
tu viendrais
il/elle viendrait
nous viendrions
vous viendriez
ils/elles viendraient

Imperfect
je venais
tu venais
il/elle venait
nous venions
vous veniez
ils/elles venaient

Present subjunctive
(que) je vienne
(que) tu viennes
(qu') il/elle vienne
(que) nous venions
(que) vous veniez
(qu') ils/elles viennent

Perfect
je suis venu/-e
tu es venu/-e
il/elle est venu/-e
nous sommes venus/-ues
vous êtes venu/-ue(s)
ils/elles sont venus/-ues

Imperfect subjunctive
(que) je vinsse
(que) tu vinsses
(qu') il/elle vînt
(que) nous vinssions
(que) vous vinssiez
(qu') ils/elles vinssent

Some common verbs that follow the same pattern

convenir	to suit/agree	prévenir✧	to warn
devenir	to become	provenir de	to come from
intervenir	to take place/	revenir	to come back
	intervene	se souvenir	to remember
		survenir	to occur

✧conjugates with **avoir** in perfect, pluperfect, and future perfect tenses

How the verb works

le plombier vient jeudi	the plumber's coming on Thursday
elle vient d'où?	where does she come from?
elle vient de Dijon	she comes from Dijon
nous venons ici tous les vendredis	we come here every Friday
viens quand tu veux	come whenever you like
il a dit qu'il viendrait dès que possible	he said he would come as soon as possible

● *followed by infinitive*

ils sont venus nous voir	they came/have come to see us
il faut que tu viennes me voir	you must come and see me
elle est venue s'excuser le lendemain	she came and apologized the next day

● *followed by 'de + infinitive'*

elle vient de partir	she's just left
nous venons de manger	we've just eaten
elle venait de se coucher quand le téléphone a sonné	she had just gone to bed when the phone rang

Language in use

allez, viens!	come on!
nous avons fait venir le plombier	we got the plumber in
le nom ne me vient pas à l'esprit	the name escapes me
ça ne m'est jamais venu à l'idée	it never occurred to me
l'année qui vient	the coming year

74 vêtir to dress

irregular verb
conjugates with avoir in compound tenses

Imperative	Present participle	Past participle
vêts (tu)	vêtant	vêtu
vêtons (nous)		
vêtez (vous)		

Present
je vêts
tu vêts
il/elle vêt
nous vêtons
vous vêtez
ils/elles vêtent

Past Historic
je vêtis
tu vêtis
il/elle vêtit
nous vêtîmes
vous vêtîtes
ils/elles vêtirent

Future
je vêtirai
tu vêtiras
il/elle vêtira
nous vêtirons
vous vêtirez
ils/elles vêtiront

Conditional
je vêtirais
tu vêtirais
il/elle vêtirait
nous vêtirions
vous vêtiriez
ils/elles vêtiraient

Imperfect
je vêtais
tu vêtais
il/elle vêtait
nous vêtions
vous vêtiez
ils/elles vêtaient

Present subjunctive
(que) je vête
(que) tu vêtes
(qu') il/elle vête
(que) nous vêtions
(que) vous vêtiez
(qu') ils/elles vêtent

Perfect
j'ai vêtu
tu as vêtu
il/elle a vêtu
nous avons vêtu
vous avez vêtu
ils/elles ont vêtu

Imperfect subjunctive
(que) je vêtisse
(que) tu vêtisses
(qu') il/elle vêtît
(que) nous vêtissions
(que) vous vêtissiez
(qu') ils/elles vêtissent

Following the same pattern

dévêtir   *to take off*   revêtir   *to put on*

How the verb works

elle s'était vêtue de plumes	*she had dressed herself in feathers*
il est arrivé, tout de blanc vêtu	*he arrived dressed all in white*
les enfants étaient tous vêtus de neuf	*the children were all wearing brand new clothes*
elle est toujours mal vêtue	*she's always badly dressed*

Language in use

il s'est dévêtu lentement	*he got undressed slowly*
leur père avait revêtu son uniforme pour l'occasion	*their father had put on his uniform for the occasion*
elle s'est revêtue d'une robe bleue	*she put on a blue dress*
nous allons revêtir les murs du salon de tissu	*we're going to cover the sitting room walls in fabric*
ce serait plus joli si vous revêtiez les murs de papier peint	*it would look nicer if you papered the walls*
l'affaire revêt de l'importance pour le gouvernement	*the affair holds importance for the government*
le débat a revêtu une nouvelle signification	*the debate has taken on a new meaning*

75 **vivre** to live

irregular verb
*conjugates with **avoir** in compound tenses*

Imperative	Present participle	Past participle
vis (tu)	vivant	vécu
vivons (nous)		
vivez (vous)		

Present
je vis
tu vis
il/elle vit
nous vivons
vous vivez
ils/elles vivent

Past Historic
je vécus
tu vécus
il/elle vécut
nous vécûmes
vous vécûtes
ils/elles vécurent

Future
je vivrai
tu vivras
il/elle vivra
nous vivrons
vous vivrez
ils/elles vivront

Conditional
je vivrais
tu vivrais
il/elle vivrait
nous vivrions
vous vivriez
ils/elles vivraient

Imperfect
je vivais
tu vivais
il/elle vivait
nous vivions
vous viviez
ils/elles vivaient

Present subjunctive
(que) je vive
(que) tu vives
(qu') il/elle vive
(que) nous vivions
(que) vous viviez
(qu') ils/elles vivent

Perfect
j'ai vécu
tu as vécu
il/elle a vécu
nous avons vécu
vous avez vécu
ils/elles ont vécu

Imperfect subjunctive
(que) je vécusse
(que) tu vécusses
(qu') il/elle vécût
(que) nous vécussions
(que) vous vécussiez
(qu') ils/elles vécussent

Following the same pattern

revivre   *to relive*   survivre   *to survive*

How the verb works

les tortues peuvent vivre très longtemps	*tortoises can live for a very long time*
je n'aimerais pas vivre à la campagne	*I wouldn't like to live in the country*
ils ont vécu longtemps à l'étranger	*they lived abroad for a long time*
il vit avec une Allemande	*he's living with a German woman*

Language in use

ils ont vécu une période difficile	*they went/have been through a difficult period*
il faut apprendre à vivre sa vie	*one has to learn to live one's own life*
vive les vacances!	*hooray for the holidays!*
ce sont des gens qui savent vivre	*they know how to enjoy life*
ils vivent avec presque rien	*they live on next to nothing*
nous ne sommes pas riches, mais nous avons de quoi vivre	*we're not rich but we have enough to live on*
il doit être difficile à vivre	*he must be difficult to live with*
je pourrais vivre de légumes	*I could live on vegetables*
l'air frais m'a fait revivre	*the fresh air has revived me*
seuls quatre passagers ont survécu	*only four passengers survived*
trois personnes ont survécu à l'accident	*three people survived the accident*

76 **voir** to see

irregular verb
conjugates with **avoir** *in compound tenses*

Imperative	Present participle	Past participle
vois (tu)	voyant	vu
voyons (nous)		
voyez (vous)		

Present
je vois
tu vois
il/elle voit
nous voyons
vous voyez
ils/elles voient

Past Historic
je vis
tu vis
il/elle vit
nous vîmes
vous vîtes
ils/elles virent

Future
je verrai
tu verras
il/elle verra
nous verrons
vous verrez
ils/elles verront

Conditional
je verrais
tu verrais
il/elle verrait
nous verrions
vous verriez
ils/elles verraient

Imperfect
je voyais
tu voyais
il/elle voyait
nous voyions
vous voyiez
ils/elles voyaient

Present subjunctive
(que) je voie
(que) tu voies
(qu') il/elle voie
(que) nous voyions
(que) vous voyiez
(qu') ils/elles voient

Perfect
j'ai vu
tu as vu
il/elle a vu
nous avons vu
vous avez vu
ils/elles ont vu

Imperfect subjunctive
(que) je visse
(que) tu visses
(qu') il/elle vît
(que) nous vissions
(que) vous vissiez
(qu') ils/elles vissent

Following the same pattern

entrevoir   *to glimpse*   revoir   *to see again*

How the verb works

qu'est-ce que tu vois?	*what can you see?*
je ne vois rien	*I can't see anything*
j'ai vu ton frère hier	*I saw your brother yesterday*
est-ce que tu as vu son nouveau film?	*have you seen his/her new film?*
je l'ai vue partir	*I saw her leave*
j'irai la voir demain	*I'll go and see her tomorrow*
voir page 32	*see page 32*

voir page 32

Language in use

fais voir ta nouvelle robe!	*let's have a look at your new dress!*
on n'a jamais vu ça!	*it's unheard of!*
et tu n'as encore rien vu!	*you ain't seen nothing yet!*
voyez-moi ça!	*just look at that!*
on voit mal comment il va le finir avant lundi	*it's hard to see how he's going to finish it by Monday*
c'est à toi de voir	*it's up to you to decide*
je vois ce que tu veux dire	*I see what you mean*
je ne vois pas l'intérêt d'attendre	*I can't see the point in waiting*
on voit bien qu'il ne sait pas ce qu'il fait	*it's obvious he doesn't know what he's doing*
à ce que je vois	*from what I can see*
c'est à voir	*that remains to be seen*
ça ne se voit pas	*it doesn't show*
je ne peux pas le voir!	*I can't stand him!*
je l'ai entrevue à la réception	*I caught a glimpse of her at the reception*
je l'ai revu le lendemain	*I saw him again the next day*

77 vouloir to want

irregular verb
conjugates with **avoir** *in compound tenses*

Imperative	Present participle	Past participle
veuille (tu)	voul**ant**	voul**u**
veuillons (nous)		
veuillez (vous)		

Present
je veux
tu veux
il/elle veut
nous voul**ons**
vous voul**ez**
ils/elles veulent

Past Historic
je voul**us**
tu voul**us**
il/elle voul**ut**
nous voul**ûmes**
vous voul**ûtes**
ils/elles voul**urent**

Future
je voudrai
tu voudras
il/elle voudra
nous voudrons
vous voudrez
ils/elles voudront

Conditional
je voudrais
tu voudrais
il/elle voudrait
nous voudrions
vous voudriez
ils/elles voudraient

Imperfect
je voul**ais**
tu voul**ais**
il/elle voul**ait**
nous voul**ions**
vous voul**iez**
ils/elles voul**aient**

Present subjunctive
(que) je veuille
(que) tu veuilles
(qu') il/elle veuille
(que) nous voul**ions**
(que) vous voul**iez**
(qu') ils/elles veuillent

Perfect
j'**ai** voulu
tu **as** voulu
il/elle **a** voulu
nous **avons** voulu
vous **avez** voulu
ils/elles **ont** voulu

Imperfect subjunctive
(que) je voul**usse**
(que) tu voul**usses**
(qu') il/elle voul**ût**
(que) nous voul**ussions**
(que) vous voul**ussiez**
(qu') ils/elles voul**ussent**

How the verb works

je veux un vélo	*I want a bike*
elle veut partir samedi	*she wants to leave on Saturday*
il voulait acheter une maison	*he wanted to buy a house*
nous voudrions habiter en France	*we'd like to live in France*
qu'est-ce que tu veux?	*what do you want?/what would you like?*
je voudrais un café	*I'd like a coffee*
je voudrais un kilo de tomates, s'il vous plaît	*I'd like a kilo of tomatoes please*
je n'en veux pas	*I don't want any*
elle veut être médecin	*she wants to be a doctor*
je voulais vous dire que...	*I wanted to tell you that...*
je voudrais bien rester mais...	*I'd like to stay but...*
je voudrais bien qu'on finisse avant lundi	*I'd like us to finish before Monday*

Language in use

viens quand tu veux	*come whenever you like*
mange autant que tu veux	*eat as much/many as you like*
tu veux que je t'aide?	*do you want me to help you?*
fais comme tu veux	*do as you like*
que veux-tu que j'y fasse?	*what do you expect me to do about it?*
veux-tu fermer la fenêtre, s'il te plaît?	*would you shut the window, please?*
la voiture ne veut pas démarrer	*the car won't start*
si tu veux	*if you like*
qu'est-ce que ça veut dire?	*what does that mean?*
je ne leur en veux pas	*I don't hold it against them*

Defective verbs

78 déchoir to decay

defective irregular verb
conjugates with **avoir** *in compound tenses*

Imperative	Present participle	Past participle
déchois (tu)	no form: but	déchu
déchoyez (vous)	**échéant**	
déchoyons (nous)		

Present
je déchois...

Conditional
je déchoirais...

Future
je déchoirai...

Present subjunctive
(que) je déchoie...

Imperfect
je déchoyais

Imperfect subjunctive
(que) je déchusse...

Past Historic
je déchus...

79 gésir to lie

defective irregular verb

Present participle	Present	Imperfect
gisant	je gis	je gisais...
	tu gis	
	il/elle gît	
	nous gisons	
	vous gisez	
	ils/elles gisent	

Verb Directory

Verb Directory

Verb directory

accumuler AVOIR *to store up* .... aimer 3
accuser AVOIR *to accuse* .... aimer 3
acharner (s') ÊTRE *to persevere* .... aimer 3
acheminer AVOIR *to transport* .... aimer 3
acheter AVOIR *to buy* .... acheter 1
achever AVOIR *to finish* .... lever 40
acquérir AVOIR *to acquire* .... acquérir 2
acquerrai, etc., acquiers, etc. .... acquérir 2
acquiescer AVOIR *to acquiesce* .... placer 54
acquis, etc. .... acquérir 2
acquitter AVOIR *to acquit* .... aimer 3
actionner AVOIR *to activate* .... aimer 3
activer AVOIR *to speed up* .... aimer 3
actualiser AVOIR *to update* .... aimer 3
adapter AVOIR *to adapt* .... aimer 3
additionner AVOIR *to add* .... aimer 3
adhérer AVOIR *to stick/join* .... céder 13
adjoindre AVOIR *to assign* .... joindre 39
adjuger AVOIR *to auction* .... manger 42
adjurer AVOIR *to implore* .... aimer 3
admettre AVOIR *to admit* .... mettre 45
administrer AVOIR *to administer* .... aimer 3
admirer AVOIR *to admire* .... aimer 3
admonester AVOIR *to admonish* .... aimer 3
adonner (s') ÊTRE *to devote* .... aimer 3
adorer AVOIR *to adore* .... aimer 3
adosser AVOIR *to lean* .... aimer 3
adoucir AVOIR *to soften* .... finir 34
adresser AVOIR *to send* .... aimer 3
aduler AVOIR *to worship* .... aimer 3
advenir ÊTRE *to happen* .... venir 73
aérer AVOIR *to air* .... céder 13
affabuler AVOIR *to tell tall stories* .... aimer 3
affaiblir AVOIR *to weaken* .... finir 34
affairer (s') ÊTRE *to bustle about* .... aimer 3
affaisser (s') ÊTRE *to sag* .... aimer 3
affaler (s') ÊTRE *to collapse* .... aimer 3
affamer AVOIR *to starve* .... aimer 3
affecter AVOIR *to affect* .... aimer 3
affectionner AVOIR *to be very fond of* .... aimer 3
affermir AVOIR *to strengthen* .... finir 34
afficher AVOIR *to display* .... aimer 3
affilier AVOIR *to affiliate* .... plier 57
affiner AVOIR *to refine* .... aimer 3
affirmer AVOIR *to assert* .... aimer 3
affliger AVOIR *to afflict* .... manger 42
affluer AVOIR *to flood in* .... aimer 3
affoler AVOIR *to throw into a panic* .... aimer 3
affranchir AVOIR *to stamp* .... finir 34
affréter AVOIR *to charter* .... céder 13
affronter AVOIR *to face* .... aimer 3

Verb directory

affûter	AVOIR	*to sharpen*	aimer	3
agacer	AVOIR	*to annoy*	placer	54
agencer	AVOIR	*to lay out*	placer	54
agenouiller (s')	ÊTRE	*to kneel down*	aimer	3
agglomérer	AVOIR	*to agglomerate*	céder	13
agglutiner	AVOIR	*to agglutinate*	aimer	3
aggraver	AVOIR	*to aggravate*	aimer	3
agir	AVOIR	*to act*	finir	34
agiter	AVOIR	*to shake*	aimer	3
agneler	AVOIR	*to lamb*	appeler	5
agonir	AVOIR	*to tell off*	finir	34
agoniser	AVOIR	*to be dying*	aimer	3
agrafer	AVOIR	*to staple*	aimer	3
agrandir	AVOIR	*to enlarge*	finir	34
agréer	AVOIR	*to agree*	créer	22
agréger (s')	ÊTRE	*to aggregate*	assiéger	8
agrémenter	AVOIR	*to brighten up*	aimer	3
agresser	AVOIR	*to assault*	aimer	3
agripper	AVOIR	*to grab*	aimer	3
aguerrir	AVOIR	*to harden*	finir	34
ahurir	AVOIR	*to stun*	finir	34
a, ai, aie, aies, ait, as			avoir	9
aider	AVOIR	*to help*	aimer	3
aigrir	AVOIR	*to embitter*	finir	34
aiguiller	AVOIR	*to direct*	aimer	3
aiguiser	AVOIR	*to sharpen*	aimer	3
ailler	AVOIR	*to put garlic into*	aimer	3
aimanter	AVOIR	*to magnetize*	aimer	3
aimer	AVOIR	*to love*	aimer	3
ajourer	AVOIR	*to hemstitch*	aimer	3
ajourner	AVOIR	*to postpone*	aimer	3
ajouter	AVOIR	*to add*	aimer	3
ajuster	AVOIR	*to adjust*	aimer	3
alarmer	AVOIR	*to alarm*	aimer	3
alcooliser	AVOIR	*to alcoholize*	aimer	3
alerter	AVOIR	*to alert*	aimer	3
aléser	AVOIR	*to bore*	céder	13
aliéner	AVOIR	*to alienate*	céder	13
aligner	AVOIR	*to put in a line*	aimer	3
alimenter	AVOIR	*to feed*	aimer	3
aliter (s')	ÊTRE	*to take to one's bed*	aimer	3
allaiter	AVOIR	*to breastfeed*	aimer	3
allécher	AVOIR	*to tempt*	céder	13
alléger	AVOIR	*to lighten*	assiéger	8
alléguer	AVOIR	*to invoke*	céder	13
aller	ÊTRE	*to go*	aller	4
allier	AVOIR	*to combine*	plier	57
allonger	AVOIR	*to lay down*	manger	42
allouer	AVOIR	*to allocate*	aimer	3
allumer	AVOIR	*to light*	aimer	3
alourdir	AVOIR	*to weigh down*	finir	34

Verb directory

alphabétiser	AVOIR	*to teach to read and write*	aimer	3
altérer	AVOIR	*to impair*	céder	13
alterner	AVOIR	*to alternate*	aimer	3
alunir	AVOIR	*to land on the moon*	finir	34
amadouer	AVOIR	*to coax*	aimer	3
amaigrir	AVOIR	*to make thinner*	finir	34
amalgamer	AVOIR	*to mix*	aimer	3
amarrer	AVOIR	*to moor*	aimer	3
amasser	AVOIR	*to amass*	aimer	3
améliorer	AVOIR	*to improve*	aimer	3
aménager	AVOIR	*to convert*	manger	42
amender	AVOIR	*to amend*	aimer	3
amener	AVOIR	*to take/bring*	lever	40
amenuiser	AVOIR	*to reduce*	aimer	3
américaniser	AVOIR	*to americanize*	aimer	3
amerrir	AVOIR	*to land on water*	finir	34
ameuter	AVOIR	*to bring out*	aimer	3
amidonner	AVOIR	*to starch*	aimer	3
amincir	AVOIR	*to make look slimmer*	finir	34
amnistier	AVOIR	*to grant amnesty*	plier	57
amocher	AVOIR	*to bash up*	aimer	3
amoindrir	AVOIR	*to weaken*	finir	34
amollir	AVOIR	*to soften*	finir	34
amorcer	AVOIR	*to begin*	placer	54
amortir	AVOIR	*to cushion/pay off*	finir	34
amouracher (s')	ÊTRE	*to become infatuated*	aimer	3
amplifier	AVOIR	*to amplify*	plier	57
amputer	AVOIR	*to amputate*	aimer	3
amuser	AVOIR	*to entertain*	aimer	3
analyser	AVOIR	*to analyse*	aimer	3
ancrer	AVOIR	*to anchor*	aimer	3
anéantir	AVOIR	*to ruin*	finir	34
anémier	AVOIR	*to make anaemic*	plier	57
anesthésier	AVOIR	*to anaesthetize*	plier	57
angliciser	AVOIR	*to anglicize*	aimer	3
angoisser	AVOIR	*to worry*	aimer	3
animer	AVOIR	*to liven up/lead*	aimer	3
ankyloser	AVOIR	*to get stiff*	aimer	3
annexer	AVOIR	*to annex*	aimer	3
annihiler	AVOIR	*to destroy*	aimer	3
annoncer	AVOIR	*to announce*	placer	54
annoter	AVOIR	*to annotate*	aimer	3
annuler	AVOIR	*to cancel*	aimer	3
anoblir	AVOIR	*to ennoble*	finir	34
ânonner	AVOIR	*to read in a drone*	aimer	3
anticiper	AVOIR	*to anticipate*	aimer	3
antiparasiter	AVOIR	*to fit a suppressor to*	aimer	3
apaiser	AVOIR	*to pacify*	aimer	3
apercevoir	AVOIR	*to see*	recevoir	62
apitoyer	AVOIR	*to move to pity*	employer	28
aplatir	AVOIR	*to flatten*	finir	34

Verb directory

Verb directory

Verb directory

autodéterminer (s') ÊTRE *to exercise self-determination* .... aimer 3
autofinancer (s') ÊTRE *to be self-financing* .... aimer 3
autogérer (s') ÊTRE *to be run on a cooperative basis* .... céder 13
automatiser AVOIR *to automate* .... aimer 3
autoriser AVOIR *to authorize* .... aimer 3
avachir (s') ÊTRE *to sag* .... finir 34
avais, avait, avaient .... avoir 9
avaler AVOIR *to swallow* .... aimer 3
avancer AVOIR *to move forward* .... placer 54
avantager AVOIR *to favour* .... manger 42
avarier AVOIR *to damage* .... plier 57
aventurer AVOIR *to risk* .... aimer 3
avérer (s') ÊTRE *to prove to be* .... céder 13
avertir AVOIR *to inform* .... finir 34
aveugler AVOIR *to blind* .... aimer 3
avez, aviez, avions .... avoir 9
aviser AVOIR *to notify* .... aimer 3
avoir AVOIR *to have* .... avoir 9
avoisiner AVOIR *to be close to* .... aimer 3
avons .... avoir 9
avorter AVOIR *to have an abortion/abort* .... aimer 3
avouer AVOIR *to confess* .... aimer 3
ayez, ayant, ayons .... avoir 9
babiller AVOIR *to babble* .... aimer 3
bâcher AVOIR *to cover with tarpaulin* .... aimer 3
bachoter AVOIR *to cram* .... aimer 3
bâcler AVOIR *to botch up* .... aimer 3
badigeonner AVOIR *to daub* .... aimer 3
bafouer AVOIR *to scorn* .... aimer 3
bafouiller AVOIR *to mumble* .... aimer 3
bâfrer AVOIR *to gorge oneself* .... aimer 3
bagarrer AVOIR *to fight* .... aimer 3
baguenauder AVOIR *to stroll about* .... aimer 3
baguer AVOIR *to ring* .... aimer 3
baigner AVOIR *to bathe* .... aimer 3
bâiller AVOIR *to yawn* .... aimer 3
bâillonner AVOIR *to gag* .... aimer 3
baiser AVOIR *to kiss* .... aimer 3
baisser AVOIR *to lower* .... aimer 3
balader AVOIR *to take for a walk* .... aimer 3
balancer AVOIR *to swing* .... placer 54
balayer AVOIR *to sweep* .... payer 52
balbutier AVOIR *to stammer* .... plier 57
ballonner AVOIR *to bloat* .... aimer 3
banaliser AVOIR *to trivialize* .... aimer 3
bander AVOIR *to bandage* .... aimer 3
bannir AVOIR *to banish* .... finir 34
baptiser AVOIR *to christen* .... aimer 3
baratiner AVOIR *to give the spiel* .... aimer 3
barber AVOIR *to bore* .... aimer 3
barbouiller AVOIR *to smear/daub* .... aimer 3

Verb directory

barrer	AVOIR	*to block*	aimer	3
barricader	AVOIR	*to barricade*	aimer	3
barrir	AVOIR	*to trumpet*	finir	34
basculer	AVOIR	*to topple over*	aimer	3
baser	AVOIR	*to base*	aimer	3
bat, bats			battre	10
batailler	AVOIR	*to fight*	aimer	3
bâter	AVOIR	*to put a pack-saddle on*	aimer	3
batifoler	AVOIR	*to romp about*	aimer	3
bâtir	AVOIR	*to build*	finir	34
battre	AVOIR	*to beat*	battre	10
bavarder	AVOIR	*to chatter*	aimer	3
baver	AVOIR	*to dribble*	aimer	3
béatifier	AVOIR	*to beatify*	plier	57
bêcher	AVOIR	*to dig*	aimer	3
bécoter	AVOIR	*to bill and coo*	aimer	3
becqueter	AVOIR	*to peck at/eat*	jeter	38
béer	AVOIR	*to gape*	créer	22
bégayer	AVOIR	*to stammer*	payer	52
bêler	AVOIR	*to bleat*	aimer	3
bénéficier	AVOIR	*to benefit from*	plier	57
bénir	AVOIR	*to bless*	finir	34
bercer	AVOIR	*to rock*	placer	54
bêtifier	AVOIR	*to say stupid things*	plier	57
beugler	AVOIR	*to bellow out*	aimer	3
beurrer	AVOIR	*to butter*	aimer	3
biaiser	AVOIR	*to hedge*	aimer	3
bidonner (se)	ÊTRE	*to laugh*	aimer	3
bidouiller	AVOIR	*to fiddle with*	aimer	3
biffer	AVOIR	*to cross out*	aimer	3
bifurquer	AVOIR	*to fork*	aimer	3
biler (se)	ÊTRE	*to worry*	aimer	3
biner	AVOIR	*to hoe*	aimer	3
biper	AVOIR	*to beep*	aimer	3
biseauter	AVOIR	*to bevel*	aimer	3
bisquer	AVOIR	*to be mad*	aimer	3
bisser	AVOIR	*to encore*	aimer	3
bitumer	AVOIR	*to asphalt*	aimer	3
biturer (se)	ÊTRE	*to get drunk*	aimer	3
bivouaquer	AVOIR	*to bivouac*	aimer	3
bizuter	AVOIR	*to rag*	aimer	3
blaguer	AVOIR	*to joke*	aimer	3
blairer	AVOIR	*to stand*	aimer	3
blâmer	AVOIR	*to criticize*	aimer	3
blanchir	AVOIR	*to whiten*	finir	34
blaser	AVOIR	*to make blasé*	aimer	3
blasphémer	AVOIR	*to blaspheme*	céder	13
blêmir	AVOIR	*to pale*	finir	34
blesser	AVOIR	*to injure*	aimer	3
blettir	AVOIR	*to overripen*	finir	34
bleuir	AVOIR	*to turn blue*	finir	34

Verb directory

blinder AVOIR *to reinforce*	aimer	3
blondir AVOIR *to turn blonde*	finir	34
bloquer AVOIR *to block*	aimer	3
blottir AVOIR *to nestle*	finir	34
blouser AVOIR *to take for a ride*	aimer	3
bluffer AVOIR *to bluff*	aimer	3
boire AVOIR *to drink*	boire	11
boiter AVOIR *to limp*	aimer	3
boitiller AVOIR *to limp slightly*	aimer	3
bombarder AVOIR *to bomb*	aimer	3
bondir AVOIR *to leap*	finir	34
bonifier AVOIR *to improve*	plier	57
border AVOIR *to line*	aimer	3
borner AVOIR *to limit*	aimer	3
bosseler AVOIR *to dent*	appeler	5
bosser AVOIR *to work on*	aimer	3
botter AVOIR *to kick*	aimer	3
boucher AVOIR *to cork*	aimer	3
boucler AVOIR *to fasten/curl*	aimer	3
bouder AVOIR *to sulk*	aimer	3
bouffer AVOIR *to eat*	aimer	3
bouffir AVOIR *to make puffy*	finir	34
bouger AVOIR *to move*	manger	42
bougonner AVOIR *to grumble*	aimer	3
bouillir AVOIR *to boil*	bouillir	12
bouillonner AVOIR *to bubble*	aimer	3
bouleverser AVOIR *to move deeply*	aimer	3
boulonner AVOIR *to bolt on*	aimer	3
bouquiner AVOIR *to read*	aimer	3
bourdonner AVOIR *to buzz*	aimer	3
bourgeonner AVOIR *to bud*	aimer	3
bourlinguer AVOIR *to travel around*	aimer	3
bourrer AVOIR *to cram*	aimer	3
boursicoter AVOIR *to dabble in shares*	aimer	3
boursoufler AVOIR *to cause to swell*	aimer	3
bous, bout	bouillir	12
bousculer AVOIR *to bump into*	aimer	3
bousiller AVOIR *to botch/ruin*	aimer	3
boutonner AVOIR *to button*	aimer	3
boxer AVOIR *to box*	aimer	3
boycotter AVOIR *to boycott*	aimer	3
braconner AVOIR *to poach*	aimer	3
brader AVOIR *to sell cheaply*	aimer	3
brailler AVOIR *to yell out*	aimer	3
braire AVOIR *to bray*	traire	70
braiser AVOIR *to braise*	aimer	3
bramer AVOIR *to bell*	aimer	3
brancher AVOIR *to plug in*	aimer	3
brandir AVOIR *to brandish*	finir	34
branler AVOIR *to wobble*	aimer	3
braquer AVOIR *to point*	aimer	3

Verb directory

brasser	AVOIR	*to toss*	aimer	3
braver	AVOIR	*to defy*	aimer	3
bredouiller	AVOIR	*to mumble*	aimer	3
breveter	AVOIR	*to patent*	jeter	38
bricoler	AVOIR	*to do DIY*	aimer	3
briguer	AVOIR	*to crave*	aimer	3
briller	AVOIR	*to shine*	aimer	3
brimer	AVOIR	*to bully*	aimer	3
briser	AVOIR	*to break*	aimer	3
brocarder	AVOIR	*to ridicule*	aimer	3
broder	AVOIR	*to embroider*	aimer	3
broncher	AVOIR	*to stumble*	aimer	3
bronzer	AVOIR	*to tan*	aimer	3
brosser	AVOIR	*to brush*	aimer	3
brouillasser	AVOIR	*to drizzle*	aimer	3
brouiller	AVOIR	*to blur*	aimer	3
brouter	AVOIR	*to graze*	aimer	3
broyer	AVOIR	*to grind*	employer	28
bruiner	AVOIR	*to drizzle*	aimer	3
bruire	AVOIR	*to rustle*	finir	34
brûler	AVOIR	*to burn*	aimer	3
brunir	AVOIR	*to tan*	finir	34
brusquer	AVOIR	*to rush*	aimer	3
brutaliser	AVOIR	*to ill-treat*	aimer	3
bu, buvez, buvons, etc.			boire	11
bûcher	AVOIR	*to slog away*	aimer	3
budgétiser	AVOIR	*to budget for*	aimer	3
bureaucratiser	AVOIR	*to bureaucratize*	aimer	3
buter	AVOIR	*to trip*	aimer	3
butiner	AVOIR	*to gather pollen*	aimer	3
butter	AVOIR	*to earth up*	aimer	3
câbler	AVOIR	*to wire*	aimer	3
cabosser	AVOIR	*to dent*	aimer	3
cabrer	AVOIR	*to rear up*	aimer	3
cabrioler	AVOIR	*to caper about*	aimer	3
cacher	AVOIR	*to hide*	aimer	3
cacheter	AVOIR	*to seal*	jeter	38
cadenasser	AVOIR	*to padlock*	aimer	3
cadencer	AVOIR	*to put rhythm into*	placer	54
cadrer	AVOIR	*to centre*	aimer	3
cafarder	AVOIR	*to tell on*	aimer	3
cafouiller	AVOIR	*to get flustered*	aimer	3
cailler	AVOIR	*to curdle*	aimer	3
cajoler	AVOIR	*to make a fuss of*	aimer	3
calciner	AVOIR	*to char*	aimer	3
calculer	AVOIR	*to calculate*	aimer	3
caler	AVOIR	*to wedge*	aimer	3
calfater	AVOIR	*to caulk*	aimer	3
calfeutrer	AVOIR	*to seal*	aimer	3
calibrer	AVOIR	*to calibrate*	aimer	3
câliner	AVOIR	*to cuddle*	aimer	3

Verb directory

calligraphier AVOIR *to write in a decorative hand*	plier	57
calmer AVOIR *to calm*	aimer	3
calomnier AVOIR *to slander*	plier	57
calquer AVOIR *to copy*	aimer	3
cambrer AVOIR *to arch*	aimer	3
cambrioler AVOIR *to burgle*	aimer	3
camer (se) ÊTRE *to be on drugs*	aimer	3
camoufler AVOIR *to camouflage*	aimer	3
camper AVOIR *to camp*	aimer	3
canaliser AVOIR *to canalize*	aimer	3
cancaner AVOIR *to gossip*	aimer	3
cancériser (se) ÊTRE *to become cancerous*	aimer	3
caner AVOIR *to knacker out/die*	aimer	3
canner AVOIR *to cane*	aimer	3
cannibaliser AVOIR *to cannibalize*	aimer	3
canoniser AVOIR *to canonize*	aimer	3
canonner AVOIR *to bombard*	aimer	3
caoutchouter AVOIR *to rubberize*	aimer	3
capitaliser AVOIR *to capitalize*	aimer	3
capitonner AVOIR *to pad*	aimer	3
capituler AVOIR *to capitulate*	aimer	3
capter AVOIR *to capture*	aimer	3
captiver AVOIR *to captivate*	aimer	3
capturer AVOIR *to capture*	aimer	3
caqueter AVOIR *to cackle*	jeter	38
caracoler AVOIR *to prance*	aimer	3
caractériser AVOIR *to characterize*	aimer	3
caraméliser AVOIR *to caramelize*	aimer	3
carboniser AVOIR *to carbonize*	aimer	3
carburer AVOIR *to carburize*	aimer	3
carder AVOIR *to card*	aimer	3
caréner AVOIR *to careen*	céder	13
caresser AVOIR *to stroke*	aimer	3
caricaturer AVOIR *to caricature*	aimer	3
carier AVOIR *to decay*	plier	57
carillonner AVOIR *to chime*	aimer	3
carreler AVOIR *to tile*	appeler	5
caser AVOIR *to put/marry off*	aimer	3
casser AVOIR *to break*	aimer	3
castrer AVOIR *to castrate*	aimer	3
cataloguer AVOIR *to catalogue*	aimer	3
catalyser AVOIR *to catalyse*	aimer	3
catapulter AVOIR *to catapult*	aimer	3
catastropher AVOIR *to devastate*	aimer	3
catéchiser AVOIR *to catechize*	aimer	3
catégoriser AVOIR *to categorize*	aimer	3
cauchemarder AVOIR *to have nightmares*	aimer	3
causer AVOIR *to cause*	aimer	3
cautériser AVOIR *to cauterize*	aimer	3
cautionner AVOIR *to give one's support to*	aimer	3
cavaler AVOIR *to rush about*	aimer	3

Verb directory

Verb directory

chômer AVOIR *to be idle/out of work*		aimer	3
choper AVOIR *to catch*		aimer	3
choquer AVOIR *to shock*		aimer	3
chorégraphier AVOIR *to choreograph*		plier	57
chosifier AVOIR *to reify*		plier	57
chouchouter AVOIR *to pamper*		aimer	3
choyer AVOIR *to pamper*		employer	28
christianiser AVOIR *to christianize*		aimer	3
chronométrer AVOIR *to time*		céder	13
chuchoter AVOIR *to whisper*		aimer	3
chuinter AVOIR *to hiss gently*		aimer	3
chuter AVOIR *to fall*		aimer	3
cibler AVOIR *to target*		aimer	3
cicatriser AVOIR *to heal*		aimer	3
ciller AVOIR *to blink*		aimer	3
cimenter AVOIR *to concrete*		aimer	3
cingler AVOIR *to sting*		aimer	3
circoncire AVOIR *to circumcise*		suffire	68
circonscrire AVOIR *to circumscribe/limit*		écrire	27
circonvenir AVOIR *to circumvent/get round*		venir	73
circuler AVOIR *to run/circulate*		aimer	3
cirer AVOIR *to polish*		aimer	3
cisailler AVOIR *to shear*		aimer	3
ciseler AVOIR *to chisel*		geler	36
citer AVOIR *to quote*		aimer	3
civiliser AVOIR *to civilize*		aimer	3
claironner AVOIR *to shout from the rooftops*		aimer	3
clamer AVOIR *to proclaim*		aimer	3
clapoter AVOIR *to lap*		aimer	3
claquer AVOIR *to slam*		aimer	3
clarifier AVOIR *to clarify*		plier	57
classer AVOIR *to classify*		aimer	3
classifier AVOIR *to classify*		plier	57
cligner AVOIR *to wink*		aimer	3
clignoter AVOIR *to flash on and off*		aimer	3
climatiser AVOIR *to air-condition*		aimer	3
cliquer AVOIR *to click*		aimer	3
cliqueter AVOIR *to jingle*		jeter	38
clochardiser (se) ÊTRE *to be reduced to vagrancy*		aimer	3
clocher AVOIR *to be faulty*		aimer	3
cloisonner AVOIR *to partition*		aimer	3
cloîtrer AVOIR *to shut away*		aimer	3
cloner AVOIR *to clone*		aimer	3
clore AVOIR *to close*		clore	14
clos, closant, etc.		clore	14
clôt		clore	14
clôturer AVOIR *to enclose*		aimer	3
clouer AVOIR *to nail down*		aimer	3
coaguler AVOIR *to coagulate*		aimer	3
coaliser AVOIR *to unite*		aimer	3
coasser AVOIR *to croak*		aimer	3

Verb directory

cocher AVOIR *to tick*	....	aimer	3
cocotter AVOIR *to stink*	....	aimer	3
cocufier AVOIR *to be unfaithful to*	....	plier	57
coder AVOIR *to code*	....	aimer	3
codifier AVOIR *to codify*	....	plier	57
coexister AVOIR *to coexist*	....	aimer	3
cogérer AVOIR *to co-manage*	....	céder	13
cogiter AVOIR *to cogitate*	....	aimer	3
cogner AVOIR *to knock*	....	aimer	3
cohabiter AVOIR *to live together*	....	aimer	3
coiffer AVOIR *to put on*	....	aimer	3
coincer AVOIR *to wedge/jam*	....	placer	54
coïncider AVOIR *to coincide*	....	aimer	3
collaborer AVOIR *to collaborate*	....	aimer	3
collationner AVOIR *to collate*	....	aimer	3
collecter AVOIR *to collect*	....	aimer	3
collectionner AVOIR *to collect*	....	aimer	3
collectiviser AVOIR *to collectivize*	....	aimer	3
coller AVOIR *to stick*	....	aimer	3
colmater AVOIR *to seal off*	....	aimer	3
coloniser AVOIR *to colonize*	....	aimer	3
colorier AVOIR *to colour*	....	plier	57
colporter AVOIR *to peddle*	....	aimer	3
combattre AVOIR *to fight*	....	battre	10
combiner AVOIR *to combine*	....	aimer	3
combler AVOIR *to fill in/fulfil*	....	aimer	3
commander AVOIR *to order*	....	aimer	3
commanditer AVOIR *to support/finance*	....	aimer	3
commémorer AVOIR *to commemorate*	....	aimer	3
commencer AVOIR *to start*	....	placer	54
commenter AVOIR *to comment on*	....	aimer	3
commercer AVOIR *to trade*	....	placer	54
commercialiser AVOIR *to market*	....	aimer	3
commettre AVOIR *to commit*	....	mettre	45
commissionner AVOIR *to commission*	....	aimer	3
commotionner AVOIR *to concuss*	....	aimer	3
commuer AVOIR *to commute*	....	aimer	3
communier AVOIR *to take Communion*	....	plier	57
communiquer AVOIR *to communicate*	....	aimer	3
commuter AVOIR *to commute*	....	aimer	3
comparaître AVOIR *to appear*	....	connaître	17
comparer AVOIR *to compare*	....	aimer	3
compatir AVOIR *to sympathize*	....	finir	34
compenser AVOIR *to compensate*	....	aimer	3
complaire (se) ÊTRE *to delight in*	....	plaire	55
compléter AVOIR *to complete*	....	céder	13
complexer AVOIR *to give a complex to*	....	aimer	3
complexifier AVOIR *to make more complex*	....	plier	57
complimenter AVOIR *to compliment*	....	aimer	3
compliquer AVOIR *to complicate*	....	aimer	3
comploter AVOIR *to plot*	....	aimer	3

Verb directory

comporter AVOIR *to include* . . . . aimer 3
composer AVOIR *to make up/compose* . . . . aimer 3
composter AVOIR *to stamp* . . . . aimer 3
comprendre AVOIR *to understand* . . . . prendre 60
compresser AVOIR *to compress* . . . . aimer 3
comprimer AVOIR *to constrict* . . . . aimer 3
compromettre AVOIR *to compromise* . . . . mettre 45
comptabiliser AVOIR *to count* . . . . aimer 3
compter AVOIR *to count* . . . . aimer 3
compulser AVOIR *to consult* . . . . aimer 3
concéder AVOIR *to grant* . . . . céder 13
concentrer AVOIR *to concentrate* . . . . aimer 3
conceptualiser AVOIR *to conceptualize* . . . . aimer 3
concerner AVOIR *to concern* . . . . aimer 3
concerter AVOIR *to plan* . . . . aimer 3
concevoir AVOIR *to design/conceive* . . . . recevoir 62
concilier AVOIR *to reconcile* . . . . plier 57
conclure AVOIR *to conclude* . . . . conclure 15
concocter AVOIR *to concoct* . . . . aimer 3
concorder AVOIR *to tally* . . . . aimer 3
concourir AVOIR *to compete* . . . . courir 19
concrétiser AVOIR *to give concrete form to* . . . . aimer 3
concurrencer AVOIR *to compete with* . . . . placer 54
condamner AVOIR *to sentence/condemn* . . . . aimer 3
condenser AVOIR *to condense* . . . . aimer 3
condescendre AVOIR *to condescend* . . . . rendre 63
conditionner AVOIR *to condition* . . . . aimer 3
conduire AVOIR *to drive* . . . . conduire 16
confectionner AVOIR *to prepare* . . . . aimer 3
conférer AVOIR *to confer* . . . . céder 13
confesser AVOIR *to confess* . . . . aimer 3
confier AVOIR *to entrust* . . . . plier 57
confiner AVOIR *to confine* . . . . aimer 3
confire AVOIR *to preserve in fat* . . . . suffire 68
confirmer AVOIR *to confirm* . . . . aimer 3
confisquer AVOIR *to confiscate* . . . . aimer 3
confondre AVOIR *to confuse* . . . . rompre 66
conformer AVOIR *to comply with* . . . . aimer 3
conforter AVOIR *to consolidate* . . . . aimer 3
confronter AVOIR *to confront* . . . . aimer 3
congédier AVOIR *to dismiss* . . . . plier 57
congeler AVOIR *to freeze* . . . . geler 36
congestionner AVOIR *to congest* . . . . aimer 3
conjecturer AVOIR *to speculate* . . . . aimer 3
conjuguer AVOIR *to conjugate* . . . . aimer 3
conjurer AVOIR *to ward off* . . . . aimer 3
connaître AVOIR *to know* . . . . connaître 17
connecter AVOIR *to connect* . . . . aimer 3
connu, connus, etc. . . . . connaître 17
conquérir AVOIR *to conquer* . . . . acquérir 2
consacrer AVOIR *to devote* . . . . aimer 3

Verb directory

Verb directory

convulsionner AVOIR *to convulse* .... aimer 3
coopérer AVOIR *to cooperate* .... céder 13
coopter AVOIR *to co-opt* .... aimer 3
coordonner AVOIR *to coordinate* .... aimer 3
copier AVOIR *to copy* .... plier 57
copiner AVOIR *to be friends* .... aimer 3
coproduire AVOIR *to co-produce* .... conduire 16
copuler AVOIR *to copulate* .... aimer 3
corner AVOIR *to hoot* .... aimer 3
correspondre AVOIR *to correspond* .... rendre 63
corriger AVOIR *to correct* .... manger 42
corroborer AVOIR *to corroborate* .... aimer 3
corrompre AVOIR *to bribe/corrupt* .... rompre 66
corroyer AVOIR *to curry* .... employer 28
corser AVOIR *to make more difficult* .... aimer 3
costumer (se) ÊTRE *to put on fancy dress* .... aimer 3
coter AVOIR *to quote* .... aimer 3
cotiser AVOIR *to pay one's contributions* .... aimer 3
côtoyer AVOIR *to mix with* .... employer 28
coucher AVOIR *to put to bed* .... aimer 3
coudoyer AVOIR *to mix with* .... employer 28
coudre AVOIR *to sew* .... coudre 18
couiner AVOIR *to squeak* .... aimer 3
couler AVOIR *to flow* .... aimer 3
coulisser AVOIR *to slide* .... aimer 3
couper AVOIR *to cut* .... aimer 3
courber AVOIR *to bend* .... aimer 3
courir AVOIR *to run* .... courir 19
couronner AVOIR *to crown* .... aimer 3
courtiser AVOIR *to woo* .... aimer 3
cousais, cousons, cousu, etc. .... coudre 18
coûter AVOIR *to cost* .... aimer 3
couver AVOIR *to brood* .... aimer 3
couvert .... couvrir 20
couvrir AVOIR *to cover* .... couvrir 20
cracher AVOIR *to spit out* .... aimer 3
crachiner AVOIR *to drizzle* .... aimer 3
craigne, craignez, craint, etc .... craindre 21
craindre AVOIR *to fear* .... craindre 21
cramponner AVOIR *to cling to* .... aimer 3
crâner AVOIR *to show off* .... aimer 3
cranter AVOIR *to notch/crimp* .... aimer 3
crapahuter AVOIR *to yomp* .... aimer 3
craqueler AVOIR *to crack* .... appeler 5
craquer AVOIR *to split* .... aimer 3
cravacher AVOIR *to whip* .... aimer 3
cravater AVOIR *to grab round the neck* .... aimer 3
crawler AVOIR *to swim the crawl* .... aimer 3
crayonner AVOIR *to scribble down* .... aimer 3
créditer AVOIR *to credit* .... aimer 3
créer AVOIR *to create* .... créer 22

Verb directory

créneler AVOIR *to crenellate*	appeler	5
crépir AVOIR *to render*	finir	34
crépiter AVOIR *to crackle*	aimer	3
creuser AVOIR *to dig*	aimer	3
crever AVOIR *to burst*	lever	40
cribler AVOIR *to riddle*	aimer	3
crier AVOIR *to shout*	plier	57
crisper AVOIR *to clench*	aimer	3
cristalliser AVOIR *to crystallize*	aimer	3
critiquer AVOIR *to criticize*	aimer	3
croasser AVOIR *to caw*	aimer	3
crocheter AVOIR *to crochet*	acheter	1
croire AVOIR *to believe*	croire	23
croiser AVOIR *to cross*	aimer	3
croissais, croisse, etc.	croître	24
croître AVOIR *to grow*	croître	24
croquer AVOIR *to crunch*	aimer	3
crotter AVOIR *to muddy*	aimer	3
crouler AVOIR *to collapse*	aimer	3
croupir AVOIR *to stagnate*	finir	34
croustiller AVOIR *to be crusty*	aimer	3
croyais, croyant, croyez, etc.	croire	23
cru, crus, etc.	croire	23
crû, crûs, etc.	croître	24
crucifier AVOIR *to crucify*	plier	57
cueillir AVOIR *to pick*	cueillir	25
cuire AVOIR *to cook*	conduire	16
cuisiner AVOIR *to cook*	aimer	3
cuiter (se) ÊTRE *to get plastered*	aimer	3
cuivrer AVOIR *to bronze*	aimer	3
culbuter AVOIR *to knock over*	aimer	3
culminer AVOIR *to peak*	aimer	3
culpabiliser AVOIR *to feel guilty*	aimer	3
cultiver AVOIR *to grow/cultivate*	aimer	3
cumuler AVOIR *to combine/accumulate*	aimer	3
curer AVOIR *to clean out*	aimer	3
cyanoser (se) ÊTRE *to become cyanotic*	aimer	3
dactylographier AVOIR *to type out*	plier	57
daigner AVOIR *to deign*	aimer	3
damasser AVOIR *to damask*	aimer	3
damner AVOIR *to damn*	aimer	3
dandiner (se) ÊTRE *to waddle*	aimer	3
danser AVOIR *to dance*	aimer	3
dater AVOIR *to date*	aimer	3
déambuler AVOIR *to wander*	aimer	3
déballer AVOIR *to unpack*	aimer	3
débaptiser AVOIR *to change the name of*	aimer	3
débarbouiller AVOIR *to wash*	aimer	3
débarder AVOIR *to haul*	aimer	3
débarquer AVOIR *to unload*	aimer	3
débarrasser AVOIR *to clear*	aimer	3

Verb directory

Verb directory

déchiqueter AVOIR *to tear to pieces*	jeter	38
déchirer AVOIR *to tear up*	aimer	3
déchoir AVOIR *to strip of*	déchoir	78
décider AVOIR *to decide*	aimer	3
décimer AVOIR *to decimate*	aimer	3
déclamer AVOIR *to declaim*	aimer	3
déclarer AVOIR *to declare*	aimer	3
déclencher AVOIR *to set off*	aimer	3
décliner AVOIR *to decline*	aimer	3
décocher AVOIR *to shoot*	aimer	3
décoder AVOIR *to decode*	aimer	3
décoiffer AVOIR *to ruffle sb's hair*	aimer	3
décoincer AVOIR *to unjam*	placer	54
décolérer AVOIR *to let up*	céder	13
décoller AVOIR *to unstick/peel off*	aimer	3
décoloniser AVOIR *to decolonize*	aimer	3
décolorer AVOIR *to bleach*	aimer	3
décommander AVOIR *to call off*	aimer	3
décomposer AVOIR *to break down*	aimer	3
décompresser AVOIR *to unwind*	aimer	3
décomprimer AVOIR *to decompress*	aimer	3
décompter AVOIR *to deduct*	aimer	3
déconcerter AVOIR *to disconcert*	aimer	3
décongeler AVOIR *to defrost*	geler	36
décongestionner AVOIR *to clear*	aimer	3
déconnecter AVOIR *to disconnect*	aimer	3
déconseiller AVOIR *to advise against*	aimer	3
décontaminer AVOIR *to decontaminate*	aimer	3
décontenancer AVOIR *to disconcert*	placer	54
décontracter AVOIR *to relax*	aimer	3
décorer AVOIR *to decorate*	aimer	3
décortiquer AVOIR *to shell*	aimer	3
découcher AVOIR *to spend the night away from home*	aimer	3
découdre AVOIR *to unstitch*	coudre	18
découler AVOIR *to follow*	aimer	3
découper AVOIR *to cut up/carve*	aimer	3
décourager AVOIR *to discourage*	manger	42
découvrir AVOIR *to discover*	couvrir	20
décrasser AVOIR *to clean up*	aimer	3
décréter AVOIR *to order*	céder	13
décrier AVOIR *to decry*	plier	57
décrire AVOIR *to describe*	écrire	27
décrocher AVOIR *to take down*	aimer	3
décroiser AVOIR *to uncross*	aimer	3
décroître AVOIR *to drop*	croître	24
décrypter AVOIR *to decipher*	aimer	3
déculotter AVOIR *to take off sb's trousers*	aimer	3
déculpabiliser AVOIR *to justify*	aimer	3
décupler AVOIR *to multiply by ten*	aimer	3
dédaigner AVOIR *to despise*	aimer	3
dédicacer AVOIR *to dedicate*	placer	54

Verb directory

dédier AVOIR *to dedicate*	plier	57
dédire (se) ÊTRE *to retract one's statement*	médire	44
dédommager AVOIR *to compensate*	manger	42
dédouaner AVOIR *to clear*	aimer	3
dédoubler AVOIR *to split in two*	aimer	3
dédramatiser AVOIR *to play down*	aimer	3
déduire AVOIR *to deduct*	conduire	16
défaillir AVOIR *to faint*	assaillir	6
défaire AVOIR *to undo*	faire	32
défavoriser AVOIR *to discriminate against*	aimer	3
défendre AVOIR *to defend/forbid*	rendre	63
défenestrer AVOIR *to throw out of a window*	aimer	3
déféquer AVOIR *to defecate*	céder	13
déférer AVOIR *to refer*	céder	13
déferler AVOIR *to flood in/erupt*	aimer	3
déficeler AVOIR *to untie*	appeler	5
défier AVOIR *to challenge*	plier	57
défigurer AVOIR *to disfigure*	aimer	3
défiler AVOIR *to parade*	aimer	3
définir AVOIR *to define*	finir	34
déflorer AVOIR *to deflower*	aimer	3
défoncer AVOIR *to smash*	placer	54
déformer AVOIR *to distort/bend*	aimer	3
défouler AVOIR *to release tension*	aimer	3
défraîchir AVOIR *to fade*	finir	34
défrayer AVOIR *to pay the expenses of*	payer	52
défricher AVOIR *to clear*	aimer	3
défriser AVOIR *to straighten*	aimer	3
défroisser AVOIR *to smooth out*	aimer	3
dégager AVOIR *to free*	manger	42
dégainer AVOIR *to draw*	aimer	3
déganter AVOIR *to take sb's glove off*	aimer	3
dégarnir AVOIR *to empty*	finir	34
dégeler AVOIR *to thaw*	geler	36
dégénérer AVOIR *to degenerate*	céder	13
dégivrer AVOIR *to de-ice*	aimer	3
déglacer AVOIR *to deglaze*	placer	54
déglinguer AVOIR *to break*	aimer	3
déglutir AVOIR *to swallow*	finir	34
dégobiller AVOIR *to vomit*	aimer	3
dégonfler AVOIR *to deflate*	aimer	3
dégorger AVOIR *to discharge/unblock*	manger	42
dégoter AVOIR *to find*	aimer	3
dégotter AVOIR *to find*	aimer	3
dégouliner AVOIR *to trickle*	aimer	3
dégourdir AVOIR *to warm up*	finir	34
dégoûter AVOIR *to disgust*	aimer	3
dégrader AVOIR *to damage*	aimer	3
dégrafer AVOIR *to undo*	aimer	3
dégraisser AVOIR *to dry-clean/streamline*	aimer	3
dégrever AVOIR *to relieve the tax burden on*	lever	40

Verb directory

dégringoler AVOIR *to tumble*	aimer	3
dégrossir AVOIR *to rough-hew*	finir	34
dégrouiller (se) ÊTRE *to hurry up*	aimer	3
déguerpir AVOIR *to clear off*	finir	34
dégueulasser AVOIR *to dirty*	aimer	3
dégueuler AVOIR *to vomit*	aimer	3
déguiser AVOIR *to dress up*	aimer	3
dégurgiter AVOIR *to bring up*	aimer	3
déguster AVOIR *to savour*	aimer	3
déhancher (se) ÊTRE *to sway one's hips*	aimer	3
déifier AVOIR *to deify*	plier	57
déjeuner AVOIR *to have lunch*	aimer	3
déjouer AVOIR *to foil/evade*	aimer	3
délabrer AVOIR *to ruin*	aimer	3
délacer AVOIR *to undo/unlace*	placer	54
délaisser AVOIR *to leave/abandon*	aimer	3
délasser AVOIR *to relax*	aimer	3
délaver AVOIR *to fade*	aimer	3
délayer AVOIR *to dilute*	payer	52
délecter (se) ÊTRE *to relish*	aimer	3
déléguer AVOIR *to delegate*	céder	13
délibérer AVOIR *to deliberate*	céder	13
délier AVOIR *to untie*	plier	57
délimiter AVOIR *to delimit*	aimer	3
délirer AVOIR *to be delirious*	aimer	3
délivrer AVOIR *to free*	aimer	3
déloger AVOIR *to evict*	manger	42
délurer AVOIR *to wake (sb) up a bit*	aimer	3
demander AVOIR *to ask*	aimer	3
démanger AVOIR *to be itchy*	manger	42
démanteler AVOIR *to dismantle*	geler	36
démaquiller AVOIR *to remove make-up from*	aimer	3
démarcher AVOIR *to sell door-to-door*	aimer	3
démarquer AVOIR *to mark down*	aimer	3
démarrer AVOIR *to start*	aimer	3
démasquer AVOIR *to unmask/uncover*	aimer	3
démazouter AVOIR *to clean the oil from*	aimer	3
démédicaliser AVOIR *to demedicalize*	aimer	3
démêler AVOIR *to disentangle*	aimer	3
démembrer AVOIR *to cut up*	aimer	3
déménager AVOIR *to move house*	manger	42
démener (se) ÊTRE *to thrash about/go to trouble*	lever	40
démentir AVOIR *to deny*	partir	51
démériter AVOIR *to prove oneself unworthy*	aimer	3
démettre AVOIR *to dislocate/dismiss*	mettre	45
demeurer AVOIR/ÊTRE *to reside/remain*	aimer	3
démilitariser AVOIR *to demilitarize*	aimer	3
déminer AVOIR *to clear of mines*	aimer	3
déminéraliser AVOIR *to demineralize*	aimer	3
démissionner AVOIR *to resign*	aimer	3
démobiliser AVOIR *to demobilize*	aimer	3

Verb directory

démocratiser AVOIR *to democratize* .... aimer 3
démoder (se) ÊTRE *to go out of fashion* .... aimer 3
démolir AVOIR *to demolish* .... finir 34
démonétiser AVOIR *to demonetize* .... aimer 3
démonter AVOIR *to take down* .... aimer 3
démontrer AVOIR *to demonstrate* .... aimer 3
démoraliser AVOIR *to demoralize* .... aimer 3
démordre AVOIR *to let go* .... rendre 63
démotiver AVOIR *to demotivate* .... aimer 3
démouler AVOIR *to turn out of the mould* .... aimer 3
démunir AVOIR *to divest* .... finir 34
démystifier AVOIR *to demystify* .... plier 57
dénationaliser AVOIR *to denationalize* .... aimer 3
dénaturer AVOIR *to denature* .... aimer 3
déneiger AVOIR *to clear the snow* .... manger 42
dénicher AVOIR *to dig out/discover* .... aimer 3
dénier AVOIR *to deny* .... plier 57
dénigrer AVOIR *to denigrate* .... aimer 3
dénombrer AVOIR *to count* .... aimer 3
dénommer AVOIR *to name* .... aimer 3
dénoncer AVOIR *to denounce* .... placer 54
dénoter AVOIR *to denote* .... aimer 3
dénouer AVOIR *to untie* .... aimer 3
dénoyauter AVOIR *to stone* .... aimer 3
denteler AVOIR *to pink* .... appeler 5
dénucléariser AVOIR *to denuclearize* .... aimer 3
dénuder AVOIR *to reveal/bare* .... aimer 3
dépanner AVOIR *to fix/help out* .... aimer 3
déparasiter AVOIR *to disinfest* .... aimer 3
dépareiller AVOIR *to spoil* .... aimer 3
déparer AVOIR *to spoil* .... aimer 3
départager AVOIR *to decide between* .... manger 42
dépasser AVOIR *to overtake/jut out* .... aimer 3
dépayser AVOIR *to provide with a change of scenery* .... aimer 3
dépecer AVOIR *to cut up* .... lever 40
dépêcher AVOIR *to dispatch* .... aimer 3
dépeigner AVOIR *to make (sb's) hair untidy* .... aimer 3
dépeindre AVOIR *to depict* .... peindre 53
dépénaliser AVOIR *to decriminalize* .... aimer 3
dépendre AVOIR *to depend on* .... rendre 63
dépenser AVOIR *to spend* .... aimer 3
dépérir AVOIR *to waste away/wilt* .... finir 34
dépersonnaliser AVOIR *to depersonalize* .... aimer 3
dépêtrer AVOIR *to extricate* .... aimer 3
dépeupler AVOIR *to depopulate* .... aimer 3
déphaser AVOIR *to disorientate* .... aimer 3
dépister AVOIR *to track down* .... aimer 3
dépiter AVOIR *to upset* .... aimer 3
déplacer AVOIR *to move* .... placer 54
déplaire AVOIR *to displease* .... plaire 55
déplier AVOIR *to unfold* .... plier 57

Verb directory

déplorer AVOIR *to deplore*		aimer	3
déployer AVOIR *to display*		employer	28
dépolariser AVOIR *to depolarize*		aimer	3
dépolir AVOIR *to frost*		finir	34
dépolitiser AVOIR *to depoliticize*		aimer	3
dépolluer AVOIR *to clean up*		aimer	3
déporter AVOIR *to send to a concentration camp*		aimer	3
déposer AVOIR *to put down/leave*		aimer	3
déposséder AVOIR *to dispossess*		céder	13
dépouiller AVOIR *to rob*		aimer	3
dépoussiérer AVOIR *to dust*		céder	13
dépraver AVOIR *to deprave*		aimer	3
déprécier AVOIR *to depreciate*		plier	57
déprimer AVOIR *to depress*		aimer	3
dépuceler AVOIR *to take (sb's) virginity*		appeler	5
députer AVOIR *to delegate*		aimer	3
déqualifier AVOIR *to deskill*		plier	57
déraciner AVOIR *to uproot*		aimer	3
dérailler AVOIR *to derail*		aimer	3
déraisonner AVOIR *not to be compos mentis*		aimer	3
déranger AVOIR *to disturb* . . . . manger		manger	42
déraper AVOIR *to skid/get out of control*		aimer	3
dératiser AVOIR *to clear of rats*		aimer	3
déréglementer AVOIR *to deregulate*		aimer	3
dérégler AVOIR *to affect/upset*		céder	13
déresponsabiliser AVOIR *to remove all sense of responsibility from*		aimer	3
dérider AVOIR *to cheer up*		aimer	3
dériver AVOIR *to divert*		aimer	3
dérober AVOIR *to steal*		aimer	3
déroger AVOIR *to infringe* . . . . manger		manger	42
dérouler AVOIR *to unroll*		aimer	3
dérouter AVOIR *to puzzle*		aimer	3
désabuser AVOIR *to disenchant*		aimer	3
désaccorder AVOIR *to make go out of tune*		aimer	3
désaccoutumer AVOIR *to disaccustom*		aimer	3
désacraliser AVOIR *to destroy the sacred aura surrounding*		aimer	3
désactiver AVOIR *to deactivate*		aimer	3
désagréger AVOIR *to disintegrate*		assiéger	8
désaltérer AVOIR *to quench (sb's) thirst*		céder	13
désamorcer AVOIR *to defuse*		placer	54
désappointer AVOIR *to disappoint*		aimer	3
désapprendre AVOIR *to forget/unlearn*		prendre	60
désapprouver AVOIR *to disapprove of*		aimer	3
désarçonner AVOIR *to throw/take aback*		aimer	3
désargenter AVOIR *to take the silver plating off*		aimer	3
désarmer AVOIR *to disarm*		aimer	3
désarticuler AVOIR *to dislocate*		aimer	3
désavantager AVOIR *to disadvantage*		manger	42
désavouer AVOIR *to deny*		aimer	3
désaxer AVOIR *to put out of true*		aimer	3
desceller AVOIR *to unseal*		aimer	3

Verb directory

Verb directory

desseller AVOIR *to unsaddle*		aimer	3
desserrer AVOIR *to loosen*		aimer	3
desservir AVOIR *to serve/lead to*		partir	51
dessiner AVOIR *to draw*		aimer	3
dessoûler AVOIR *to sober up*		aimer	3
déstabiliser AVOIR *to unsettle*		aimer	3
destiner AVOIR *to intend/design*		aimer	3
destituer AVOIR *to discharge*		aimer	3
désunir AVOIR *to divide*		finir	34
détacher AVOIR *to untie*		aimer	3
détailler AVOIR *to detail*		aimer	3
détaler AVOIR *to bolt*		aimer	3
détartrer AVOIR *to descale*		aimer	3
détecter AVOIR *to detect*		aimer	3
déteindre AVOIR *to fade*		peindre	53
dételer AVOIR *to unharness*		appeler	5
détendre AVOIR *to release*		rendre	63
détenir AVOIR *to keep*		venir	73
détériorer AVOIR *to damage*		aimer	3
déterminer AVOIR *to determine*		aimer	3
déterrer AVOIR *to dig up*		aimer	3
détester AVOIR *to detest*		aimer	3
détoner AVOIR *to detonate*		aimer	3
détonner AVOIR *to be out of place*		aimer	3
détourner AVOIR *to divert/hijack*		aimer	3
détraquer AVOIR *to break/upset*		aimer	3
détremper AVOIR *to saturate*		aimer	3
détromper AVOIR *to disabuse*		aimer	3
détrôner AVOIR *to dethrone*		aimer	3
détruire AVOIR *to destroy*		conduire	16
dévaler AVOIR *to hurtle down*		aimer	3
dévaliser AVOIR *to rob*		aimer	3
dévaloriser AVOIR *to depreciate*		aimer	3
dévaluer AVOIR *to devalue*		aimer	3
devancer AVOIR *to be ahead of*		placer	54
dévaster AVOIR *to destroy*		aimer	3
développer AVOIR *to develop*		aimer	3
devenir ÊTRE *to become*		venir	73
dévergonder (se) ÊTRE *to lead a debauched life*		aimer	3
déverser AVOIR *to pour*		aimer	3
dévêtir AVOIR *to undress*		vêtir	74
dévier AVOIR *to deflect*		plier	57
deviner AVOIR *to guess*		aimer	3
dévisager AVOIR *to stare at*		manger	42
deviser AVOIR *to converse*		aimer	3
dévisser AVOIR *to unscrew*		aimer	3
dévitaliser AVOIR *to do root canal work on*		aimer	3
dévoiler AVOIR *to unveil*		aimer	3
devoir AVOIR *to have to*		devoir	26
dévorer AVOIR *to devour*		aimer	3
dévouer (se) ÊTRE *to devote oneself*		aimer	3

Verb directory

dévoyer	AVOIR	to deprave	employer	28
diagnostiquer	AVOIR	to diagnose	aimer	3
dialoguer	AVOIR	to have talks	aimer	3
dialyser	AVOIR	to perform dialysis on	aimer	3
dicter	AVOIR	to dictate	aimer	3
diffamer	AVOIR	to slander	aimer	3
différencier	AVOIR	to differentiate	plier	57
différer	AVOIR	to postpone	céder	13
diffuser	AVOIR	to broadcast	aimer	3
digérer	AVOIR	to digest	céder	13
digitaliser	AVOIR	to digitize	aimer	3
dilapider	AVOIR	to squander	aimer	3
dilater	AVOIR	to dilate	aimer	3
diluer	AVOIR	to dilute	aimer	3
diminuer	AVOIR	to reduce	aimer	3
dîner	AVOIR	to have dinner/dine	aimer	3
diplômer	AVOIR	to award a diploma to	aimer	3
dire	AVOIR	to say	médire	44
diriger	AVOIR	to run/steer/direct	manger	42
discerner	AVOIR	to make out	aimer	3
discipliner	AVOIR	to discipline	aimer	3
discontinuer	AVOIR	to stop	aimer	3
disconvenir	ÊTRE	to deny	venir	73
discourir	AVOIR	to hold forth	courir	19
discréditer	AVOIR	to discredit	aimer	3
discriminer	AVOIR	to categorize	aimer	3
disculper	AVOIR	to exculpate	aimer	3
discuter	AVOIR	to discuss	aimer	3
disgracier	AVOIR	to reject	plier	57
disjoindre	AVOIR	to loosen	joindre	39
disjoncter	AVOIR	to trip	aimer	3
disloquer	AVOIR	to dismember/dislocate	aimer	3
disparaître	AVOIR/ÊTRE	to disappear	connaître	17
dispenser	AVOIR	to give/exempt	aimer	3
disperser	AVOIR	to scatter	aimer	3
disposer	AVOIR	to arrange	aimer	3
disputer	AVOIR	to compete	aimer	3
disqualifier	AVOIR	to disqualify	plier	57
disséminer	AVOIR	to spread	aimer	3
disséquer	AVOIR	to dissect	céder	13
disserter	AVOIR	to speak	aimer	3
dissimuler	AVOIR	to conceal	aimer	3
dissiper	AVOIR	to dispel	aimer	3
dissocier	AVOIR	to dissociate	plier	57
dissoudre	AVOIR	to dissolve	résoudre	64
dissuader	AVOIR	to dissuade	aimer	3
distancer	AVOIR	to outdistance	placer	54
distendre	AVOIR	to distend	rendre	63
distiller	AVOIR	to distil	aimer	3
distinguer	AVOIR	to distinguish	aimer	3
distordre	AVOIR	to distort	rendre	63

Verb directory

Verb directory

écailler AVOIR *to scale* .... aimer 3
écarquiller AVOIR *to open wide* .... aimer 3
écarteler AVOIR *to tear apart* .... geler 36
écarter AVOIR *to move apart* .... aimer 3
échafauder AVOIR *to put together* .... aimer 3
échanger AVOIR *to exchange* .... manger 42
échantillonner AVOIR *to sample* .... aimer 3
échapper AVOIR *to escape* .... aimer 3
écharper AVOIR *to tear to pieces* .... aimer 3
échauder AVOIR *to put (sb) off* .... aimer 3
échauffer AVOIR *to warm up* .... aimer 3
échelonner AVOIR *to space out* .... aimer 3
écheveler AVOIR *to ruffle (sb's) hair* .... appeler 5
échiner (s') ÊTRE *to make a great effort* .... aimer 3
échoir AVOIR/ÊTRE *to fall to (sb's) share/fall du* .... déchoir 78
échouer AVOIR *to fail/beach* .... aimer 3
éclabousser AVOIR *to splash* .... aimer 3
éclaircir AVOIR *to lighten* .... finir 34
éclairer AVOIR *to light* .... aimer 3
éclater AVOIR *to burst* .... aimer 3
éclipser AVOIR *to eclipse* .... aimer 3
éclore AVOIR/ÊTRE *to hatch* .... clore 14
écœurer AVOIR *to make (sb) feel sick* .... aimer 3
éconduire AVOIR *to turn (sb) away* .... conduire 16
économiser AVOIR *to save* .... aimer 3
écoper AVOIR *to bail out* .... aimer 3
écorcer AVOIR *to strip the bark from* .... placer 54
écorcher AVOIR *to graze/ skin* .... aimer 3
écorner AVOIR *to take the edge off* .... aimer 3
écosser AVOIR *to shell* .... aimer 3
écouler AVOIR *to sell* .... aimer 3
écourter AVOIR *to shorten* .... aimer 3
écouter AVOIR *to listen* .... aimer 3
écraser AVOIR *to crush* .... aimer 3
écrémer AVOIR *to skim* .... céder 13
écrier (s') ÊTRE *to exclaim* .... plier 57
écrire AVOIR *to write* .... écrire 27
écrive, écrivez, etc. .... écrire 27
écrouer AVOIR *to commit to prison* .... aimer 3
écrouler (s') ÊTRE *to collapse* .... aimer 3
écumer AVOIR *to skim/foam* .... aimer 3
édenter AVOIR *to break the teeth of* .... aimer 3
édifier AVOIR *to build* .... plier 57
éditer AVOIR *to publish* .... aimer 3
édulcorer AVOIR *to sweeten* .... aimer 3
éduquer AVOIR *to educate* .... aimer 3
effacer AVOIR *to erase* .... placer 54
effarer AVOIR *to alarm* .... aimer 3
effaroucher AVOIR *to frighten away* .... aimer 3
effectuer AVOIR *to carry out* .... aimer 3
effeuiller AVOIR *to thin out the leaves of* .... aimer 3

Verb directory

effilocher	AVOIR *to shred*	aimer	3
effleurer	AVOIR *to touch lightly*	aimer	3
effondrer (s')	ÊTRE *to collapse*	aimer	3
effrayer	AVOIR *to frighten*	payer	52
égaler	AVOIR *to equal*	aimer	3
égaliser	AVOIR *to level out/equalize*	aimer	3
égarer	AVOIR *to lead astray/to mislay*	aimer	3
égayer	AVOIR *to enliven*	payer	52
égorger	AVOIR *to cut (sb's) throat*	manger	42
égosiller (s')	ÊTRE *to shout oneself hoarse*	aimer	3
égoutter	AVOIR *to drain*	aimer	3
égratigner	AVOIR *to scratch*	aimer	3
égrener	AVOIR *to shell*	lever	40
éjaculer	AVOIR *to ejaculate*	aimer	3
éjecter	AVOIR *to eject*	aimer	3
élaborer	AVOIR *to devise*	aimer	3
élaguer	AVOIR *to lop*	aimer	3
élancer	AVOIR *to have a throbbing pain*	placer	54
élargir	AVOIR *to widen*	finir	34
électrifier	AVOIR *to bring electricity to*	plier	57
électrocuter	AVOIR *to electrocute*	aimer	3
élever	AVOIR *to put up/bring up/raise*	lever	40
élider	AVOIR *to elide*	aimer	3
élimer	AVOIR *to wear thin*	aimer	3
éliminer	AVOIR *to eliminate*	aimer	3
élire	AVOIR *to elect*	lire	41
éloigner	AVOIR *to move away*	aimer	3
élucider	AVOIR *to solve*	aimer	3
éluder	AVOIR *to evade*	aimer	3
émacier	AVOIR *to emaciate*	plier	57
émanciper	AVOIR *to emancipate*	aimer	3
émaner	AVOIR *to emanate*	aimer	3
émasculer	AVOIR *to emasculate*	aimer	3
emballer	AVOIR *to pack*	aimer	3
embarquer	AVOIR *to load/board*	aimer	3
embarrasser	AVOIR *to embarrass*	aimer	3
embastiller	AVOIR *to imprison*	aimer	3
embaucher	AVOIR *to hire*	aimer	3
embaumer	AVOIR *to embalm/smell of*	aimer	3
embellir	AVOIR *to embellish*	finir	34
emberlificoter	AVOIR *to entangle*	aimer	3
embêter	AVOIR *to bother*	aimer	3
emboîter	AVOIR *to fit together*	aimer	3
embourber	AVOIR *to get (sth) stuck in the mud*	aimer	3
embourgeoiser (s')	ÊTRE *to become middle-class*	aimer	3
embouteiller	AVOIR *to clog*	aimer	3
emboutir	AVOIR *to stamp/crash into*	finir	34
embraser	AVOIR *to set ablaze*	aimer	3
embrasser	AVOIR *to kiss*	aimer	3
embrayer	AVOIR *to engage the clutch*	payer	52
embrigader	AVOIR *to recruit*	aimer	3

Verb directory

embrocher AVOIR *to put on a spit*		aimer	3
embrouiller AVOIR *to tangle*		aimer	3
embuer AVOIR *to mist up*		aimer	3
embusquer AVOIR *to place in ambush*		aimer	3
émerger AVOIR *to emerge*		manger	42
émerveiller AVOIR *to fill with wonder*		aimer	3
émettre AVOIR *to express/emit*		mettre	45
émietter AVOIR *to crumble*		aimer	3
émigrer AVOIR *to emigrate*		aimer	3
émincer AVOIR *to slice thinly*		placer	54
emmagasiner AVOIR *to store*		aimer	3
emmailloter AVOIR *to swaddle*		aimer	3
emmancher AVOIR *to fit a handle to*		aimer	3
emmêler AVOIR *to tangle*		aimer	3
emménager AVOIR *to move in*		manger	42
emmener AVOIR *to take*		lever	40
emmerder AVOIR *to hassle*		aimer	3
emmitoufler AVOIR *to wrap up warmly*		aimer	3
émousser AVOIR *to blunt*		aimer	3
émoustiller AVOIR *to exhilarate*		aimer	3
émouvoir AVOIR *to move/touch*		mouvoir	48
empailler AVOIR *to seat with straw/stuff*		aimer	3
empaler AVOIR *to impale*		aimer	3
empaqueter AVOIR *to package*		jeter	38
emparer (s') de ÊTRE *to take over*		aimer	3
empâter AVOIR *to fur up*		aimer	3
empêcher AVOIR *to prevent*		aimer	3
empeser AVOIR *to starch*		lever	40
empester AVOIR *to stink out*		aimer	3
empêtrer AVOIR *to get (sb) mixed up*		aimer	3
empiéter AVOIR *to encroach*		céder	13
empiffrer (s') ÊTRE *to stuff oneself*		aimer	3
empiler AVOIR *to pile up*		aimer	3
empirer AVOIR *to get worse*		aimer	3
emplir AVOIR *to fill*		finir	34
emploie, emploies, etc.		employer	28
employer AVOIR *to employ*		employer	28
empocher AVOIR *to pocket*		aimer	3
empoigner AVOIR *to grab*		aimer	3
empoisonner AVOIR *to poison*		aimer	3
emporter AVOIR *to take*		aimer	3
empoter AVOIR *to pot*		aimer	3
empoussiérer AVOIR *to cover with dust*		céder	13
empreindre AVOIR *to imprint*		peindre	53
empresser (s') ÊTRE *to hasten*		aimer	3
emprisonner AVOIR *to imprison*		aimer	3
emprunter AVOIR *to borrow*		aimer	3
empuantir AVOIR *to stink out*		finir	34
émuler AVOIR *to emulate*		aimer	3
encadrer AVOIR *to frame/supervise*		aimer	3
encaisser AVOIR *to cash*		aimer	3

Verb directory

encanailler (s') ÊTRE *to slum it*		aimer	3
encastrer AVOIR *to build in*		aimer	3
encaustiquer AVOIR *to wax-polish*		aimer	3
enceindre AVOIR *to encircle*		peindre	53
encenser AVOIR *to acclaim/cense*		aimer	3
encercler AVOIR *to surround*		aimer	3
enchaîner AVOIR *to chain up*		aimer	3
enchanter AVOIR *to delight*		aimer	3
enchérir AVOIR *to bid*		finir	34
enchevêtrer AVOIR *to tangle up*		aimer	3
enclencher AVOIR *to launch*		aimer	3
enclore AVOIR *to enclose*		clore	14
encoller AVOIR *to paste*		aimer	3
encombrer AVOIR *to clutter up*		aimer	3
encourager AVOIR *to encourage*		manger	42
encourir AVOIR *to incur*		courir	19
encrasser AVOIR *to clog up*		aimer	3
encrer AVOIR *to ink*		aimer	3
encroûter (s') ÊTRE *to get in a rut*		aimer	3
enculer AVOIR *to bugger*		aimer	3
endetter AVOIR *to put into debt*		aimer	3
endeuiller AVOIR *to plunge (sb) into mourning*		aimer	3
endiguer AVOIR *to contain*		aimer	3
endoctriner AVOIR *to indoctrinate*		aimer	3
endolorir AVOIR *to make ache*		finir	34
endommager AVOIR *to damage*		manger	42
endormir AVOIR *to send to sleep*		partir	51
endosser AVOIR *to put on*		aimer	3
enduire AVOIR *to coat*		conduire	16
endurcir AVOIR *to strengthen*		finir	34
endurer AVOIR *to endure*		aimer	3
énerver AVOIR *to irritate*		aimer	3
enfanter AVOIR *to give birth*		aimer	3
enfermer AVOIR *to shut in*		aimer	3
enfiévrer AVOIR *to excite*		céder	13
enfiler AVOIR *to slip on*		aimer	3
enflammer AVOIR *to set fire to*		aimer	3
enfler AVOIR *to exaggerate*		aimer	3
enfoncer AVOIR *to push in*		placer	54
enfouir AVOIR *to bury*		finir	34
enfourcher AVOIR *to mount*		aimer	3
enfourner AVOIR *to put in the oven*		aimer	3
enfreindre AVOIR *to infringe*		peindre	53
enfuir ('s) ÊTRE *to run away*		fuir	35
engager AVOIR *to hire*		manger	42
engendrer AVOIR *to engender*		aimer	3
englober AVOIR *to include*		aimer	3
engloutir AVOIR *to swallow up*		finir	34
engluer AVOIR *to lime*		aimer	3
engorger AVOIR *to block*		manger	42
engourdir AVOIR *to make numb*		finir	34

Verb directory

engraisser AVOIR *to fatten*	aimer	3
engranger AVOIR *to gather in*	manger	42
engueuler AVOIR *to tell off*	aimer	3
enhardir AVOIR *to embolden*	finir	34
enivrer AVOIR *to intoxicate*	aimer	3
enjamber AVOIR *to step over*	aimer	3
enjoindre AVOIR *to enjoin*	joindre	39
enjoliver AVOIR *to embellish*	aimer	3
enlacer AVOIR *to embrace*	placer	54
enlaidir AVOIR *to spoil*	finir	34
enlever AVOIR *to remove*	lever	40
enliser AVOIR *to get (sth) stuck*	aimer	3
enluminer AVOIR *to illuminate*	aimer	3
ennoblir AVOIR *to ennoble*	finir	34
ennuyer AVOIR *to bore*	essuyer	30
énoncer AVOIR *to pronounce*	placer	54
enorgueillir AVOIR *to make proud*	finir	34
enquérir (s') ÊTRE *to inquire*	acquérir	2
enquêter AVOIR *to investigate*	aimer	3
enquiquiner AVOIR *to pester*	aimer	3
enraciner AVOIR *to root*	aimer	3
enrager AVOIR *to be furious*	manger	42
enrayer AVOIR *to check*	payer	52
enregistrer AVOIR *to record*	aimer	3
enrhumer AVOIR *to give (sb) a cold*	aimer	3
enrichir AVOIR *to make rich*	finir	34
enrober AVOIR *to coat*	aimer	3
enrôler AVOIR *to recruit*	aimer	3
enrouer AVOIR *to make hoarse*	aimer	3
enrouler AVOIR *to wind*	aimer	3
ensabler AVOIR *to get stuck in the sand*	aimer	3
ensanglanter AVOIR *to cover with blood*	aimer	3
enseigner AVOIR *to teach*	aimer	3
ensemencer AVOIR *to sow*	placer	54
enserrer AVOIR *to fit tightly round*	aimer	3
ensevelir AVOIR *to bury*	finir	34
ensorceler AVOIR *to cast a spell on*	appeler	5
ensuivre (s') ÊTRE *to follow*	suivre	69
entamer AVOIR *to start*	aimer	3
entartrer AVOIR *to scale up*	aimer	3
entasser AVOIR *to pile*	aimer	3
entendre AVOIR *to hear*	rendre	63
enter AVOIR *to graft*	aimer	3
entériner AVOIR *to ratify*	aimer	3
enterrer AVOIR *to bury*	aimer	3
entêter (s') ÊTRE *to be stubborn*	aimer	3
enthousiasmer AVOIR *to fill with enthusiasm*	aimer	3
enticher (s') ÊTRE *to become infatuated*	aimer	3
entonner AVOIR *to start singing*	aimer	3
entortiller AVOIR *to wind*	aimer	3
entourer AVOIR *to surround*	aimer	3

Verb directory

entraider (s') ÊTRE *to help each other* . . . . aimer 3
entraîner AVOIR *to train/lead to* . . . . aimer 3
entraver AVOIR *to hinder* . . . . aimer 3
entrebâiller AVOIR *to half-open* . . . . aimer 3
entrechoquer AVOIR *to clatter* . . . . aimer 3
entrecouper AVOIR *to punctuate* . . . . aimer 3
entrecroiser AVOIR *to intertwine* . . . . aimer 3
entre-déchirer (s') ÊTRE *to tear each other to pieces* . . . . aimer 3
entrelacer AVOIR *to intertwine* . . . . placer 54
entremêler AVOIR *to mix* . . . . aimer 3
entremettre (s') ÊTRE *to act as mediator* . . . . mettre 45
entreposer AVOIR *to store* . . . . aimer 3
entreprendre AVOIR *to start* . . . . prendre 60
entrer AVOIR/ÊTRE *to take in/to go/come in* . . . . aimer 3
entretenir AVOIR *to look after* . . . . venir 73
entre-tuer (s') ÊTRE *to kill each other* . . . . aimer 3
entrevoir AVOIR *to catch a glimpse* . . . . voir 76
entrouvrir AVOIR *to open a little* . . . . couvrir 20
énumérer AVOIR *to enumerate* . . . . céder 13
envahir AVOIR *to invade* . . . . finir 34
envelopper AVOIR *to wrap up* . . . . aimer 3
envenimer AVOIR *to inflame* . . . . aimer 3
envier AVOIR *to envy* . . . . plier 57
environner AVOIR *to surround* . . . . aimer 3
envisager AVOIR *to plan* . . . . manger 42
envoler (s') ÊTRE *to fly off* . . . . aimer 3
envoûter AVOIR *to bewitch* . . . . aimer 3
envoyer AVOIR *to send* . . . . envoyer 29
épaissir AVOIR *to thicken* . . . . finir 34
épancher AVOIR *to pour out* . . . . aimer 3
épandre AVOIR *to spread* . . . . rendre 63
épanouir AVOIR *to open out* . . . . finir 34
épargner AVOIR *to save/spare* . . . . aimer 3
éparpiller AVOIR *to scatter* . . . . aimer 3
épater AVOIR *to impress* . . . . aimer 3
épauler AVOIR *to help* . . . . aimer 3
épeler AVOIR *to spell* . . . . appeler 5
épépiner AVOIR *to seed* . . . . aimer 3
épicer AVOIR *to spice* . . . . placer 54
épier AVOIR *to spy on* . . . . plier 57
épiler AVOIR *to depilate* . . . . aimer 3
épingler AVOIR *to pin* . . . . aimer 3
éplucher AVOIR *to peel* . . . . aimer 3
éponger AVOIR *to mop up* . . . . manger 42
épouser AVOIR *to marry* . . . . aimer 3
épousseter AVOIR *to dust* . . . . jeter 38
époustoufler AVOIR *to amaze* . . . . aimer 3
épouvanter AVOIR *to terrify* . . . . aimer 3
éprendre (s') ÊTRE *to become enamoured* . . . . prendre 60
éprouver AVOIR *to feel* . . . . aimer 3
épuiser AVOIR *to exhaust* . . . . aimer 3

Verb directory

épurer	AVOIR	to purify	aimer	3
équilibrer	AVOIR	to balance	aimer	3
équiper	AVOIR	to equip	aimer	3
équivaloir	AVOIR	to be equivalent to	valoir	72
éradiquer	AVOIR	to eradicate	aimer	3
érafler	AVOIR	to scratch	aimer	3
érailler	AVOIR	to scratch	aimer	3
éreinter	AVOIR	to exhaust	aimer	3
ergoter	AVOIR	to quibble	aimer	3
ériger	AVOIR	to erect	manger	42
éroder	AVOIR	to erode	aimer	3
érotiser	AVOIR	to eroticize	aimer	3
errer	AVOIR	to wander	aimer	3
éructer	AVOIR	to eructate	aimer	3
escalader	AVOIR	to climb	aimer	3
escamoter	AVOIR	to make disappear	aimer	3
esclaffer (s')	ÊTRE	to burst out laughing	aimer	3
escompter	AVOIR	to discount	aimer	3
escorter	AVOIR	to escort	aimer	3
escroquer	AVOIR	to swindle	aimer	3
espacer	AVOIR	to space out	placer	54
espérer	AVOIR	to hope	céder	13
espionner	AVOIR	to spy on	aimer	3
esquinter	AVOIR	to damage	aimer	3
esquisser	AVOIR	to sketch	aimer	3
esquiver	AVOIR	to dodge	aimer	3
essaimer	AVOIR	to swarm	aimer	3
essayer	AVOIR	to try	payer	52
essorer	AVOIR	to wring	aimer	3
essouffler	AVOIR	to leave breathless	aimer	3
essuie, essuies, etc.			essuyer	30
essuyer	AVOIR	to dry/wipe	essuyer	30
estimer	AVOIR	to feel/estimate	aimer	3
estomaquer	AVOIR	to flabbergast	aimer	3
estomper	AVOIR	to shade off	aimer	3
estropier	AVOIR	to maim	plier	57
établir	AVOIR	to set up	finir	34
étager	AVOIR	to plant in tiers/stagger	manger	42
étais, été, était, étions, etc.			être	
étaler	AVOIR	to spread out	aimer	3
étancher	AVOIR	to make watertight/quench	aimer	3
étatiser	AVOIR	to bring under state control	aimer	3
étayer	AVOIR	to prop up/support	payer	52
éteindre	AVOIR	to switch off/put out	peindre	53
étendre	AVOIR	to stretch	rendre	63
éterniser	AVOIR	to prolong	aimer	3
éternuer	AVOIR	to sneeze	aimer	3
étinceler	AVOIR	to twinkle	appeler	5
étiqueter	AVOIR	to label	jeter	38
étirer	AVOIR	to stretch	aimer	3
étoffer	AVOIR	to flesh out	aimer	3

Verb directory

étonner	AVOIR	*to surprise*	aimer	3
étouffer	AVOIR	*to stifle*	aimer	3
étourdir	AVOIR	*to stun*	finir	34
étrangler	AVOIR	*to strangle*	aimer	3
être	AVOIR	*to be*	être	31
étreindre	AVOIR	*to embrace*	peindre	53
étrenner	AVOIR	*to wear for the first time*	aimer	3
étudier	AVOIR	*to study*	plier	57
eu, eûmes, eusse, eût, etc.			avoir	9
européaniser	AVOIR	*to europeanize*	aimer	3
évacuer	AVOIR	*to evacuate*	aimer	3
évader (s')	ÊTRE	*to escape*	aimer	3
évaluer	AVOIR	*to estimate*	aimer	3
évangéliser	AVOIR	*to evangelize*	aimer	3
évanouir (s')	ÊTRE	*to faint*	finir	34
évaporer (s')	ÊTRE	*to evaporate*	aimer	3
évaser	AVOIR	*to flare*	aimer	3
éveiller	AVOIR	*to stimulate*	aimer	3
éventer	AVOIR	*to discover*	aimer	3
éventrer	AVOIR	*to disembowel*	aimer	3
évertuer (s')	ÊTRE	*to try one's best*	aimer	3
évincer	AVOIR	*to oust*	placer	54
éviter	AVOIR	*to avoid*	aimer	3
évoluer	AVOIR	*to evolve*	aimer	3
évoquer	AVOIR	*to recall*	aimer	3
exacerber	AVOIR	*to exacerbate*	aimer	3
exagérer	AVOIR	*to exaggerate*	céder	13
exalter	AVOIR	*to elate*	aimer	3
examiner	AVOIR	*to examine*	aimer	3
exaspérer	AVOIR	*to exasperate*	céder	13
exaucer	AVOIR	*to grant*	placer	54
excéder	AVOIR	*to exceed*	céder	13
exceller	AVOIR	*to excel*	aimer	3
exciser	AVOIR	*to excise*	aimer	3
exciter	AVOIR	*to stir up*	aimer	3
exclamer (s')	ÊTRE	*to exclaim*	aimer	3
exclure	AVOIR	*to exclude*	conclure	15
excommunier	AVOIR	*to excommunicate*	plier	57
excréter	AVOIR	*to excrete*	céder	13
excuser	AVOIR	*to forgive*	aimer	3
exécrer	AVOIR	*to loathe*	céder	13
exécuter	AVOIR	*to carry out*	aimer	3
exemplifier	AVOIR	*to exemplify*	plier	57
exempter	AVOIR	*to exempt*	aimer	3
exercer	AVOIR	*to exercise*	placer	54
exhausser	AVOIR	*to raise*	aimer	3
exhiber	AVOIR	*to flaunt*	aimer	3
exhorter	AVOIR	*to motivate*	aimer	3
exhumer	AVOIR	*to exhume*	aimer	3
exiger	AVOIR	*to demand*	manger	42
exiler	AVOIR	*to exile*	aimer	3

Verb directory

Verb directory

fatiguer AVOIR *to make tired*	aimer	3
faucher AVOIR *to mow*	aimer	3
faudra, faudrait	falloir	33
faufiler AVOIR *to baste*	aimer	3
fausser AVOIR *to distort*	aimer	3
faut	falloir	33
fauter AVOIR *to sin*	aimer	3
favoriser AVOIR *to favour*	aimer	3
faxer AVOIR *to fax*	aimer	3
féconder AVOIR *to fertilize*	aimer	3
fédérer AVOIR *to federate*	céder	13
feindre AVOIR *to feign*	peindre	53
feinter AVOIR *to make a feint*	aimer	3
fêler AVOIR *to crack*	aimer	3
féliciter AVOIR *to congratulate*	aimer	3
féminiser AVOIR *to open up to women*	aimer	3
fendiller AVOIR *to chap/craze*	aimer	3
fendre AVOIR *to chop*	rendre	63
fera, ferais, ferions, etc.	faire	32
fermenter AVOIR *to ferment*	aimer	3
fermer AVOIR *to close*	aimer	3
ferrer AVOIR *to shoe*	aimer	3
fertiliser AVOIR *to fertilize*	aimer	3
festoyer AVOIR *to feast*	employer	28
fêter AVOIR *to celebrate*	aimer	3
feuilleter AVOIR *to leaf through*	jeter	38
fiancer (se) ÊTRE *to get engaged*	placer	54
ficeler AVOIR *to tie up*	appeler	5
ficher AVOIR *to put on a file/do*	aimer	3
fidéliser AVOIR *to secure the loyalty of*	aimer	3
fier (se) ÊTRE *to trust*	plier	57
figer AVOIR *to congeal*	manger	42
fignoler AVOIR *to put the finishing touches to*	aimer	3
figurer AVOIR *to represent*	aimer	3
filer AVOIR *to spin/go off*	aimer	3
fileter AVOIR *to thread*	acheter	1
filmer AVOIR *to film*	aimer	3
filtrer AVOIR *to filter*	aimer	3
finaliser AVOIR *to finalize*	aimer	3
financer AVOIR *to finance*	placer	54
finasser AVOIR *to scheme*	aimer	3
finir AVOIR *to finish*	finir	34
fiscaliser AVOIR *to tax*	aimer	3
fisse, fissions, etc.	faire	32
fissionner AVOIR *to split*	aimer	3
fissurer AVOIR *to crack*	aimer	3
fixer AVOIR *to fix*	aimer	3
flageller AVOIR *to flog*	aimer	3
flageoler AVOIR *to crumble*	aimer	3
flagorner AVOIR *to fawn on*	aimer	3
flairer AVOIR *to sniff*	aimer	3

Verb directory

flamber AVOIR *to burn/flambé*	....	aimer	3
flamboyer AVOIR *to blaze*	....	employer	28
flancher AVOIR *to crack up*	....	aimer	3
flâner AVOIR *to stroll*	....	aimer	3
flanquer AVOIR *to flank/give*	....	aimer	3
flatter AVOIR *to flatter*	....	aimer	3
flécher AVOIR *to signpost*	....	céder	13
fléchir AVOIR *to bend*	....	finir	34
flemmarder AVOIR *to loaf around*	....	aimer	3
flétrir AVOIR *to fade*	....	finir	34
fleurir AVOIR *to flower*	....	finir	34
flinguer AVOIR *to shoot*	....	aimer	3
flipper AVOIR *to freak out*	....	aimer	3
flirter AVOIR *to flirt*	....	aimer	3
flotter AVOIR *to float*	....	aimer	3
fluctuer AVOIR *to fluctuate*	....	aimer	3
fluidifier AVOIR *to thin*	....	plier	57
focaliser AVOIR *to focus*	....	aimer	3
foirer AVOIR *to be a complete disaster*	....	aimer	3
foisonner AVOIR *to abound*	....	aimer	3
foncer AVOIR *to rush/darken*	....	placer	54
fonctionner AVOIR *to work*	....	aimer	3
fonder AVOIR *to found*	....	aimer	3
fondre AVOIR *to melt*	....	rendre	63
forcer AVOIR *to force*	....	placer	54
forcir AVOIR *to become stronger*	....	finir	34
forer AVOIR *to drill*	....	aimer	3
forfaire AVOIR *to be false to*	....	faire	32
forger AVOIR *to forge*	....	manger	42
formaliser AVOIR *to formalize*	....	aimer	3
formater AVOIR *to format*	....	aimer	3
former AVOIR *to form*	....	aimer	3
formuler AVOIR *to express*	....	aimer	3
forniquer AVOIR *to fornicate*	....	aimer	3
fortifier AVOIR *to strengthen*	....	plier	57
foudroyer AVOIR *to strike down*	....	employer	28
fouetter AVOIR *to flog*	....	aimer	3
fouiller AVOIR *to search*	....	aimer	3
fouiner AVOIR *to forage about*	....	aimer	3
fouler AVOIR *to tread*	....	aimer	3
fourguer AVOIR *to flog*	....	aimer	3
fourmiller AVOIR *to abound*	....	aimer	3
fournir AVOIR *to supply*	....	finir	34
fourrer AVOIR *to stuff/line*	....	aimer	3
fourvoyer AVOIR *to mislead*	....	employer	28
foutre AVOIR *to do*	....	rendre	63
fracasser AVOIR *to smash*	....	aimer	3
fractionner AVOIR *to divide up*	....	aimer	3
fracturer AVOIR *to fracture*	....	aimer	3
fragiliser AVOIR *to weaken*	....	aimer	3
fragmenter AVOIR *to break up*	....	aimer	3

Verb directory

fraîchir AVOIR *to get cooler* .... finir 34
franchir AVOIR *to cross* .... finir 34
franchiser AVOIR *to franchise* .... aimer 3
franciser AVOIR *to frenchify* .... aimer 3
franger AVOIR *to fringe* .... manger 42
frapper AVOIR *to hit* .... aimer 3
fraterniser AVOIR *to fraternize* .... aimer 3
frauder AVOIR *to cheat* .... aimer 3
frayer AVOIR *to spawn* .... payer 52
fredonner AVOIR *to hum* .... aimer 3
freiner AVOIR *to brake* .... aimer 3
frémir AVOIR *to quiver* .... finir 34
fréquenter AVOIR *to associate with* .... aimer 3
frétiller AVOIR *to wriggle* .... aimer 3
fricoter AVOIR *to cook up* .... aimer 3
frictionner AVOIR *to rub* .... aimer 3
frigorifier AVOIR *to freeze* .... plier 57
frimer AVOIR *to show off* .... aimer 3
fringuer (se) ÊTRE *to dress* .... aimer 3
friper AVOIR *to crease* .... aimer 3
frire AVOIR *to fry* .... suffire 68
friser AVOIR *to curl* .... aimer 3
frissonner AVOIR *to shiver* .... aimer 3
froisser AVOIR *to crumple/hurt* .... aimer 3
frôler AVOIR *to brush* .... aimer 3
froncer AVOIR *to gather* .... placer 54
frotter AVOIR *to scrub* .... aimer 3
fructifier AVOIR *to bear fruit* .... plier 57
frustrer AVOIR *to frustrate* .... aimer 3
fuguer AVOIR *to run away* .... aimer 3
fuir AVOIR *to flee* .... fuir 35
fulminer AVOIR *to fulminate* .... aimer 3
fumer AVOIR *to smoke* .... aimer 3
fureter AVOIR *to rummage* .... acheter 1
fûmes, fus, fusse, etc. .... être 31
fuser AVOIR *to rocket/fuse* .... aimer 3
fusiller AVOIR *to shoot* .... aimer 3
fusionner AVOIR *to merge* .... aimer 3
fustiger AVOIR *to castigate* .... manger 42
fuyant, fuyez, fuyant, fuyons, etc. .... fuir 35
gâcher AVOIR *to waste* .... aimer 3
gaffer AVOIR *to blunder* .... aimer 3
gager AVOIR *to suppose/pawn* .... manger 42
gagner AVOIR *to win* .... aimer 3
gainer AVOIR *to sheathe* .... aimer 3
galérer AVOIR *to have a hard time* .... céder 13
galoper AVOIR *to canter* .... aimer 3
galvaniser AVOIR *to galvanize* .... aimer 3
galvauder AVOIR *to sully* .... aimer 3
gambader AVOIR *to gambol* .... aimer 3
gamberger AVOIR *to think hard* .... manger 42

Verb directory

gangrener AVOIR *to corrupt* .... lever 40
garantir AVOIR *to guarantee* .... finir 34
garder AVOIR *to keep* .... aimer 3
garer AVOIR *to park* .... aimer 3
gargariser (se) ÊTRE *to gargle* .... aimer 3
gargouiller AVOIR *to gurgle* .... aimer 3
garnir AVOIR *to fill* .... finir 34
gaspiller AVOIR *to waste* .... aimer 3
gâter AVOIR *to spoil* .... aimer 3
gauchir AVOIR *to warp* .... finir 34
gaufrer AVOIR *to emboss* .... aimer 3
gaver AVOIR *to force-feed* .... aimer 3
gazéifier AVOIR *to carbonate* .... plier 57
gazer AVOIR *to gas* .... aimer 3
gazouiller AVOIR *to twitter* .... aimer 3
geindre AVOIR *to moan* .... peindre 53
geler AVOIR *to freeze* .... geler 36
gélifier AVOIR *to gel* .... plier 57
gémir AVOIR *to moan* .... finir 34
gendarmer (se) ÊTRE *to protest* .... aimer 3
gêner AVOIR *to disturb* .... aimer 3
généraliser AVOIR *to generalize* .... aimer 3
générer AVOIR *to generate* .... céder 13
gerber AVOIR *to bind/vomit* .... aimer 3
gercer AVOIR *to chap* .... placer 54
gérer AVOIR *to manage* .... céder 13
germaniser AVOIR *to germanize* .... aimer 3
germer AVOIR *to sprout/form* .... aimer 3
gésir *to be lying* .... gésir 79
gesticuler AVOIR *to fidget* .... aimer 3
gicler AVOIR *to spurt/squirt* .... aimer 3
gifler AVOIR *to slap* .... aimer 3
gigoter AVOIR *to wriggle/fidget* .... aimer 3
givrer AVOIR *to frost over* .... aimer 3
glacer AVOIR *to freeze/chill* .... placer 54
glander AVOIR *to bum around* .... aimer 3
glandouiller AVOIR *to bum around* .... aimer 3
glaner AVOIR *to glean* .... aimer 3
glapir AVOIR *to yap/screech* .... finir 34
glisser AVOIR *to slip/be slippery* .... aimer 3
glorifier AVOIR *to glorify* .... plier 57
glousser AVOIR *to cluck* .... aimer 3
gober AVOIR *to swallow* .... aimer 3
goinfrer (se) ÊTRE *to stuff oneself* .... aimer 3
gommer AVOIR *to erase* .... aimer 3
gondoler AVOIR *to crinkle* .... aimer 3
gonfler AVOIR *to blow up/swell* .... aimer 3
gorger AVOIR *to force-feed* .... manger 42
goudronner AVOIR *to tarmac* .... aimer 3
goupiller AVOIR *to fix* .... aimer 3
gourer (se) ÊTRE *to make a mistake* .... aimer 3

Verb directory

goûter AVOIR to taste	......	aimer	3
goutter AVOIR to drip	......	aimer	3
gouverner AVOIR to govern	......	aimer	3
gracier AVOIR to reprieve	......	plier	57
graduer AVOIR to increase/grade	......	aimer	3
graisser AVOIR to grease	......	aimer	3
grandir AVOIR to grow	......	finir	34
grasseyer AVOIR to speak with an uvular R	......	payer	52
gratifier AVOIR to gratify	......	plier	57
gratiner AVOIR to brown	......	aimer	3
gratouiller AVOIR to make itch	......	aimer	3
gratter AVOIR to scratch	......	aimer	3
graver AVOIR to engrave	......	aimer	3
gravir AVOIR to climb up	......	finir	34
graviter AVOIR to orbit	......	aimer	3
gréer AVOIR to rig	......	créer	22
greffer AVOIR to graft/transplant	......	aimer	3
grêler AVOIR to hail	......	aimer	3
grelotter AVOIR to shiver	......	aimer	3
grésiller AVOIR to crackle	......	aimer	3
grever AVOIR to put a strain on	......	lever	40
gribouiller AVOIR to scribble	......	aimer	3
griffer AVOIR to scratch	......	aimer	3
griffonner AVOIR to scrawl	......	aimer	3
grignoter AVOIR to nibble	......	aimer	3
grillager AVOIR to put wire netting round	......	manger	42
griller AVOIR to grill	......	aimer	3
grimacer AVOIR to grimace	......	placer	54
grimer AVOIR to make up	......	aimer	3
grimper AVOIR to climb	......	aimer	3
grincer AVOIR to creak	......	placer	54
gripper AVOIR to seize up	......	aimer	3
griser AVOIR to exhilarate	......	aimer	3
grisonner AVOIR to go grey	......	aimer	3
grogner AVOIR to grumble	......	aimer	3
grommeler AVOIR to grumble	......	appeler	5
gronder AVOIR to tell off/growl	......	aimer	3
grossir AVOIR to enlarge/put on weight	......	finir	34
grouiller AVOIR to swarm about	......	aimer	3
grouper AVOIR to put together	......	aimer	3
gruger AVOIR to dupe	......	manger	42
guérir AVOIR to heal/recover	......	finir	34
guerroyer AVOIR to wage war	......	employer	28
guetter AVOIR to watch	......	aimer	3
gueuler AVOIR to yell	......	aimer	3
gueuletonner AVOIR to have a big meal	......	aimer	3
guider AVOIR to guide	......	aimer	3
guillotiner AVOIR to guillotine	......	aimer	3
guinder AVOIR to make look stiff	......	aimer	3
habiliter AVOIR to authorize	......	aimer	3
habiller AVOIR to dress	......	aimer	3

Verb directory

Verb directory

idolâtrer AVOIR *to idolize* .... aimer 3
ignifuger AVOIR *to fireproof* .... manger 42
ignorer AVOIR *to ignore/not to know* .... aimer 3
illuminer AVOIR *to illuminate* .... aimer 3
illustrer AVOIR *to illustrate* .... aimer 3
imaginer AVOIR *to imagine* .... aimer 3
imbiber AVOIR *to soak* .... aimer 3
imiter AVOIR *to imitate* .... aimer 3
immatriculer AVOIR *to register* .... aimer 3
immerger AVOIR *to immerse* .... manger 42
immigrer AVOIR *to immigrate* .... aimer 3
immiscer (s') ÊTRE *to interfere* .... placer 54
immobiliser AVOIR *to immobilize* .... aimer 3
immoler AVOIR *to immolate* .... aimer 3
immortaliser AVOIR *to immortalize* .... aimer 3
immuniser AVOIR *to immunize* .... aimer 3
impatienter AVOIR *to irritate* .... aimer 3
imperméabiliser AVOIR *to waterproof* .... aimer 3
implanter AVOIR *to establish* .... aimer 3
impliquer AVOIR *to implicate* .... aimer 3
implorer AVOIR *to implore* .... aimer 3
imploser AVOIR *to implode* .... aimer 3
importer AVOIR *to import* .... aimer 3
importuner AVOIR *to bother* .... aimer 3
imposer AVOIR *to impose* .... aimer 3
imprégner AVOIR *to impregnate* .... céder 13
impressionner AVOIR *to impress* .... aimer 3
imprimer AVOIR *to print* .... aimer 3
improviser AVOIR *to improvise* .... aimer 3
imputer AVOIR *to attribute* .... aimer 3
inaugurer AVOIR *to open/unveil* .... aimer 3
incarcérer AVOIR *to imprison* .... céder 13
incarner AVOIR *to embody* .... aimer 3
incendier AVOIR *to burn down* .... plier 57
incinérer AVOIR *to incinerate* .... céder 13
inciser AVOIR *to make an incision in* .... aimer 3
inciter AVOIR *to encourage* .... aimer 3
incliner AVOIR *to tilt* .... aimer 3
inclure AVOIR *to include* .... conclure 15
incommoder AVOIR *to bother* .... aimer 3
incorporer AVOIR *to blend in/incorporate* .... aimer 3
incriminer AVOIR *to accuse* .... aimer 3
incruster AVOIR *to inlay/scale up* .... aimer 3
incuber AVOIR *to incubate* .... aimer 3
inculper AVOIR *to charge* .... aimer 3
inculquer AVOIR *to instil* .... aimer 3
indemniser AVOIR *to compensate* .... aimer 3
indexer AVOIR *to index* .... aimer 3
indifférer AVOIR *to leave (sb) indifferent* .... céder 13
indigner AVOIR *to outrage* .... aimer 3
indiquer AVOIR *to point out* .... aimer 3

Verb directory

indisposer AVOIR *to upset* .... aimer 3
individualiser AVOIR *to individualize* .... aimer 3
induire AVOIR *to lead to/infer* .... conduire 16
industrialiser AVOIR *to industrialize* .... aimer 3
infatuer (s') ÊTRE *to become infatuated* .... aimer 3
infecter AVOIR *to infect* .... aimer 3
inférer AVOIR *to infer* .... céder 13
infester AVOIR *to infest* .... aimer 3
infiltrer AVOIR *to infiltrate* .... aimer 3
infléchir AVOIR *to inflect/soften* .... finir 34
infliger AVOIR *to inflict* .... manger 42
influencer AVOIR *to influence* .... placer 54
influer AVOIR *to have an influence* .... aimer 3
informatiser AVOIR *to computerize* .... aimer 3
informer AVOIR *to inform* .... aimer 3
infuser AVOIR *to infuse* .... aimer 3
ingurgiter AVOIR *to gulp down* .... aimer 3
inhaler AVOIR *to inhale* .... aimer 3
inhiber AVOIR *to inhibit* .... aimer 3
inhumer AVOIR *to bury* .... aimer 3
initialiser AVOIR *to initialize* .... aimer 3
initier AVOIR *to initiate* .... plier 57
injecter AVOIR *to inject* .... aimer 3
injurier AVOIR *to swear at* .... plier 57
innocenter AVOIR *to prove innocent* .... aimer 3
innover AVOIR *to innovate* .... aimer 3
inoculer AVOIR *to inoculate* .... aimer 3
inonder AVOIR *to flood* .... aimer 3
inquiéter AVOIR *to worry* .... céder 13
inscrire AVOIR *to enrol/write down* .... écrire 27
inséminer AVOIR *to inseminate* .... aimer 3
insensibiliser AVOIR *to anaesthetize* .... aimer 3
insérer AVOIR *to insert* .... céder 13
insinuer AVOIR *to insinuate* .... aimer 3
insister AVOIR *to insist* .... aimer 3
insonoriser AVOIR *to soundproof* .... aimer 3
inspecter AVOIR *to inspect* .... aimer 3
inspirer AVOIR *to inspire* .... aimer 3
installer AVOIR *to install* .... aimer 3
instaurer AVOIR *to institute/establish* .... aimer 3
instiller AVOIR *to instil* .... aimer 3
instituer AVOIR *to institute* .... aimer 3
institutionnaliser AVOIR *to institutionalize* .... aimer 3
instruire AVOIR *to teach* .... conduire 16
instrumenter AVOIR *to orchestrate* .... aimer 3
insulter AVOIR *to insult* .... aimer 3
insurger (s') ÊTRE *to rise up (against)* .... manger 42
intégrer AVOIR *to include/integrate* .... céder 13
intensifier AVOIR *to intensify* .... plier 57
intercaler AVOIR *to insert* .... aimer 3
intercéder AVOIR *to intercede* .... céder 13

Verb directory

Verb directory

jointoyer AVOIR *to point*		employer	28
joncher AVOIR *to litter*		aimer	3
jongler AVOIR *to juggle*		aimer	3
jouer AVOIR *to play*		aimer	3
jouir AVOIR *to enjoy/have an orgasm*		finir	34
jubiler AVOIR *to rejoice*		aimer	3
jucher AVOIR *to perch*		aimer	3
juger AVOIR *to judge*		manger	42
juguler AVOIR *to stamp out/curb*		aimer	3
jumeler AVOIR *to twin*		appeler	5
jurer AVOIR *to swear*		aimer	3
justifier AVOIR *to justify*		plier	57
juxtaposer AVOIR *to juxtapose*		aimer	3
kidnapper AVOIR *to kidnap*		aimer	3
klaxonner AVOIR *to hoot*		aimer	3
labourer AVOIR *to plough*		aimer	3
lacer AVOIR *to lace up*		placer	54
lacérer AVOIR *to lacerate*		céder	13
lâcher AVOIR *to drop/let go of*		aimer	3
laïciser AVOIR *to secularize*		aimer	3
laisser AVOIR *to leave*		aimer	3
lamenter (se) ÊTRE *to moan*		aimer	3
laminer AVOIR *to roll*		aimer	3
lancer AVOIR *to throw*		placer	54
lanciner AVOIR *to torment/nag*		aimer	3
langer AVOIR *to wrap in swaddling clothes*		manger	42
languir AVOIR *to languish*		finir	34
laper AVOIR *to lap*		aimer	3
lapider AVOIR *to stone*		aimer	3
laquer AVOIR *to lacquer*		aimer	3
larguer AVOIR *to launch*		aimer	3
larmoyer AVOIR *to water*		employer	28
lasser AVOIR *to bore/weary*		aimer	3
laver AVOIR *to wash*		aimer	3
lécher AVOIR *to lick*		céder	13
légaliser AVOIR *to legalize*		aimer	3
légiférer AVOIR *to legislate*		céder	13
légitimer AVOIR *to legitimate*		aimer	3
léguer AVOIR *to leave/bequeath*		céder	13
léser AVOIR *to wrong*		céder	13
lésiner AVOIR *to skimp on*		aimer	3
lessiver AVOIR *to wash*		aimer	3
leurrer AVOIR *to delude*		aimer	3
lever AVOIR *to raise*		lever	40
lézarder AVOIR *to crack/bask in the sun*		aimer	3
libeller AVOIR *to word/make out*		aimer	3
libéraliser AVOIR *to liberalize*		aimer	3
libérer AVOIR *to free*		céder	13
licencier AVOIR *to make redundant*		plier	57
lier AVOIR *to tie up*		plier	57
ligaturer AVOIR *to tie/ligature*		aimer	3

Verb directory

ligoter	AVOIR	*to truss up*	aimer	3
liguer	AVOIR	*to get (sb) to join forces against*	aimer	3
limer	AVOIR	*to file*	aimer	3
limiter	AVOIR	*to limit*	aimer	3
limoger	AVOIR	*to dismiss*	manger	42
liquéfier	AVOIR	*to liquefy*	plier	57
liquider	AVOIR	*to settle/liquidate*	aimer	3
lire	AVOIR	*to read*	lire	41
lis, lise, lisons, etc.			lire	41
lisser	AVOIR	*to smooth*	aimer	3
lister	AVOIR	*to list*	aimer	3
livrer	AVOIR	*to deliver*	aimer	3
localiser	AVOIR	*to locate*	aimer	3
loger	AVOIR	*to house/live*	manger	42
longer	AVOIR	*to go along*	manger	42
lorgner	AVOIR	*to eye up*	aimer	3
lotir	AVOIR	*to allot/share out*	finir	34
loucher	AVOIR	*to squint*	aimer	3
louer	AVOIR	*to let/rent/hire*	aimer	3
louper	AVOIR	*to miss*	aimer	3
louvoyer	AVOIR	*to tack*	employer	28
lu, lus, etc.			lire	41
lubrifier	AVOIR	*to lubricate*	plier	57
luire	AVOIR	*to shine*	conduire	16
lustrer	AVOIR	*to polish*	aimer	3
lutiner	AVOIR	*to flirt*	aimer	3
lutter	AVOIR	*to fight/struggle*	aimer	3
luxer	AVOIR	*to dislocate*	aimer	3
lyncher	AVOIR	*to lynch*	aimer	3
lyophiliser	AVOIR	*to freeze-dry*	aimer	3
macérer	AVOIR	*to soak/marinate*	céder	13
mâcher	AVOIR	*to chew*	aimer	3
mâchonner	AVOIR	*to chew*	aimer	3
mâchouiller	AVOIR	*to chew (on)*	aimer	3
maculer	AVOIR	*to spatter/smudge*	aimer	3
madériser	AVOIR	*to maderize*	aimer	3
magner (se)	ÊTRE	*to get a move on*	aimer	3
magnétiser	AVOIR	*to magnetize*	aimer	3
magnifier	AVOIR	*to idealize/glorify*	plier	57
magouiller	AVOIR	*to fiddle*	aimer	3
maigrir	AVOIR	*to lose weight*	finir	34
maintenir	AVOIR	*to maintain*	venir	73
maîtriser	AVOIR	*to control*	aimer	3
majorer	AVOIR	*to increase*	aimer	3
malaxer	AVOIR	*to knead*	aimer	3
malmener	AVOIR	*to manhandle*	lever	40
maltraiter	AVOIR	*to mistreat*	aimer	3
manager	AVOIR	*to manage*	manger	42
mandater	AVOIR	*to give a mandate to*	aimer	3
mander	AVOIR	*to summon*	aimer	3
manger	AVOIR	*to eat*	manger	42

Verb directory

manier AVOIR *to handle*	plier	57
manifester AVOIR *to show/demonstrate*	aimer	3
manigancer AVOIR *to be up to*	placer	54
manipuler AVOIR *to handle*	aimer	3
manœuvrer AVOIR *to manoeuvre*	aimer	3
manquer AVOIR *to miss*	aimer	3
manucurer AVOIR *to give a manicure to*	aimer	3
manufacturer AVOIR *to manufacture*	aimer	3
maquiller AVOIR *to make up*	aimer	3
marauder AVOIR *to pilfer*	aimer	3
marchander AVOIR *to haggle*	aimer	3
marcher AVOIR *to walk*	aimer	3
marginaliser AVOIR *to marginalize*	aimer	3
marier AVOIR *to marry*	plier	57
mariner AVOIR *to marinate*	aimer	3
marmonner AVOIR *to mumble*	aimer	3
marmotter AVOIR *to mumble*	aimer	3
marner AVOIR *to slog away/marl*	aimer	3
maronner AVOIR *to moan and groan*	aimer	3
marquer AVOIR *to mark*	aimer	3
marrer (se) ÊTRE *to have a good laugh*	aimer	3
marteler AVOIR *to beat*	geler	36
martyriser AVOIR *to torment*	aimer	3
masculiniser AVOIR *to make look masculine*	aimer	3
masquer AVOIR *to conceal*	aimer	3
massacrer AVOIR *to slaughter*	aimer	3
masser AVOIR *to massage/assemble*	aimer	3
mastiquer AVOIR *to chew*	aimer	3
masturber AVOIR *to masturbate*	aimer	3
matelasser AVOIR *to pad*	aimer	3
mater AVOIR *to take in hand*	aimer	3
matérialiser AVOIR *to realize/fulfil*	aimer	3
materner AVOIR *to mother*	aimer	3
maudire AVOIR *to curse*	maudire	43
maugréer AVOIR *to grumble*	créer	22
maximaliser AVOIR *to maximize*	aimer	3
maximiser AVOIR *to maximize*	aimer	3
mazouter AVOIR *to cover with oil*	aimer	3
méconnaître AVOIR *to misunderstand*	connaître	17
mécontenter AVOIR *to annoy*	aimer	3
médailler AVOIR *to award a medal*	aimer	3
médiatiser AVOIR *to give sth publicity*	aimer	3
médicaliser AVOIR *to medicalize*	aimer	3
médire AVOIR *to speak ill of*	médire	44
méditer AVOIR *to meditate/ponder over*	aimer	3
méduser AVOIR *to dumbfound*	aimer	3
méfier (se) ÊTRE *to be careful*	plier	57
mégoter AVOIR *to skimp*	aimer	3
méjuger AVOIR *to misjudge*	manger	42
mélanger AVOIR *to mix/blend*	manger	42
mêler AVOIR *to mix/blend*	aimer	3

Verb directory

mémoriser AVOIR *to memorize* .... aimer 3
menacer AVOIR *to threaten* .... placer 54
ménager AVOIR *to treat gently* .... manger 42
mendier AVOIR *to beg* .... plier 57
mener AVOIR *to lead* .... lever 40
mensualiser AVOIR *to pay monthly* .... aimer 3
mentionner AVOIR *to mention* .... aimer 3
mentir AVOIR *to lie* .... partir 51
méprendre (se) ÊTRE *to be mistaken* .... prendre 60
mépriser AVOIR *to despise* .... aimer 3
mériter AVOIR *to deserve* .... aimer 3
mésallier (se) ÊTRE *to marry beneath one* .... plier 57
mésestimer AVOIR *to underrate* .... aimer 3
messeoir AVOIR *to be unbecoming* .... asseoir 7
mesurer AVOIR *to measure* .... aimer 3
métamorphoser AVOIR *to transform* .... aimer 3
métisser AVOIR *to cross* .... aimer 3
métrer AVOIR *to measure in metre* .... céder 13
mettre AVOIR *to put* .... mettre 45
meubler AVOIR *to furnish* .... aimer 3
meugler AVOIR *to moo* .... aimer 3
meuler AVOIR *to grind* .... aimer 3
meure, meurs, etc. .... mourir 47
meurtrir AVOIR *to hurt* .... finir 34
meus, meut, meuvent. .... mouvoir 48
miauler AVOIR *to miaow* .... aimer 3
migrer AVOIR *to migrate* .... aimer 3
mijoter AVOIR *to simmer* .... aimer 3
militariser AVOIR *to militarize* .... aimer 3
militer AVOIR *to campaign* .... aimer 3
mimer AVOIR *to mime* .... aimer 3
minauder AVOIR *to mince about* .... aimer 3
mincir AVOIR *to lose weight* .... finir 34
miner AVOIR *to mine/sap* .... aimer 3
minéraliser AVOIR *to mineralize* .... aimer 3
miniaturiser AVOIR *to miniaturize* .... aimer 3
minimiser AVOIR *to minimize* .... aimer 3
minorer AVOIR *to reduce* .... aimer 3
minuter AVOIR *to time* .... aimer 3
mirer AVOIR *to gaze at* .... aimer 3
miroiter AVOIR *to sparkle/shimmer* .... aimer 3
mis, mise, etc. .... mettre 45
miser AVOIR *to bet* .... aimer 3
miter (se) ÊTRE *to become moth-eaten* .... aimer 3
mitonner AVOIR *to cook slowly* .... aimer 3
mitrailler AVOIR *to machine-gun* .... aimer 3
mixer AVOIR *to mix* .... aimer 3
mobiliser AVOIR *to mobilize* .... aimer 3
modeler AVOIR *to model* .... geler 36
modérer AVOIR *to moderate/curb* .... céder 13
moderniser AVOIR *to modernize* .... aimer 3

Verb directory

modifier AVOIR *to modify* .... plier 57
moduler AVOIR *to modulate* .... aimer 3
moirer AVOIR *to moiré* .... aimer 3
moisir AVOIR *to go mouldy* .... finir 34
moissonner AVOIR *to harvest* .... aimer 3
molester AVOIR *to manhandle* .... aimer 3
mollir AVOIR *to fail/go weak* .... finir 34
monder AVOIR *to hull/husk* .... aimer 3
mondialiser AVOIR *to globalize* .... aimer 3
monétiser AVOIR *to monetize* .... aimer 3
monnayer AVOIR *to convert into cash* .... payer 52
monopoliser AVOIR *to monopolize* .... aimer 3
monter AVOIR/ÊTRE *to take up/go/come up* .... aimer 3
montrer AVOIR *to show* .... aimer 3
moquer (se) ÊTRE *to make fun of* .... aimer 3
moraliser AVOIR *to moralize* .... aimer 3
morceler AVOIR *to divide up* .... appeler 5
mordre AVOIR *to bite* .... rendre 63
morfondre AVOIR *to hang around/pine* .... rendre 63
morigéner AVOIR *to reprimand* .... céder 13
mort, morte, mortes, morts .... mourir 47
mortifier AVOIR *to mortify* .... plier 57
motiver AVOIR *to motivate* .... aimer 3
moucher (se) AVOIR *to blow one's nose* .... aimer 3
moudre AVOIR *to grind* .... moudre 46
mouiller AVOIR *to wet* .... aimer 3
moulais, moulons, moulu, etc. .... moudre 46
mouler AVOIR *to mould* .... aimer 3
mouliner AVOIR *to purée* .... aimer 3
mourir ÊTRE *to die* .... mourir 47
mousser AVOIR *to bubble/foam* .... aimer 3
mouvoir AVOIR *to move* .... mouvoir 48
mû, mûmes, etc. .... mouvoir 48
muer AVOIR *to moult/slough skin* .... aimer 3
mugir AVOIR *to bellow* .... finir 34
multiplier AVOIR *to multiply* .... plier 57
munir AVOIR *to provide* .... finir 34
murer AVOIR *to wall up* .... aimer 3
mûrir AVOIR *to ripen* .... finir 34
murmurer AVOIR *to murmur* .... aimer 3
muscler AVOIR *to develop the muscles* .... aimer 3
museler AVOIR *to muzzle* .... appeler 5
muter AVOIR *to transfer/mutate* .... aimer 3
mutiler AVOIR *to mutilate* .... aimer 3
mutiner (se) ÊTRE *to mutiny* .... aimer 3
mystifier AVOIR *to fool* .... plier 57
nager AVOIR *to swim* .... manger 42
naissais, naissons, etc. .... naître 49
naître ÊTRE *to be born* .... naître 49
nantir AVOIR *to provide* .... finir 34
napper AVOIR *to coat* .... aimer 3

Verb directory

Verb directory

occulter	AVOIR	*to eclipse*	aimer	3
occuper	AVOIR	*to occupy*	aimer	3
octroyer	AVOIR	*to grant*	employer	28
œuvrer	AVOIR	*to work*	aimer	3
offenser	AVOIR	*to offend*	aimer	3
offert			offrir	50
officialiser	AVOIR	*to make sth official*	aimer	3
officier	AVOIR	*to officiate*	plier	57
offrir	AVOIR	*to give/offer*	offrir	50
offusquer	AVOIR	*to offend*	aimer	3
omettre	AVOIR	*to omit*	mettre	45
ondoyer	AVOIR	*to undulate*	employer	28
onduler	AVOIR	*to curl/roll*	aimer	3
ont			avoir	9
opérer	AVOIR	*to operate (on)*	céder	13
opposer	AVOIR	*to oppose/divide*	aimer	3
oppresser	AVOIR	*to oppress*	aimer	3
opprimer	AVOIR	*to oppress*	aimer	3
opter	AVOIR	*to opt*	aimer	3
optimiser	AVOIR	*to optimize*	aimer	3
ordonner	AVOIR	*to order/prescribe*	aimer	3
organiser	AVOIR	*to organize*	aimer	3
orienter	AVOIR	*to direct*	aimer	3
orner	AVOIR	*to decorate*	aimer	3
orthographier	AVOIR	*to spell*	plier	57
osciller	AVOIR	*to swing/oscillate*	aimer	3
oser	AVOIR	*to dare*	aimer	3
ossifier	AVOIR	*to ossify*	plier	57
ôter	AVOIR	*to take off*	aimer	3
ouater	AVOIR	*to wad*	aimer	3
oublier	AVOIR	*to forget*	plier	57
ouïr	AVOIR	*to hear*	fuir	35
ourdir	AVOIR	*to hatch*	finir	34
outrager	AVOIR	*to offend*	manger	42
outrepasser	AVOIR	*to exceed*	aimer	3
outrer	AVOIR	*to outrage*	aimer	3
ouvrir	AVOIR	*to open*	couvrir	20
ovuler	AVOIR	*to ovulate*	aimer	3
oxyder	AVOIR	*to oxidize*	aimer	3
oxygéner	AVOIR	*to oxygenate*	céder	13
pacifier	AVOIR	*to pacify*	plier	57
pactiser	AVOIR	*to treat*	aimer	3
pagayer	AVOIR	*to paddle*	payer	52
paginer	AVOIR	*to paginate*	aimer	3
paie, paierai, paies, etc.			payer	52
paître	AVOIR	*to graze*	naître	49
palabrer	AVOIR	*to discuss*	aimer	3
pâlir	AVOIR	*to fade/grow pale*	finir	34
pallier	AVOIR	*to compensate for*	plier	57
palper	AVOIR	*to palpate*	aimer	3
palpiter	AVOIR	*to beat*	aimer	3

Verb directory

paner	AVOIR	*to coat with breadcrumbs*	aimer	3
paniquer	AVOIR	*to panic*	aimer	3
panser	AVOIR	*to dress/bandage*	aimer	3
papoter	AVOIR	*to chatter*	aimer	3
parachuter	AVOIR	*to parachute*	aimer	3
parader	AVOIR	*to strut about*	aimer	3
paraître	AVOIR	*to appear/seem* ÊTRE *to be published*	connaître	17
paralyser	AVOIR	*to paralyse*	aimer	3
parapher	AVOIR	*to initial*	aimer	3
parasiter	AVOIR	*to live as a parasite*	aimer	3
parcourir	AVOIR	*to travel all over/cover*	courir	19
pardonner	AVOIR	*to forgive*	aimer	3
parer	AVOIR	*to ward off*	aimer	3
paresser	AVOIR	*to laze*	aimer	3
parfaire	AVOIR	*to complete/perfect*	faire	32
parfumer	AVOIR	*to put scent in/flavour*	aimer	3
parier	AVOIR	*to bet*	plier	57
parlementer	AVOIR	*to negotiate*	aimer	3
parler	AVOIR	*to speak/talk*	aimer	3
parodier	AVOIR	*to parody*	plier	57
parquer	AVOIR	*to pen/park*	aimer	3
parqueter	AVOIR	*to lay parquet in*	aimer	3
parrainer	AVOIR	*to sponsor*	aimer	3
pars, part			partir	51
parsemer	AVOIR	*to sprinkle*	lever	40
partager	AVOIR	*to share/divide*	manger	42
participer	AVOIR	*to take part in/contribute to*	aimer	3
partir	ÊTRE	*to leave*	partir	51
parvenir	ÊTRE	*to reach*	venir	73
passer	AVOIR/ÊTRE	*to spend/go through/pass*	aimer	3
passionner	AVOIR	*to fascinate*	aimer	3
pasteuriser	AVOIR	*to pasteurize*	aimer	3
patauger	AVOIR	*to splash about*	manger	42
patienter	AVOIR	*to wait*	aimer	3
patiner	AVOIR	*to skate*	aimer	3
pâtir	AVOIR	*to suffer*	finir	34
patrouiller	AVOIR	*to patrol*	aimer	3
paumer	AVOIR	*to lose*	aimer	3
paupériser	AVOIR	*to pauperize*	aimer	3
paver	AVOIR	*to strut about*	aimer	3
pavoiser	AVOIR	*to be jubilant*	aimer	3
payer	AVOIR	*to pay*	payer	52
pécher	AVOIR	*to sin*	céder	13
pêcher	AVOIR	*to fish*	aimer	3
pédaler	AVOIR	*to pedal*	aimer	3
peigner	AVOIR	*to comb*	aimer	3
peindre	AVOIR	*to paint*	peindre	53
peiner	AVOIR	*to sadden*	aimer	3
peler	AVOIR	*to peel*	geler	36
pelotonner	AVOIR	*to wind into a ball*	aimer	3
pelucher	AVOIR	*to become fluffy*	aimer	3

Verb directory

pénaliser AVOIR *to penalize*	aimer	3
pencher AVOIR *to tilt/lean*	aimer	3
pendre AVOIR *to hang*	rendre	63
pénétrer AVOIR *to penetrate/enter*	céder	13
penser AVOIR *to think*	aimer	3
percer AVOIR *to pierce*	placer	54
percevoir AVOIR *to receive/perceive*	recevoir	62
percher AVOIR *to perch*	aimer	3
percuter AVOIR *to hit*	aimer	3
perdre AVOIR *to lose*	rendre	63
perdurer AVOIR *to continue*	aimer	3
perfectionner AVOIR *to perfect*	aimer	3
perforer AVOIR *to perforate*	aimer	3
périr AVOIR *to die/perish*	finir	34
permettre AVOIR *to allow*	mettre	45
permuter AVOIR *to switch around*	aimer	3
pérorer AVOIR *to hold forth*	aimer	3
perpétrer AVOIR *to perpetrate*	céder	13
perpétuer AVOIR *to perpetuate*	aimer	3
perquisitionner AVOIR *to search*	aimer	3
persécuter AVOIR *to persecute*	aimer	3
persévérer AVOIR *to persevere*	céder	13
persifler AVOIR *to mock*	aimer	3
persister AVOIR *to persist*	aimer	3
personnaliser AVOIR *to customize*	aimer	3
personnifier AVOIR *to personify*	plier	57
persuader AVOIR *to persuade*	aimer	3
perturber AVOIR *to disrupt*	aimer	3
pervertir AVOIR *to corrupt*	finir	34
peser AVOIR *to weigh*	lever	40
pester AVOIR *to curse*	aimer	3
pétarader AVOIR *to backfire*	aimer	3
péter AVOIR *to break/fart*	céder	13
pétiller AVOIR *to fizz/sparkle*	aimer	3
pétrifier AVOIR *to petrify*	plier	57
pétrir AVOIR *to knead*	finir	34
peupler AVOIR *to populate*	aimer	3
peut, peux	pouvoir	59
philosopher AVOIR *to philosophize*	aimer	3
photocopier AVOIR *to photocopy*	plier	57
photographier AVOIR *to photograph*	plier	57
piaffer AVOIR *to paw the ground*	aimer	3
piailler AVOIR *to chirp*	aimer	3
pianoter AVOIR *to tinkle*	aimer	3
picoler AVOIR *to booze*	aimer	3
picorer AVOIR *to peck about*	aimer	3
picoter AVOIR *to sting*	aimer	3
piéger AVOIR *to trap*	assiéger	8
piétiner AVOIR *to trample*	aimer	3
pieuter AVOIR *to kip*	aimer	3
pifer AVOIR *to stand*	aimer	3

Verb directory

piger AVOIR *to understand* .... manger 42
pigmenter AVOIR *to alter the pigmentation of* .... aimer 3
piler AVOIR *to crush* .... aimer 3
piller AVOIR *to pillage* .... aimer 3
pilonner AVOIR *to bombard* .... aimer 3
piloter AVOIR *to pilot* .... aimer 3
pimenter AVOIR *to spice* .... aimer 3
pinailler AVOIR *to split hairs* .... aimer 3
pincer AVOIR *to pinch* .... placer 54
piocher AVOIR *to dig* .... aimer 3
pique-niquer AVOIR *to picnic* .... aimer 3
piquer AVOIR *to sting* .... aimer 3
pisser AVOIR *to pee* .... aimer 3
pister AVOIR *to trail* .... aimer 3
pistonner AVOIR *to pull strings for* .... aimer 3
pivoter AVOIR *to pivot* .... aimer 3
placarder AVOIR *to post* .... aimer 3
placer AVOIR *to put/place* .... placer 54
plafonner AVOIR *to reach a ceiling* .... aimer 3
plagier AVOIR *to plagiarize* .... plier 57
plaider AVOIR *to plead* .... aimer 3
plaindre AVOIR *to pity* .... craindre 21
plaire AVOIR *to please* .... plaire 55
plaisanter AVOIR *to joke* .... aimer 3
planer AVOIR *to glide* .... aimer 3
planifier AVOIR *to plan* .... plier 57
planquer AVOIR *to hide* .... aimer 3
planter AVOIR *to plant* .... aimer 3
plaquer AVOIR *to veneer/flatten* .... aimer 3
plastifier AVOIR *to plastic-coat* .... plier 57
plâtrer AVOIR *to plaster* .... aimer 3
plébisciter AVOIR *to acclaim* .... aimer 3
pleurer AVOIR *to cry* .... aimer 3
pleurnicher AVOIR *to snivel* .... aimer 3
pleuvoir AVOIR *to rain* .... pleuvoir 56
pleuvoter AVOIR *to drizzle* .... aimer 3
plier AVOIR *to fold* .... plier 57
plisser AVOIR *to pleat* .... aimer 3
plonger AVOIR *to dive* .... manger 42
ployer AVOIR *to bow/bend* .... employer 28
plu .... plaire/pleuvoir 55/56
plumer AVOIR *to pluck* .... aimer 3
pluviner AVOIR *to drizzle* .... aimer 3
pocher AVOIR *to poach* .... aimer 3
poêler AVOIR *to fry* .... aimer 3
poignarder AVOIR *to stab* .... aimer 3
poinçonner AVOIR *to punch* .... aimer 3
poindre AVOIR *to dawn/break* .... joindre 39
pointer AVOIR *to point/clock in/out* .... aimer 3
poivrer AVOIR *to add pepper to* .... aimer 3
polariser AVOIR *to polarize/focus* .... aimer 3

Verb directory

Verb directory

Verb directory

promouvoir AVOIR *to promote*	mouvoir	48
promulguer AVOIR *to promulgate*	aimer	3
prôner AVOIR *to advocate*	aimer	3
prononcer AVOIR *to pronounce*	placer	54
propager AVOIR *to spread*	manger	42
proposer AVOIR *to suggest/offer*	aimer	3
propulser AVOIR *to propel*	aimer	3
proroger AVOIR *to defer*	manger	42
proscrire AVOIR *to ban*	écrire	27
prospecter AVOIR *to prospect*	aimer	3
prospérer AVOIR *to thrive*	céder	13
prosterner (se) ÊTRE *to prostrate oneself*	aimer	3
prostituer (se) ÊTRE *to prostitute oneself*	aimer	3
protéger AVOIR *to protect*	assiéger	8
protester AVOIR *to protest*	aimer	3
prouver AVOIR *to prove*	aimer	3
provenir ÊTRE *to come*	venir	73
provoquer AVOIR *to cause/provoke*	aimer	3
publier AVOIR *to publish*	plier	57
pu, pus, etc.	pouvoir	59
puer AVOIR *to stink (of)*	aimer	3
puiser AVOIR *to draw*	aimer	3
puisse, puisses.	pouvoir	59
pulluler AVOIR *to proliferate*	aimer	3
pulvériser AVOIR *to spray*	aimer	3
punir AVOIR *to punish*	finir	34
purger AVOIR *to purge*	manger	42
purifier AVOIR *to purify*	plier	57
pu, pus, put, pûmes, pûtes, etc.	pouvoir	59
putréfier (se) ÊTRE *to putrefy*	plier	57
quadrupler AVOIR *to quadruple*	aimer	3
qualifier AVOIR *to describe/qualify*	plier	57
quantifier AVOIR *to quantify*	plier	57
quémander AVOIR *to beg*	aimer	3
quereller (se) ÊTRE *to quarrel*	aimer	3
quérir AVOIR *to fetch*	acquérir	2
questionner AVOIR *to question*	aimer	3
quêter AVOIR *to seek/take the collection*	aimer	3
quintupler AVOIR *to quintuple*	aimer	3
quitter AVOIR *to leave*	aimer	3
rabâcher AVOIR *to keep repeating*	aimer	3
rabaisser AVOIR *to lower*	aimer	3
rabattre AVOIR *to pull down*	battre	10
rabrouer AVOIR *to snub*	aimer	3
raccommoder AVOIR *to mend*	aimer	3
raccompagner AVOIR *to walk (sb) back home*	aimer	3
raccorder AVOIR *to connect*	aimer	3
raccourcir AVOIR *to shorten*	finir	34
raccrocher AVOIR *to hang up*	aimer	3
racheter AVOIR *to buy back*	acheter	1
racketter AVOIR *to extort money from*	aimer	3

Verb directory

racler	AVOIR	*to scrape off*	aimer	3
racoler	AVOIR	*to tout for*	aimer	3
raconter	AVOIR	*to tell*	aimer	3
racornir	AVOIR	*to harden/stiffen*	finir	34
radier	AVOIR	*to remove/strike off*	plier	57
radiodiffuser	AVOIR	*to broadcast*	aimer	3
radiographier	AVOIR	*to x-ray*	plier	57
radoter	AVOIR	*to ramble on*	aimer	3
radoucir	AVOIR	*to soften*	finir	34
raffermir	AVOIR	*to tone*	finir	34
raffiner	AVOIR	*to refine*	aimer	3
raffoler	AVOIR	*to be crazy about*	aimer	3
rafistoler	AVOIR	*to patch up*	aimer	3
rafler	AVOIR	*to swipe*	aimer	3
rafraîchir	AVOIR	*to cool*	finir	34
ragaillardir	AVOIR	*to cheer up*	finir	34
rager	AVOIR	*to rage*	manger	42
raidir	AVOIR	*to tighten*	finir	34
raisonner	AVOIR	*to reason with/think*	aimer	3
rajeunir	AVOIR	*to feel younger*	finir	34
rajouter	AVOIR	*to add*	aimer	3
rajuster	AVOIR	*to straighten*	aimer	3
ralentir	AVOIR	*to slow down*	finir	34
râler	AVOIR	*to moan*	aimer	3
rallier	AVOIR	*to rally*	plier	57
rallonger	AVOIR	*to extend*	manger	42
rallumer	AVOIR	*to relight*	aimer	3
ramasser	AVOIR	*to collect/pick up*	aimer	3
ramener	AVOIR	*to bring back*	lever	40
ramer	AVOIR	*to row*	aimer	3
rameuter	AVOIR	*to round up*	aimer	3
ramifier (se)	ÊTRE	*to branch*	plier	57
ramollir	AVOIR	*to soften*	finir	34
ramoner	AVOIR	*to sweep*	aimer	3
ramper	AVOIR	*to crawl*	aimer	3
rancir	AVOIR	*to go rancid*	finir	34
rancarder	AVOIR	*to arrange to meet*	aimer	3
rançonner	AVOIR	*to rob*	aimer	3
ranger	AVOIR	*to put away/tidy up*	manger	42
ranimer	AVOIR	*to resuscitate*	aimer	3
rapatrier	AVOIR	*to repatriate*	plier	57
râper	AVOIR	*to grate*	aimer	3
rapetisser	AVOIR	*to shrink*	aimer	3
rapiécer	AVOIR	*to patch*	céder	13
rappeler	AVOIR	*to remind*	appeler	5
rappliquer	AVOIR	*to turn up*	aimer	3
rapporter	AVOIR	*to bring back/be lucrative*	aimer	3
rapprocher	AVOIR	*to move closer*	aimer	3
raréfier	AVOIR	*to rarefy*	plier	57
raser	AVOIR	*to shave*	aimer	3
rassasier	AVOIR	*to fill up*	plier	57

Verb directory

rassembler AVOIR *to gather*	....	aimer	3
rasséréner AVOIR *to reassure*	....	céder	13
rassir AVOIR *to go stale*	....	finir	34
rassurer AVOIR *to reassure*	....	aimer	3
rater AVOIR *to fail/miss*	....	aimer	3
ratifier AVOIR *to ratify*	....	plier	57
rationaliser AVOIR *to rationalize*	....	aimer	3
rationner AVOIR *to ration*	....	aimer	3
ratisser AVOIR *to rake over*	....	aimer	3
rattacher AVOIR *to attach*	....	aimer	3
rattraper AVOIR *to catch up with*	....	aimer	3
raturer AVOIR *to cross out*	....	aimer	3
ravager AVOIR *to devastate*	....	manger	42
ravaler AVOIR *to renovate/swallow*	....	aimer	3
ravigoter AVOIR *to invigorate*	....	aimer	3
ravir AVOIR *to delight*	....	finir	34
ravitailler AVOIR *to refuel*	....	aimer	3
ravoir AVOIR *to get (sth) back/clean*	....	avoir	9
rayer AVOIR *to cross out*	....	payer	52
réactiver AVOIR *to rekindle*	....	aimer	3
réactualiser AVOIR *to update*	....	aimer	3
réadapter AVOIR *to readjust*	....	aimer	3
réagir AVOIR *to react*	....	finir	34
réajuster AVOIR *to readjust*	....	aimer	3
réaliser AVOIR *to fulfil/realize*	....	aimer	3
réaménager AVOIR *to redevelop*	....	manger	42
réanimer AVOIR *to resuscitate*	....	aimer	3
réapparaître AVOIR ÊTRE *to reappear*	....	connaître	17
réarmer AVOIR *to rearm*	....	aimer	3
réassortir AVOIR *to match up*	....	finir	34
rebâtir AVOIR *to rebuild*	....	finir	34
rebattre AVOIR *to reshuffle*	....	battre	10
rebeller (se) ÊTRE *to rebel*	....	aimer	3
rebiffer (se) ÊTRE *to rebel*	....	aimer	3
reboiser AVOIR *to reforest*	....	aimer	3
rebondir AVOIR *to bounce*	....	finir	34
rebuter AVOIR *to repel*	....	aimer	3
recaler AVOIR *to fail*	....	aimer	3
récapituler AVOIR *to recapitulate*	....	aimer	3
recéder AVOIR *to give back*	....	céder	13
receler AVOIR *to conceal/contain*	....	geler	36
recenser AVOIR *to take a census of*	....	aimer	3
recevoir AVOIR *to receive*	....	recevoir	62
rechaper AVOIR *to retread*	....	aimer	3
réchapper AVOIR *to come through*	....	aimer	3
recharger AVOIR *to reload*	....	manger	42
réchauffer AVOIR *to heat up*	....	aimer	3
rechercher AVOIR *to look for*	....	aimer	3
rechigner AVOIR *to grumble*	....	aimer	3
récidiver AVOIR *to re-offend*	....	aimer	3
réciter AVOIR *to recite*	....	aimer	3

Verb directory

réclamer AVOIR *to ask/complain* .... aimer 3
récolter AVOIR *to harvest* .... aimer 3
recommander AVOIR *to advise* .... aimer 3
recommencer AVOIR *to start again* .... placer 54
récompenser AVOIR *to reward* .... aimer 3
réconcilier AVOIR *to reconcile* .... plier 57
reconduire AVOIR *to see (sb) out* .... conduire 16
réconforter AVOIR *to comfort* .... aimer 3
reconnaître AVOIR *to recognize* .... connaître 17
reconquérir AVOIR *to reconquer* .... acquérir 2
reconstituer AVOIR *to reform* .... aimer 3
reconstruire AVOIR *to reconstruct* .... conduire 16
reconvertir AVOIR *to convert* .... finir 34
recopier AVOIR *to copy out* .... plier 57
recoudre AVOIR *to sew up* .... coudre 18
recourber AVOIR *to bend back* .... aimer 3
recourir AVOIR *to resort (to)/run again* .... courir 19
recouvrer AVOIR *to recover* .... aimer 3
recouvrir AVOIR *to cover* .... couvrir 20
recracher AVOIR *to spit out* .... aimer 3
récrier (se) ÊTRE *to exclaim* .... plier 57
récriminer AVOIR *to rail* .... aimer 3
ré(é)crire AVOIR *to rewrite* .... écrire 27
recroqueviller (se) ÊTRE *to huddle up* .... aimer 3
recruter AVOIR *to recruit* .... aimer 3
rectifier AVOIR *to rectify* .... plier 57
reçu .... recevoir 62
recueillir AVOIR *to collect* .... cueillir 25
reculer AVOIR *to move back* .... aimer 3
récupérer AVOIR *to get back* .... céder 13
récurer AVOIR *to scour* .... aimer 3
récuser AVOIR *to challenge* .... aimer 3
recycler AVOIR *to recycle* .... aimer 3
redécouvrir AVOIR *to rediscover* .... couvrir 20
redéfinir AVOIR *to redefine* .... finir 34
redescendre AVOIR/ÊTRE *to take/go/come down again* .... rendre 63
redevenir ÊTRE *to become again* .... venir 73
rédiger AVOIR *to write* .... manger 42
redire AVOIR *to repeat* .... médire 44
redoubler AVOIR *to repeat a year* .... aimer 3
redouter AVOIR *to fear* .... aimer 3
redresser AVOIR *to straighten up* .... aimer 3
réduire AVOIR *to reduce* .... conduire 16
rééduquer AVOIR *to rehabilitate* .... aimer 3
réélire AVOIR *to reelect* .... lire 41
réemployer AVOIR *to reuse/re-employ* .... employer 28
rééquilibrer AVOIR *to readjust* .... aimer 3
réessayer AVOIR *to try again* .... payer 52
réévaluer AVOIR *to revalue* .... aimer 3
réexaminer AVOIR *to re-examine* .... aimer 3
réexpédier AVOIR *to forward* .... plier 57

Verb directory

Verb directory

relancer AVOIR *to throw again* .... placer 54
relater AVOIR *to recount* .... aimer 3
relativiser AVOIR *to put into perspective* .... aimer 3
relaxer AVOIR *to relax/discharge* .... aimer 3
relayer AVOIR *to take over from* .... payer 52
reléguer AVOIR *to relegate* .... céder 13
relever AVOIR *to raise/pick up* .... lever 40
relier AVOIR *to link up* .... plier 57
relire AVOIR *to reread/proofread* .... lire 41
reluire AVOIR *to shine* .... conduire 16
remâcher AVOIR *to chew again* .... aimer 3
remailler AVOIR *to mend the mesh of* .... aimer 3
remanier AVOIR *to revise/reorganize* .... plier 57
remarier AVOIR *to remarry* .... plier 57
remarquer AVOIR *to point out/notice* .... aimer 3
remballer AVOIR *to pack up again* .... aimer 3
rembarquer AVOIR *to re-embark* .... aimer 3
rembarrer AVOIR *to send packing* .... aimer 3
remblaver AVOIR *to resow* .... aimer 3
rembourrer AVOIR *to stuff/pad* .... aimer 3
rembourser AVOIR *to pay off/refund* .... aimer 3
rembrunir (se) ÊTRE *to darken* .... finir 34
remédier AVOIR *to remedy* .... plier 57
remémorer (se) ÊTRE *to recall* .... aimer 3
remercier AVOIR *to thank* .... plier 57
remettre AVOIR *to put back* .... mettre 45
remiser AVOIR *to put away* .... aimer 3
remmener AVOIR *to take back* .... lever 40
remodeler AVOIR *to restructure* .... geler 36
remonter AVOIR/ÊTRE *to take/go/come* .... aimer 3
remontrer AVOIR *to show again* .... aimer 3
remorquer AVOIR *to tow* .... aimer 3
remouler AVOIR *to recast* .... aimer 3
rempailler AVOIR *to reseat* .... aimer 3
rempaqueter AVOIR *to pack up again* .... jeter 38
rempiler AVOIR *to restack* .... aimer 3
remplacer AVOIR *to replace* .... placer 54
remplir AVOIR *to fill* .... finir 34
remporter AVOIR *to win* .... aimer 3
remuer AVOIR *to move* .... aimer 3
rémunérer AVOIR *to pay* .... céder 13
renâcler AVOIR *to show reluctance* .... aimer 3
renaître ÊTRE *to come back to life* .... naître 49
rencarder AVOIR *to arrange to meet* .... aimer 3
renchérir AVOIR *to increase/add* .... finir 34
rencontrer AVOIR *to meet* .... aimer 3
rendormir AVOIR *to put back to sleep* .... partir 51
rendre AVOIR *to give back* .... rendre 63
renfler AVOIR *to puff out* .... aimer 3
renflouer AVOIR *to raise/bail out* .... aimer 3
renforcer AVOIR *to reinforce* .... placer 54

Verb directory

Verb directory

Verb directory

retransmettre AVOIR *to broadcast*		mettre	45
retravailler AVOIR *to revise/go back to work*		aimer	3
rétrécir AVOIR *to shrink*		finir	34
retremper (se) ÊTRE *to have another dip*		aimer	3
rétrocéder AVOIR *to retrocede*		céder	13
rétrograder AVOIR *to demote/change down*		aimer	3
rétropédaler AVOIR *to backpedal*		aimer	3
retrousser AVOIR *to hitch/roll up*		aimer	3
retrouver AVOIR *to find(again)/rediscover*		aimer	3
réunifier AVOIR *to reunify*		plier	57
réunir AVOIR *to bring together*		finir	34
réussir AVOIR *to succeed/achieve*		finir	34
réutiliser AVOIR *to reuse*		aimer	3
revaloir AVOIR *to get even*		valoir	72
revaloriser AVOIR *revalue*		aimer	3
rêvasser AVOIR *to daydream*		aimer	3
réveiller AVOIR *to wake(sb) up*		aimer	3
réveillonner AVOIR *to see Christmas or New Year in*		aimer	3
révéler AVOIR *to reveal*		céder	13
revendiquer AVOIR *to claim*		aimer	3
revendre AVOIR *to sell/retail*		rendre	63
revenir ÊTRE *to come back*		venir	73
rêver AVOIR *to dream*		aimer	3
réverbérer AVOIR *to reflect*		céder	13
reverdir AVOIR *to grow green again*		finir	34
révérer AVOIR *to revere*		céder	13
revérifier AVOIR *to double-check*		plier	57
revêtir AVOIR *to put on*		vêtir	74
revigorer AVOIR *to revive*		aimer	3
réviser AVOIR *to revise*		aimer	3
revisser AVOIR *to screw back on*		aimer	3
revitaliser AVOIR *to revitalize*		aimer	3
revivifier AVOIR *to revive*		plier	57
revivre AVOIR *to relive/come alive again*		vivre	75
revoir AVOIR *to see again/revise*		voir	76
revoler AVOIR *to fly/steal again*		aimer	3
révolter AVOIR *to appal*		aimer	3
révolutionner AVOIR *to revolutionize*		aimer	3
révoquer AVOIR *to revoke*		aimer	3
révulser AVOIR *to appal*		aimer	3
rhabiller AVOIR *to dress (again)*		aimer	3
ricaner AVOIR *to snigger*		aimer	3
ricocher AVOIR *to ricochet*		aimer	3
rider AVOIR *to wrinkle*		aimer	3
ridiculiser AVOIR *to ridicule*		aimer	3
rigidifier AVOIR *to rigidify*		plier	57
rigoler AVOIR *to laugh*		aimer	3
rimailler AVOIR *to write bad verse*		aimer	3
rimer AVOIR *to rhyme*		aimer	3
rincer AVOIR *to rinse*		placer	54
ripailler AVOIR *to feast*		aimer	3

Verb directory

riper	AVOIR	*to slip*	aimer	3
riposter	AVOIR	*to retort*	aimer	3
rire	AVOIR	*to laugh*	rire	65
risquer	AVOIR	*to face*	aimer	3
rissoler	AVOIR	*to brown*	aimer	3
ristourner	AVOIR	*to give a discount*	aimer	3
ritualiser	AVOIR	*to ritualize*	aimer	3
rivaliser	AVOIR	*to compete with*	aimer	3
river	AVOIR	*to clinch*	aimer	3
riveter	AVOIR	*to rivet*	jeter	38
robotiser	AVOIR	*to automate*	aimer	3
roder	AVOIR	*to run in*	aimer	3
rôder	AVOIR	*to prowl*	aimer	3
rogner	AVOIR	*to trim/clip*	aimer	3
romancer	AVOIR	*to romanticize*	placer	54
rompre	AVOIR	*to break*	rompre	66
ronchonner	AVOIR	*to grumble*	aimer	3
ronéoter	AVOIR	*to duplicate*	aimer	3
ronfler	AVOIR	*to snore*	aimer	3
ronger	AVOIR	*to gnaw*	manger	42
ronronner	AVOIR	*to purr*	aimer	3
rosir	AVOIR	*to turn pink*	finir	34
rosser	AVOIR	*to beat up*	aimer	3
roter	AVOIR	*to burp*	aimer	3
rôtir	AVOIR	*to roast*	finir	34
roucouler	AVOIR	*to coo*	aimer	3
rougeoyer	AVOIR	*to glow red*	employer	28
rougir	AVOIR	*to turn red/blush*	finir	34
rouiller	AVOIR	*to rust*	aimer	3
rouir	AVOIR	*to ret*	finir	34
rouler	AVOIR	*to roll*	aimer	3
roulotter	AVOIR	*to roll a hem on*	aimer	3
roupiller	AVOIR	*to sleep*	aimer	3
rouscailler	AVOIR	*to gripe*	aimer	3
rouspéter	AVOIR	*to grumble*	céder	13
roussir	AVOIR	*to go brown*	finir	34
router	AVOIR	*to sort for mailing*	aimer	3
rouvrir	AVOIR	*to reopen*	couvrir	20
rudoyer	AVOIR	*to bully*	employer	28
ruer	AVOIR	*to kick*	aimer	3
rugir	AVOIR	*to roar*	finir	34
ruiner	AVOIR	*to ruin*	aimer	3
ruisseler	AVOIR	*to stream*	appeler	5
ruminer	AVOIR	*to ruminate/brood*	aimer	3
ruser	AVOIR	*to be crafty*	aimer	3
russifier	AVOIR	*to russify*	plier	57
rutiler	AVOIR	*to gleam*	aimer	3
rythmer	AVOIR	*to put rhythm into*	aimer	3
sabler	AVOIR	*to grit*	aimer	3
saborder	AVOIR	*to scuttle/scupper*	aimer	3
saboter	AVOIR	*to sabotage*	aimer	3

Verb directory

sabrer AVOIR *to sabre* .... aimer 3
saccager AVOIR *to wreck* .... manger 42
sacquer AVOIR *to sack* .... aimer 3
sacraliser AVOIR *to make sacred* .... aimer 3
sacrer AVOIR *to crown/consecrate* .... aimer 3
sache, sachez, etc. .... savoir 67
sacrifier AVOIR *to sacrifice* .... plier 57
saigner AVOIR *to bleed* .... aimer 3
saillir AVOIR *to serve/jut out* .... assaillir 6
sais, sait. .... savoir 67
saisir AVOIR *to seize/grab* .... finir 34
saler AVOIR *to salt* .... aimer 3
salifier AVOIR *to salify* .... plier 57
salir AVOIR *to dirty* .... finir 34
saliver AVOIR *to salivate* .... aimer 3
saloper AVOIR *to botch* .... aimer 3
saluer AVOIR *to greet* .... aimer 3
sanctifier AVOIR *to sanctify* .... plier 57
sanctionner AVOIR *to punish* .... aimer 3
sangler AVOIR *to girth* .... aimer 3
sangloter AVOIR *to sob* .... aimer 3
saper AVOIR *to undermine/dress up* .... aimer 3
saponifier AVOIR *to saponify* .... plier 57
saquer AVOIR *to mark down* .... aimer 3
sarcler AVOIR *to hoe* .... aimer 3
sasser AVOIR *to sift* .... aimer 3
satelliser AVOIR *to put into orbit* .... aimer 3
satisfaire AVOIR *to satisfy* .... faire 32
saturer AVOIR *to saturate* .... aimer 3
saucer AVOIR *to wipe with a piece of bread* .... placer 54
saucissonner AVOIR *to have a snack* .... aimer 3
saupoudrer AVOIR *to sprinkle* .... aimer 3
saurai, saurais, etc. .... savoir 67
sauter AVOIR *to jump* .... aimer 3
sautiller AVOIR *to hop* .... aimer 3
sauvegarder AVOIR *to safeguard/save* .... aimer 3
sauver AVOIR *to save* .... aimer 3
savoir AVOIR *to know* .... savoir 67
savonner AVOIR *to soap* .... aimer 3
savourer AVOIR *to savour* .... aimer 3
scalper AVOIR *to scalp* .... aimer 3
scandaliser AVOIR *to outrage* .... aimer 3
scander AVOIR *to scan* .... aimer 3
scarifier AVOIR *to scarify* .... plier 57
sceller AVOIR *to seal* .... aimer 3
schématiser AVOIR *to simplify* .... aimer 3
schlinguer AVOIR *to stink* .... aimer 3
scier AVOIR *to saw* .... plier 57
scinder AVOIR *to split* .... aimer 3
scintiller AVOIR *to sparkle* .... aimer 3
scléroser AVOIR *to sclerose* .... aimer 3

Verb directory

scolariser AVOIR *to send to school*		aimer	3
scotcher AVOIR *to Sellotape™*		aimer	3
scruter AVOIR *to scrutinize*		aimer	3
sculpter AVOIR *to sculpt*		aimer	3
sécher AVOIR *to dry*		céder	13
seconder AVOIR *to assist*		aimer	3
secouer AVOIR *to shake*		aimer	3
secourir AVOIR *to help/rescue*		courir	19
sécréter AVOIR *to secrete*		céder	13
sectionner AVOIR *to sever/cut*		aimer	3
sectoriser AVOIR *to divide into sectors*		aimer	3
séculariser AVOIR *to secularize/laicize*		aimer	3
sécuriser AVOIR *to reassure*		aimer	3
sédentariser AVOIR *to settle*		aimer	3
séduire AVOIR *to appeal to/win over*		conduire	16
segmenter AVOIR *to segment*		aimer	3
séjourner AVOIR *to stay*		aimer	3
sélectionner AVOIR *to select*		aimer	3
seller AVOIR *to saddle*		aimer	3
sembler AVOIR *to seem*		aimer	3
semer AVOIR *to sow*		lever	40
sensibiliser AVOIR *to make more aware of*		aimer	3
sentir AVOIR *to smell/feel*		partir	51
seoir AVOIR *to suit/be appropriate*		asseoir	7
séparer AVOIR *to separate*		aimer	3
septupler AVOIR *to increase sevenfold*		aimer	3
séquestrer AVOIR *to hold/sequestrate*		aimer	3
sera, serai, serait, etc.		être	31
sérier AVOIR *to classify*		plier	57
seriner AVOIR *to harp on*		aimer	3
sermonner AVOIR *to lecture*		aimer	3
serpenter AVOIR *to wind*		aimer	3
serrer AVOIR *to tighten/grip*		aimer	3
sertir AVOIR *to set*		finir	34
servir AVOIR *to serve*		partir	51
sévir AVOIR *to clamp down/be rife*		finir	34
sevrer AVOIR *to wean*		lever	40
sextupler AVOIR *to increase sixfold*		aimer	3
shampouiner AVOIR *to shampoo*		aimer	3
shooter AVOIR *to shoot*		aimer	3
sidérer AVOIR *to stagger*		céder	13
siéger AVOIR *to sit*		assiéger	8
siffler AVOIR *to whistle*		aimer	3
siffloter AVOIR *to whistle to oneself*		aimer	3
signaler AVOIR *to point out/indicate*		aimer	3
signaliser AVOIR *to signpost*		aimer	3
signer AVOIR *to sign*		aimer	3
signifier AVOIR *to mean*		plier	57
silhouetter AVOIR *to draw an outline of*		aimer	3
siller AVOIR *to buzz*		aimer	3
sillonner AVOIR *to go up and down*		aimer	3

Verb directory

Verb directory

souper	AVOIR	*to have supper*	aimer	3
soupeser	AVOIR	*to heft/weigh up*	lever	40
soupirer	AVOIR	*to sigh*	aimer	3
sourciller	AVOIR	*to raise one's eyebrows*	aimer	3
sourdre	AVOIR	*to seep out/well up*	rendre	63
sourire	AVOIR	*to smile*	rire	65
souscrire	AVOIR	*to take out/sign*	écrire	27
sous-employer	AVOIR	*to underemploy*	employer	28
sous-entendre	AVOIR	*to imply*	rendre	63
sous-estimer	AVOIR	*to underestimate*	aimer	3
sous-évaluer	AVOIR	*to underestimate*	aimer	3
sous-exposer	AVOIR	*to underexpose*	aimer	3
sous-louer	AVOIR	*to sublet*	aimer	3
sous-payer	AVOIR	*to underpay*	payer	52
sous-tendre	AVOIR	*to underlie*	rendre	63
sous-titrer	AVOIR	*to subtitle*	aimer	3
soustraire	AVOIR	*to subtract*	traire	70
sous-traiter	AVOIR	*to contract out*	aimer	3
soutenir	AVOIR	*to support*	venir	73
soutirer	AVOIR	*to extract*	aimer	3
souvenir (se)	ÊTRE	*to remember*	venir	73
soviétiser	AVOIR	*to sovietize*	aimer	3
soyez, soyons			être	31
spatialiser	AVOIR	*to spatialize*	aimer	3
spécialiser	AVOIR	*to specialize*	aimer	3
spécifier	AVOIR	*to specify*	plier	57
spéculer	AVOIR	*to speculate*	aimer	3
spiritualiser	AVOIR	*to spiritualize*	aimer	3
spolier	AVOIR	*to despoil*	plier	57
sponsoriser	AVOIR	*to sponsor*	aimer	3
sprinter	AVOIR	*to sprint*	aimer	3
squatter	AVOIR	*to squat in*	aimer	3
stabiliser	AVOIR	*to stabilize*	aimer	3
stagner	AVOIR	*to stagnate*	aimer	3
standardiser	AVOIR	*to standardize*	aimer	3
stationner	AVOIR	*to park*	aimer	3
statuer	AVOIR	*to give a ruling*	aimer	3
statufier	AVOIR	*to transfix*	plier	57
sténographier	AVOIR	*to take down in shorthand*	plier	57
stériliser	AVOIR	*to sterilize*	aimer	3
stigmatiser	AVOIR	*to stigmatize*	aimer	3
stimuler	AVOIR	*to stimulate*	aimer	3
stipendier	AVOIR	*to hire*	plier	57
stipuler	AVOIR	*to stipulate*	aimer	3
stocker	AVOIR	*to stock/store*	aimer	3
stopper	AVOIR	*to stop*	aimer	3
stratifier	AVOIR	*to stratify*	plier	57
stresser	AVOIR	*to put under stress/get stressed*	aimer	3
striduler	AVOIR	*to stridulate*	aimer	3
strier	AVOIR	*to streak*	plier	57
structurer	AVOIR	*to structure*	aimer	3

Verb directory

Verb directory

surcoter AVOIR *to overvalue* .... aimer 3
surélever AVOIR *to raise the height of* .... lever 40
surenchérir AVOIR *to bid higher* .... finir 34
surentraîner AVOIR *to overtrain* .... aimer 3
suréquiper AVOIR *to overequip* .... aimer 3
surestimer AVOIR *to overvalue* .... aimer 3
surévaluer AVOIR *to overvalue* .... aimer 3
surexciter AVOIR *to overexcite* .... aimer 3
surexploiter AVOIR *to overexploit* .... aimer 3
surexposer AVOIR *to overexpose* .... aimer 3
surfacer AVOIR *to surface* .... placer 54
surfaire AVOIR *to overrate* .... faire 32
surfer AVOIR *to surf* .... aimer 3
surfiler AVOIR *to oversew* .... aimer 3
surgeler AVOIR *to deep-freeze* .... geler 36
surgir AVOIR *to appear suddenly* .... finir 34
surimposer AVOIR *to surtax* .... aimer 3
surir AVOIR *to go sour* .... finir 34
surjeter AVOIR *to oversew* .... jeter 38
surligner AVOIR *to highlight* .... aimer 3
surmener AVOIR *to overwork* .... lever 40
surmonter AVOIR *to overcome* .... aimer 3
surnager AVOIR *to float* .... manger 42
surnommer AVOIR *to nickname* .... aimer 3
surpasser AVOIR *to surpass* .... aimer 3
surpayer AVOIR *to overpay* .... payer 52
surpiquer AVOIR *to topstitch* .... aimer 3
surplomber AVOIR *to overhang* .... aimer 3
surprendre AVOIR *to surprise* .... prendre 60
sursauter AVOIR *to jump* .... aimer 3
surseoir AVOIR *to postpone* .... asseoir 7
surtaxer AVOIR *to surcharge* .... aimer 3
survaloriser AVOIR *to put too much emphasis on* .... aimer 3
surveiller AVOIR *to keep an eye on* .... aimer 3
survenir ÊTRE *to occur* .... venir 73
survirer AVOIR *to oversteer* .... aimer 3
survivre AVOIR *to survive* .... vivre 75
survoler AVOIR *to fly over* .... aimer 3
survolter AVOIR *to boost* .... aimer 3
susciter AVOIR *to spark off/create* .... aimer 3
suspecter AVOIR *to suspect* .... aimer 3
suspendre AVOIR *to hang up* .... rendre 63
sustenter (se) ÊTRE *to have a little snack* .... aimer 3
susurrer AVOIR *to whisper* .... aimer 3
suturer AVOIR *to stitch, suture* .... aimer 3
symboliser AVOIR *to symbolize* .... aimer 3
sympathiser AVOIR *to get on well* .... aimer 3
synchroniser AVOIR *to synchronize* .... aimer 3
syndiquer AVOIR *to unionize* .... aimer 3
synthétiser AVOIR *to synthetize* .... aimer 3
systématiser AVOIR *to systematize* .... aimer 3

Verb directory

tabasser	AVOIR	to beat up	aimer	3
tabler	AVOIR	to bank on	aimer	3
tacher	AVOIR	to stain	aimer	3
tâcher	AVOIR	to try	aimer	3
tacheter	AVOIR	to speckle	jeter	38
taillader	AVOIR	to slash	aimer	3
tailler	AVOIR	to cut	aimer	3
taire (se)	AVOIR	to remain silent	plaire	55
talocher	AVOIR	to clout	aimer	3
talonner	AVOIR	to follow hot on the heels of	aimer	3
talquer	AVOIR	to put talcum powder on	aimer	3
tambouriner	AVOIR	to drum on	aimer	3
tamiser	AVOIR	to sieve/sift	aimer	3
tamponner	AVOIR	to mop	aimer	3
tancer	AVOIR	to scold	placer	54
tanguer	AVOIR	to pitch	aimer	3
tanner	AVOIR	to tan	aimer	3
taper	AVOIR	to hit	aimer	3
tapiner	AVOIR	to be a hooker	aimer	3
tapir (se)	ÊTRE	to hide	finir	34
tapisser	AVOIR	to wallpaper/cover	aimer	3
tapoter	AVOIR	to tap	aimer	3
taquiner	AVOIR	to tease	aimer	3
tarabuster	AVOIR	to bother	aimer	3
tarauder	AVOIR	to torment	aimer	3
tarder	AVOIR	to delay/take time	aimer	3
tarer	AVOIR	to tare	aimer	3
targuer (se)	ÊTRE	to claim/boast	aimer	3
tarifer	AVOIR	to fix the price of	aimer	3
tarir	AVOIR	to dry up	finir	34
tartiner	AVOIR	to spread	aimer	3
tasser	AVOIR	to press down	aimer	3
tâter	AVOIR	to feel	aimer	3
tâtonner	AVOIR	to grope about	aimer	3
tatouer	AVOIR	to tattoo	aimer	3
taveler	AVOIR	to blemish	appeler	5
taxer	AVOIR	to tax	aimer	3
teindre	AVOIR	to dye/stain	peindre	53
teinter	AVOIR	to tint	aimer	3
télécharger	AVOIR	to download	manger	42
télécommander	AVOIR	to operate by remote control	aimer	3
télécopier	AVOIR	to fax	plier	57
télédiffuser	AVOIR	to broadcast	aimer	3
télégraphier	AVOIR	to telegraph	plier	57
téléguider	AVOIR	to control by radio	aimer	3
téléphoner	AVOIR	to phone	aimer	3
télescoper	AVOIR	to crush	aimer	3
télexer	AVOIR	to telex	aimer	3
témoigner	AVOIR	to testify	aimer	3
tempérer	AVOIR	to temper	céder	13
temporiser	AVOIR	to stall/temporize	aimer	3

Verb directory

Verb directory

tournebouler AVOIR *to upset*	aimer	3
tourner AVOIR *to turn*	aimer	3
tournicoter AVOIR *to hang around*	aimer	3
tournoyer AVOIR *to swirl around*	employer	28
tousser AVOIR *to cough*	aimer	3
toussoter AVOIR *to have a slight cough*	aimer	3
tracasser AVOIR *to bother*	aimer	3
tracer AVOIR *to draw*	placer	54
tracter AVOIR *to tow*	aimer	3
traduire AVOIR *to translate*	conduire	16
traficoter AVOIR *to scheme*	aimer	3
trafiquer AVOIR *to fiddle with*	aimer	3
trahir AVOIR *to betray*	finir	34
traînailler AVOIR *to loaf about*	aimer	3
traînasser AVOIR *to loaf about*	aimer	3
traîner AVOIR *to drag/hang around*	aimer	3
traire AVOIR *to milk*	traire	70
traiter AVOIR *to treat*	aimer	3
tramer AVOIR *to weave*	aimer	3
trancher AVOIR *to slice*	aimer	3
tranquilliser AVOIR *to reassure*	aimer	3
transbahuter AVOIR *to shift*	aimer	3
transborder AVOIR *to transship*	aimer	3
transcender AVOIR *to transcend*	aimer	3
transcoder AVOIR *to transcode*	aimer	3
transcrire AVOIR *to transcribe*	écrire	27
transférer AVOIR *to transfer*	céder	13
transfigurer AVOIR *to transform*	aimer	3
transformer AVOIR *to change*	aimer	3
transfuser AVOIR *to give a blood transfusion to*	aimer	3
transgresser AVOIR *to contravene*	aimer	3
transhumer AVOIR *to move to summer pastures*	aimer	3
transiger AVOIR *to compromise*	manger	42
transir AVOIR *to paralyse*	finir	34
transiter AVOIR *to pass through*	aimer	3
translater AVOIR *to translate*	aimer	3
translittérer AVOIR *to transliterate*	céder	13
transmettre AVOIR *to pass on/transmit*	mettre	45
transmuter AVOIR *to transmute*	aimer	3
transparaître AVOIR *to show through*	connaître	17
transpercer AVOIR *to pierce*	placer	54
transpirer AVOIR *to sweat*	aimer	3
transplanter AVOIR *to transplant*	aimer	3
transporter AVOIR *to carry/transport*	aimer	3
transposer AVOIR *to transpose*	aimer	3
transvaser AVOIR *to decant*	aimer	3
traquer AVOIR *to track down*	aimer	3
traumatiser AVOIR *to traumatize*	aimer	3
travailler AVOIR *to work*	aimer	3
traverser AVOIR *to cross*	aimer	3
travestir AVOIR *to dress up*	finir	34

Verb directory

trayais, trayons, etc.		traire	70
trébucher	AVOIR *to stumble*	aimer	3
trembler	AVOIR *to shake*	aimer	3
trembloter	AVOIR *to tremble*	aimer	3
trémousser (se)	ÊTRE *to wiggle around*	aimer	3
tremper	AVOIR *to soak/dip*	aimer	3
trépaner	AVOIR *to trephine*	aimer	3
trépasser	AVOIR ÊTRE *to pass away*	aimer	3
trépider	AVOIR *to shake/vibrate*	aimer	3
trépigner	AVOIR *to stamp one's feet*	aimer	3
tressaillir	AVOIR *to start/quiver*	assaillir	6
tressauter	AVOIR *to start/jolt*	aimer	3
tresser	AVOIR *to plait*	aimer	3
tricher	AVOIR *to cheat*	aimer	3
tricoter	AVOIR *to knit*	aimer	3
trier	AVOIR *to sort*	plier	57
trifouiller	AVOIR *to rummage/tinker with*	aimer	3
trimbaler	AVOIR *to drag around*	aimer	3
trimer	AVOIR *to slave away*	aimer	3
tringler	AVOIR *to chalk a line on*	aimer	3
trinquer	AVOIR *to clink glasses*	aimer	3
triompher	AVOIR *to triumph*	aimer	3
tripatouiller	AVOIR *to fiddle with*	aimer	3
tripler	AVOIR *to treble*	aimer	3
tripoter	AVOIR *to grope*	aimer	3
triturer	AVOIR *to twist/fiddle with*	aimer	3
tromper	AVOIR *to deceive*	aimer	3
tronçonner	AVOIR *to saw up*	aimer	3
trôner	AVOIR *to sit enthroned*	aimer	3
tronquer	AVOIR *to truncate*	aimer	3
troquer	AVOIR *to barter*	aimer	3
trotter	AVOIR *to trot*	aimer	3
trottiner	AVOIR *to jog*	aimer	3
troubler	AVOIR *to cloud/disturb*	aimer	3
trouer	AVOIR *to make a hole in*	aimer	3
trousser	AVOIR *to truss/tuck up*	aimer	3
trouver	AVOIR *to find*	aimer	3
truander	AVOIR *to cheat*	aimer	3
trucider	AVOIR *to kill*	aimer	3
truffer	AVOIR *to stuff with truffles*	aimer	3
truquer	AVOIR *to fiddle*	aimer	3
tuber	AVOIR *to tube*	aimer	3
tuer	AVOIR *to kill*	aimer	3
tuméfier	AVOIR *to make swell up*	plier	57
turbiner	AVOIR *to slog away*	aimer	3
turlupiner	AVOIR *to bother*	aimer	3
tutoyer	AVOIR *to address (sb) as 'tu'*	employer	28
tuyauter	AVOIR *to tip/flute*	aimer	3
twister	AVOIR *to twist*	aimer	3
tyranniser	AVOIR *to tyrannize*	aimer	3
ulcérer	AVOIR *to revolt*	céder	13

Verb directory

ululer AVOIR *to hoot*	aimer	3
unifier AVOIR *to unify*	plier	57
uniformiser AVOIR *to standardize*	aimer	3
unir AVOIR *to unite*	finir	34
universaliser AVOIR *to universalize*	aimer	3
urbaniser AVOIR *to urbanize*	aimer	3
urger AVOIR *to be urgent*	manger	42
uriner AVOIR *to urinate*	aimer	3
user AVOIR *to wear out*	aimer	3
usiner AVOIR *to machine*	aimer	3
usurper AVOIR *to usurp*	aimer	3
utiliser AVOIR *to use*	aimer	3
va, vais, vas	aller	4
vacciner AVOIR *to vaccinate*	aimer	3
vaciller AVOIR *to sway*	aimer	3
vadrouiller AVOIR *to wander around*	aimer	3
vagabonder AVOIR *to wander*	aimer	3
vagir AVOIR *to wail*	finir	34
vaille, vailles	valoir	72
vaincre AVOIR *to defeat*	vaincre	71
vainquais, vainquons, etc.	vaincre	71
valdinguer AVOIR *to go flying*	aimer	3
valider AVOIR *to stamp*	aimer	3
valoir AVOIR *to be worth*	valoir	72
valoriser AVOIR *to promote*	aimer	3
valser AVOIR *to waltz*	aimer	3
vampiriser AVOIR *to suck the lifeblood from*	aimer	3
vandaliser AVOIR *to vandalize*	aimer	3
vanner AVOIR *to winnow*	aimer	3
vanter AVOIR *to praise*	aimer	3
vaporiser AVOIR *to spray*	aimer	3
vaquer à AVOIR *to attend to*	aimer	3
varier AVOIR *to vary*	plier	57
vasouiller AVOIR *to flounder*	aimer	3
vaticiner AVOIR *to soothsay*	aimer	3
vaudrai, vaudrait, vaut, vaux, etc.	valoir	72
vautrer (se) ÊTRE *to sprawl*	aimer	3
vécu, vécus, etc.	vivre	75
végéter AVOIR *to vegetate*	céder	13
véhiculer AVOIR *to carry/transport*	aimer	3
veiller AVOIR *to watch over*	aimer	3
vêler AVOIR *to calve*	aimer	3
vendanger AVOIR *to harvest the grapes*	manger	42
vendre AVOIR *to sell*	rendre	63
vénérer AVOIR *to venerate*	céder	13
venger AVOIR *to avenge*	manger	42
venir ÊTRE *to come*	venir	73
venter AVOIR *to blow*	aimer	3
ventiler AVOIR *to ventilate*	aimer	3
verbaliser AVOIR *to record an offence*	aimer	3
verdir AVOIR *to turn green*	finir	34

Verb directory

Verb directory

Also available from Oxford University Press

Oxford Take off in French
Language learning course with almost 5 hours of audio
Book and 4 cassettes 0–19–860274–x
Book and 4 CDs 0–19–860298–7
Book only 0–19–860299–5

Oxford Take off in French Dictionary
48,000 words and phrases
0–19–860331–2
(available in the UK only)

Pocket Oxford-Hachette French Dictionary
The ideal dictionary for higher examinations
0–19–860279–0

The Oxford Colour French Dictionary
Colour headwords throughout
0–19–860191–3
0–19–860190–5 (US edition)

The Oxford Starter French Dictionary
Designed for absolute beginners
0–19–860328–2

Oxford French Wordpack
0–19–860335–5

Oxford French Grammar
Clear explanations of modern French usage
0–19–860341–x